DATE DUE			

D1010557

AFTER SUCH KNOWLEDGE

After Such Knowledge

MEMORY, HISTORY,

AND THE

LEGACY

OF THE

HOLOCAUST

Eva Hoffman

PUBLICAFFAIRS

NEW YORK

Published in the United States by PublicAffairs™, a member of the Perseus Books Group.

BOOK DESIGN AND COMPOSITION BY JENNY DOSSIN. TEXT SET IN ADOBE GARAMOND.

Library of Congress Cataloging-in-Publication Data
Hoffman, Eva, 1945–
After such knowledge: memory, history, and the legacy of the Holocaust / Eva Hoffman.
p. cm.
Includes bibliographical references and index.
ISBN 1–58648–046–4
1. Holocaust, Jewish (1939–1945)—Historiography. 2. Holocaust, Jewish (1939–1945)—In-
fluence. 3. Holocaust, Jewish (1939–1945)—Psychological aspects. 4. Memory. I. Title
D804.348.H64 2004   2003066443

FIRST EDITION
10 9 8 7 6 5 4 3 2 1

To my sister Alina, fellow inheritor of the legacy.

AND

Rafael (Felek) Scharf,
who knew how to transmit knowledge.

CONTENTS

INTRODUCTION

And so, after all, the Holocaust.

Sixty years after the Holocaust took place, our reckoning with this defining event is far from over. Indeed, as this immense catastrophe recedes from us in time, our preoccupation with it seems only to increase. We are ever more intent to penetrate its dark lessons, to excavate every datum concerning its origins and execution, to try to rectify, however belatedly, some of its injustices.

At the same time, even as our fascination intensifies, we inevitably contemplate the Shoah from an ever-growing distance—temporal, geographical, cultural—with all the risks of simplification implicit in such remoteness. It has become routine to speak of the "memory" of the Holocaust and to give this putative faculty privileged status; but most of us, of course, do not have memories of the Shoah, nor, often, sufficient means for apprehending that event. How should we, then, from our distance, apprehend it? What meanings does the Holocaust hold for us today—and how are we going to pass on those meanings to subsequent generations?

I had grown up with a consciousness of the Shoah from the beginning. My parents had emerged from its crucible shortly before my birth. They had survived, in what was then the Polish part of the Ukraine, with the help of Polish and Ukrainian neighbors; but their entire families perished. Those were the inescapable facts—the inescapable knowledge—I had come into. But the knowledge had not always been equally active, nor did I always want to make the inheritance defining.

Indeed, it was not until I started writing about it in my first book, *Lost in Translation,* that I began discerning, amidst other threads, the Holocaust strand of my history. I had carried this part of my psychic past within me all my life; but it was only now, as I began pondering it from a longer distance and through the clarifying process of writing, that what had been an inchoate, obscure knowledge appeared to me as a powerful theme and influence in my life. Until then, it had not occurred to me that I was in effect a receptacle of a historical legacy, or that its burden had a significance and weight that needed to be acknowledged. Now, personal memory appeared to me clearly linked to larger history, and the heavy dimensions of this inheritance started becoming fully apparent.

Several developments led me to feel that I wanted to return to and foreground further this aspect of my own and my generational history. Some of the recent manifestations, and proliferations, of the "memory cult" have left me uneasy. At the same time, my parents died; the survivors as a group were reaching the end of their natural life span. I had listened to their stories throughout my life. Now, I felt more and more palpably that the legacy of the Shoah was being passed on to us, its symbolic descendants and next of kin. We were the closest to its memories; we had touched upon its horror and its human scars. If I did not want the "memory" of the Holocaust to be flattened out through distance or ignorance, if I wanted to preserve some of the pulsing complexity I had felt in survivors' own perceptions, then it was up to me.

At the same time, it seemed to me that if I wanted to understand the significance of the Holocaust inheritance for those who come after, then I needed to reflect on my own and my peers' link to that legacy, to excavate our generational story from under its weight and shadow—to retrieve it from that "secondariness" which many of us have felt in relation to a formidable and forbidding past. In a sense, I needed to address frontally what I had thought about obliquely: the profound effects of a traumatic history, and its paradoxical richness; the kinds of knowledge which the Shoah has bequeathed to us, and the knowledge we might derive from it.

Within the larger history of postwar responses to the Holocaust, the direct descendants of survivors—the so-called second generation—form a particular subset and story. The existence of the "second generation" was probably announced in 1979 with the publication of Helen Epstein's seminal book *Children of the Holocaust: Conversations with Sons and Daughters of Survivors.* All of Epstein's interlocutors had been deeply affected by their parents' experiences, whether these were spoken about or not. But for many of the book's subjects, the interviews were the first time they had looked at the post-Holocaust aspect of their stories as something distinct and significant, or had articulated the impact of their parents' histories on the parents themselves, the family dynamics, or their own inner and outer lives.

Since then, however, the "second generation" has crystallized into a recognized entity, and a self-conscious "identity." Children of survivors by now comprise a defined, if hybrid, collectivity which holds international meetings and conferences and which has given rise to a growing body of writing, ranging from highly personal to highly theoretical.

This book is emphatically not a sociological study, nor a work of specialist scholarship. I have not tried to encompass all the aspects of the second-generation phenomenon, nor have I conducted systematic interviews. Nevertheless, it seemed to me that the second generation's story is a strong case study in the deep and long-lasting impact of atrocity; and that children of survivors' very personal transactions with the past are a strong clue to the problems we must grapple with if we would grasp the meanings and consequences of historical horror. In their mediated but immediate relation to the Holocaust, children of survivors have had to live out and struggle with some of the defining issues that follow from atrocity: the internal impact of gratuitous violence and the transmission of traumatic experience across generations; the emotional intricacies of dealing with victims of persecution and the moral quandaries implicit in dialogues with perpetrators; the difficulties of witnessing the pain of others and of thinking about tragic pasts; and the relationship of private memory to a broader understanding of history.

The text which follows is an extended essay, or a series of reflections on such themes, informed by long-standing personal and intellectual engagement and composed of several interwoven motifs. On one level, I use the thread of my own and my family's story to probe and convey the subjective aftereffects of the Holocaust, the impact of its transferred legacy, and that legacy's later vicissitudes. At the same time, this book has grown out of continuous readings (and occasional writings) on the Holocaust and its aftermath: the growing body of personal testimony, memoirs, and fiction produced by children of survivors, as well as survivors themselves; psychoanalytic case studies, historical documentation, and the hefty corpus of cultural theory and philosophical speculation which continues to accumulate in this area. In my explorations of the subject, I draw on disparate disciplines and forms of literature to explore the broader psychological, moral, and philosophical implications of the "second-generation" story.

Indeed, it is part of my aim in this book to attempt a kind of informal synthesis, to bring the various approaches to this vast subject into dynamic interaction. Most scholarly works on the impact of the Holocaust and its "reception" in the postwar world emphasize either the psychocultural or the sociopolitical aspects of the problem. I wanted to bring them together under the roof of one book, partly because it seems to me that, while such categories of explanation may exist separately on our maps of ideas, they are not easily distinguishable as forms of experience. Morality is not separable from affect, or politics from psyche—at least not in relation to experiences as potent and raveled as those following from the Holocaust.

In another vein, I wanted to introduce, insofar as possible, a comparative perspective to a subject which is usually treated, in effect, from a monocultural vantage point. Whether the Holocaust is or is not unique is not here the issue. Like all history-shattering events, the Shoah needs to be understood first of all in its full factuality and specificity. But the very extremity of this paradigmatic catastrophe and the depth at which it has been examined means that it can, and has, served as a template for thinking about other tragic events. At the same time, the question is whether insight into other modes of atrocity, or a cross-cultural understanding of, say, ethnic conflict, or reactions to human catastrophe, can illuminate the broader sources and patterns of such events.

Finally, this book is also the result of conversations I have had over many years with survivors and second-generation peers, with Poles and Germans of all ages, and with yet others who have brought insights into violent events in other parts of the world. It may be that a cross-cultural, or cross-situational, understanding here, too, may be illuminating; and that the testimony and study of the post-Holocaust "second generation" may be useful to second generations elsewhere, and emerging from other difficult histories.

After Such Knowledge is divided into seven short sections, roughly corresponding to the chronological trajectory of the second generation and postwar response to the Holocaust. At the same time, the sections delineate the stages of understanding, or the modalities of knowledge, which children of survivors move through as they struggle with the burden of a powerful psychic inheritance and which are available to all of us as we try to unpack the daunting burden of meanings bequeathed to us by the Holocaust. Throughout the text, I use the terms "Holocaust" (meaning, approximately, "burnt offering") and the Hebrew "Shoah" (meaning "calamity") interchangeably, as they have come to be used in both colloquial and scholarly discourse.

The title of this book is taken from a line in a poem by T. S. Eliot: "After such knowledge, what forgiveness?" The poem is "Gerontion," and it is marred by anti-Semitic overtones. Nevertheless, the line, and even the verse to which it belongs, seemed exactly appropriate for my theme; and it may be that the inclusion of disturbing anti-Semitic or other prejudicial elements in an otherwise beautiful and masterly work is part of the knowledge with which we have to contend.

The guardianship of the Holocaust is being passed on to us. The second generation is the hinge generation in which received, transferred knowledge of events is transmuted into history, or into myth. It is also the generation in which we can think about certain questions arising from the Shoah with a sense of a living connection. This is one person's meditation on such questions, and on a long reckoning with the long aftermath of atrocity.

I

FROM EVENT TO FABLE

In the beginning was the war. That was my childhood theory of origins, akin perhaps to certain childhood theories of sexuality. For me, the world as I knew it and the people in it emerged not from the womb, but from war. The theory was perhaps understandable, for I was born in Poland, in 1945, that is, on the site of the Second World War's greatest ravages; and so soon after the cataclysm as to conflate it with the causes of my own birth.

Even in Cracow, where I grew up and which had escaped physical destruction, traces of war were everywhere visible: in the injured bodies of war veterans; in the orphaned children I met on our street, and whose condition seemed to me the most pitiable; in the pervasive presence and consciousness of death. Everyone I knew had lost relatives, intimates, friends. My parents lost their entire families: their own parents, sisters, brothers, cousins, uncles, and aunts. On the Jewish high holidays, when our small family went to one of Cracow's old synagogues, we met a community in mourning. The facts of death were so

ubiquitous that they seemed both to precede and to supersede
the facts of life.

When I was about five, my father took me to Warsaw, a city
still lying largely in ruins. We walked along stretches of smooth
pavement, but all around us there was stony rubble and skeletal
scaffoldings. Metal columns stuck through jagged remains of
walls. Window frames gaped, revealing rooms cut in half and
filled with debris. Sometimes, the pavement along which we
walked gave out as well, and my father and I stumbled as we
picked our way across rubble-covered streets. The greyness, the
mounds and crumbling hillocks of stone, had an almost lyrical
picturesqueness; but the scene was also profoundly, piercingly
sad.

Along with the Renaissance architecture of Cracow and the
flowering meadows and forests of the Polish countryside, the ruined cities were part of my primal landscape—as, through films
and photographs, they became part of my generation's primal
iconography. Some of us grew up in or near ruined cities, some
of us knew them only through tale and imagery. But all of us
born in those first years came into a torn, ravaged world. It is no
wonder that so many postwar artists have found fascination in
abandoned sites, decayed structures, rust, rubble, peeling paint;
the signs and traces of destruction. And it is no wonder that so
many have been tempted to see in such subjects a kind of
melancholy beauty.

War penetrated the very fabric of my childhood. It interwove
itself into other, more sunny sensations with a somber poetry of
its own. But it was also the heavy ground of being, the natural
condition to which the world tended, and could at any moment
revert. Everything else was a precarious aftermath, or maybe an

interregnum. In retrospect, I can see that I spent much of my childhood waiting for the war. Waiting for it to manifest itself again, to emerge from where it lurked with its violent, ravaging claws. Waiting for danger and destruction, which were the fundamental human condition, to trample the fragile coverlet of peace. I kept anticipating, with a fearful anxiety I took as normal, the death of my parents. After all, every one of the adults who had once formed our family group, and to whom my parents so often referred, was dead. Life itself, for children born into families like mine, could seem a tenuous condition, a buffeted island in the infinite ocean of death. The Holocaust was not yet distinguished from "war" in anyone's mind; but the intimations of mortality that followed from it were part of my earliest perceptions of the world as I transformed the felt traces of a historical event into a kind of story about the basic elements and shape of the world, a childish mythos or fable.

.   .   .

My parents endured the terrible years in the small town of Załośce, situated about two hundred miles east of Lvóv (now Lviv), in what was before the war the Polish part of the Ukraine. That was where they had both grown up, in their still Orthodox, premodern shtetl families; and that was where they remained, through the war and the annihilation of their families and community. They survived with the help of local Ukrainian and Polish people, and by eluding the hostility of others. During much of the war, they were hidden in the attic of a primitive cottage belonging to Ukrainian peasants who were risking their own lives in order to shelter my parents. Their survival was

wrested from the most improbable odds. The statistics of extermination in their region of Europe were among the worst.
When the war ended and Załośce, with all of Polish-Ukrainian
territory, was declared to be part of the Soviet Union, my parents made the wise decision to head for the nearest Polish city,
which happened to be Cracow. They had just gone through an
inferno of hiding and hunger, of fear and hairsbreadth escapes,
of hearing regular, devastating news about the murders of their
closest and most loved relatives. I was born several months later.

It is no exaggeration to say that I have spent much of my life
struggling with this compressed cluster of facts. They were
transmitted to me as my first knowledge, a sort of supercon-
densed pellet of primal information—the kind from which
everything else grows, or explodes, or follows, and which it takes
a lifetime to unpack and decode. The facts seemed to be such an
inescapable part of my inner world as to belong to me, to my
own experience. But of course, they didn't; and in that elision,
that caesura, much of the postgeneration's problematic can be
found.

The Holocaust, in my first, childish reception, was a deeply
internalized but strangely unknown past. It has become routine
to speak of the "memory" of the Holocaust, and to adduce to
this faculty a moral, even a spiritual value. But it is important to
be precise: We who came after do not have memories of the
Holocaust. Even from my most intimate proximity I could not
form "memories" of the Shoah or take my parents' memories as
my own. Rather, I took in that first information as a sort of fairy
tale deriving not so much from another world as from the center of the cosmos: an enigmatic but real fable.

Nor was it exactly memories that were expressed at first by

the survivors themselves. Rather, it was something both more potent and less lucid; something closer to enactment of experience, to emanations or sometimes nearly embodiments of psychic matter—of material too awful to be processed and assimilated into the stream of consciousness, or memory, or intelligible feeling.

Not that my parents or others within the war-ravaged community wanted to dwell on the recent past. The war—it was not yet the Holocaust—was not my parents' or their friends' main theme or conscious focus. Their energies, their efforts, were pointed towards the present. That mix of carpe diem energy and carpe diem cynicism that was the characteristic postwar mood was reflected in particular personalities, and I think that many of us second-generation children were awed by our elders' vitality in those postwar years. After emerging from their hidden hells, after making their epic treks and their escapes, the survivors wanted to snatch experience somehow and anyhow, to live and create new lives. People who lost families started new ones. Those who lost homes found new places of habitation. From my childhood, I remember the merriment of conversation when my parents got together with their Jewish friends, the zest with which they talked of books and clothes (so scarce and valued in Poland of that time), and the films they had seen. To those who had lived through the war, the difference between life and death must have seemed extremely well marked just then— even as it seemed very liminal to those of us who had just come into the world.

In the world at large, one could also sense a dynamism—perhaps the sheer surge of a collective life-instinct coming through after so much death—that coexisted with the sadness so closely as to be braided into it. In Poland, as in all of Eastern Europe, there was also a kind of official optimism, a sense of hardship overcome, and of triumphant, Soviet-sponsored victory. On the fifteen-minute newsreels shown before the movies we went to on Sunday mornings, the ruined skeletons of buildings were replaced by images of buildings going up, filmed against sunny skies, with teams of purposeful and thick-muscled workers placing brick upon brick with euphoric, Stakhanovite speed, and sometimes straightening up to look far into the horizon, masculine hand put up against the brow to shield the eyes from the promise of the sun. Rebuilding, reconstruction: the mood, or idea, that governed much of the postwar world, though not everywhere as tendentiously, as cynically in fact, as in Eastern Europe. Much of the globe, after all, had just emerged from an orgy of killing and was ready to start again with a strange, almost euphoric vitality.

But there were also—the postwar mood was potently complex—images of brute mute tanks on the newsreels, making their slow progress between enfilades of cheering people; and there was footage of soldiers on parade, marching to the accompaniment of the peculiarly energetic tones of that period's news commentary, voices whose theatrical decisiveness suggested that the times called for vigilance and iron resolve. Armies were still very much with us, and the fear of war, it seemed to me, was always in the air, although the adults often tried to reassure us children that nobody would go to war so soon after the cataclysm had ended; that people had suffered too much from its evils; that perhaps, after what had happened, no one would go to war ever again.

A charged, mixed atmosphere, then, a determined turn to life despite and against all other evidence. But for those who had actually endured the Shoah, the ghastly evidence could not be fully suppressed, the affirmation (or was it a denial?) could be sustained only so far. The overwhelming experiences, still raw, still palpably present, kept breaking through into the ordinary day. It is increasingly clear that the myth of survivors' muteness, of a blank, blanket silence, was largely a misconception. A few survivors were determined never to talk about what they had lived through; but others wanted to give expression to the horror, or perhaps couldn't help doing so. Whether the world wanted to listen was another question. Much of it didn't; and so, survivors, or at least those among them who were willing to touch on their experiences in words, tended to talk among those from whom they could hope for some understanding—fellow survivors, or others whom they could trust.

But they also spoke—how could they help it?—to their immediate intimates, to spouses and siblings, and yes, to their children. There, they spoke in the language of family—a form of expression that is both more direct and more ruthless than social or public speech. I do not know what form my parents' wartime stories took in conversation with their friends. But in our small apartment, it was a chaos of emotion that emerged from their words rather than any coherent narration. Or rather, the emotion, direct and tormented, was enacted through the words, the form of their utterances. The memories—no, not memories but emanations—of wartime experiences kept erupting in flashes of imagery; in abrupt, fragmented phrases; in repetitious, broken refrains. They kept manifesting themselves with a frightening immediacy in that most private and potent of family languages—the language of the body. In my home, as in so many others, the past broke through in the sounds of night-mares, the idiom of sighs and illness, of tears and the acute aches that were the legacy of the damp attic and of the conditions my parents endured during their hiding.

In the midst of her daily round, my mother would suddenly be overcome by a sharp, terrible image, or by tears. On other subjects, she was robustly articulate; but when sudden recall of her loved ones punctured her mind's protective membrane, speech came in frail phrases, in litanies of sorrow. There were the images she returned to again and again, the dark amulets: how she and my father spent their days in a forest bunker, and how she waited for him, alone, as he went out to forage or plead for food in the night. How they later sat in a peasant's attic for two years, in wet straw, shivering from cold in the winter and from hunger in all seasons. How her sister—this was the heart of grief—had been murdered. She was shot into a mass grave in Załośce, not far from where my parents were hiding. A witness later told my mother that the Jews rounded up for that particular massacre had to dig the pit into which their bodies were subsequently thrown, sometimes still quivering with remainders of life. She was just nineteen, my mother would say about her sister, and begin to cry.

On the most painful matters, my father was silent. The moments he could bear to remember, or to articulate, presented themselves as episodes in an ultimate adventure, a game literally of life and death. There was the time when he was arraigned by two strong Ukrainian peasants on a bridge at night, and was being dragged by them undoubtedly to the local Gestapo station. Instead, with all his strength—my father always made a violent gesture with his powerful arms when he told this story—he threw the two youths against the railing of the bridge and then jumped into the icy river; there he stayed until he could be sure that the danger had passed, under the cover of watery darkness, ice floes floating around him. There was the crucial night when he made his hairsbreadth escape from a German convoy truck transporting their Jewish "catch" to a nearby concentration camp. After making his way through the snowy forest, my father found himself, in the early dawn, near the same concentration camp for which he had been destined. He knocked on the door of a peasant's hut. He was too tired to go on, even if what the hut held was death. But he was lucky. He was let in and sheltered.

Many others who grew up in households like mine remember the torn, incoherent character of those first communications about the Holocaust, the speech broken under the pressure of pain. The episodes, the talismanic litanies, were repeated but never elaborated upon. They remained compressed, packed, sharp. I suppose the inassimilable character of the experiences they referred to was expressed—and passed on—through this form. For it was precisely the indigestibility of these utterances, their fearful weight of densely packed feeling, as much as any specific content, that I took in as a child. The fragmentary phrases lodged themselves in my mind like shards, like the deadly needles I remember from certain fairy tales, which pricked your flesh and could never be extracted again.

Indeed, in my childish mind, the hypervivid moments summoned by my parents registered themselves as half awful reality, half wondrous fairy tale. A peasant's hut, holding the riddle of life or death; a snowy forest, which confounds the senses and sense of direction. A hayloft in which one sits, awaiting fate, while a stranger downstairs, who is really a good fairy in disguise, is fending off that fate by muttering invocations under her breath and bringing to the hiding place a bowl of soup. The sister, young, innocent, and loved, standing naked above a pit that is soon to become her own mass grave . . . Brutal-faced Germans with large vicious dogs. Humiliating orders shouted in a harsh language. ("You should have seen their faces," my mother said. "They were not really human.") The pursuit of powerless people, bent silhouettes running desperately through an exposed landscape, trying to make it into the bordering woods. ("We were hunted from all sides. There was nowhere to escape to.") Fields, trenches, pits of death. For others, barbed wire, skeletal figures, smoke, intimations of mass death. Every survivor's child has such images available right behind the eyelids. Later, through literature and film, through memoirs and oral testimony, these components of horror became part of a whole generation's store of imagery and narration, the icons and sagas of the post-Holocaust world. In retrospect, and as knowledge about the Holocaust has grown, we can see that every survivor has lived through a mythic trial, an epic, an odyssey.

But at first, these were not epics. They were humble, homely, disconnected units of narration, the most dread-inducing of family stories, a fable or myth about the beginnings or foundations of the world. As I decode it in retrospect, the mythology passed on in this way conveyed a universe of absolute forces and absolute unreason, a world in which ultimate things happened without cause or motive, where life was saved or lost routinely and through reflex movement, and where the border between life and death was dangerously permeable. Irrational as the world that my parents endured had been, I made of it something more utterly irrational still.

Beyond the suction hole of unreason, beyond the threshold of the war, there seemed to be no reality and no past. It was true of my parents, as it was of many survivors, that they did not talk much about their prewar lives. Perhaps the impact of the subsequent events overwhelmed and deleted everything else. Or perhaps to remember the world before would have made the losses even more piercing. In my own family, the cut from the past was complete. There was one frayed photograph with an indistinct image of my mother's sister that somehow made it from one universe to the other. But no objects had managed to travel across the time gap and, of course, no persons. When my parents did allude to their lives in Załośce, it was as if they were talking about a very remote, quaint world seen through a diminishing telescope. The six years of the war had created a geological fissure in time and removed the world before to another era. There was nothing to help me imagine time extending backwards. The cut reinforced the conviction that the war, the Holocaust, was the dark root from which the world sprang.

The mythology had its implicit morality within which the good was closely equated with suffering. Or rather, perhaps it is more accurate to say that the early awareness of suffering created an unconscious, or preconscious, ethics, and that in this system, just as war was the ground of being, so pain was the ground of personhood. The presence of suffering was powerful enough so that it had to be absorbed; but there was also an imperative to remain loyal to it, to make up for it, to provide solace. This was clear to me from the beginning, as it must have been to those many children of survivors who later testified to their need to protect their parents. Perhaps there is something in us, an antidote to the selfish gene, that respects a creature in pain. Or perhaps I understood the sacredness of suffering, its untouchable, dark delicacy, because, with a childish receptivity, I absorbed my parents' unhappiness through channels that seemed nearly physical. The pain of their psyches reverberated in my body almost as if it were mine. Whatever the cause, I certainly understood in the marrow of my bones that, no matter how I might want to hurt my parents, or how much I felt they hurt me, I couldn't touch them in the wounded places; I couldn't violate by the slightest indelicacy their mourning and their deep, embodied anguish.

The other side of these primitive (or nascent) ethics was the equation of evil with brutal power, and a choked, breathless hatred of "the Germans," an almost physical urgency of rage accompanied by the pressing need not only to discard everything they stood for but to proclaim the utter wrongness of their vile work. "The Germans" were the demonic force in the universe, and the duty to abhor them was almost as strong and as morally tinctured as the obligation to respect those on whom their cruelties were inflicted.

Perhaps these twinned imperatives of loyalty and hate were not disconnected from the difficulty of comprehending the structure of parental stories. The loyalty meant that the moments, the images, the phrases bequeathed to me through my parents' utterances demanded to be preserved in their unaltered integrity. There was a deeply internalized duty not to let diffusion, or forgetfulness, or imaginative transformation, dilute the condensed communications. After all, I was the designated carrier for the cargo of awesome knowledge transferred to me by my parents, and its burden had to be transported carefully, with all the iterated accounts literally intact. Moreover, there was a kind of prohibition on the very quality of coherence. To make a sequential narrative of what happened would have been to make indecently rational what had been obscenely irrational. It would have been to normalize through familiar form an utterly aberrant content. One was not to make a nice story out of loathsome cruelty and of piercing, causeless hurt.

.   .   .

That everybody died; that my parents survived by dint of my father's resourcefulness and my mother's fatalistic fearlessness; that there were people in whose hands one could place one's life, and others who set vicious dogs on humans: Those were the givens. More than for our parents, the Holocaust, for us, was the paradoxical fundament. Dan Bar-On, an Israeli psychoanalyst who has written about the effect of the Holocaust on three generations, puts this succinctly: "My parents' generation grew up in a world without a Holocaust," he writes, "but for us there could be no such world."

To start with the Holocaust as the foundation was, potentially, a premise for a nihilistic or a wholly unillusioned philosophy; and perhaps the Shoah is the hidden basis for the metaphysics of nullity and absence, for the urge to deconstruct all meanings and reach a vacuous center, so salient in postwar visions of the world. But in childhood, the awareness of loss and death was not yet philosophy. Instead, like all children, I took the character of the recent past entirely for granted; that is, I took the conditions of the war and the Holocaust as a kind of mythology and the norm.

It was, however, an irony attendant on this that, although we postwar children were the closest to wartime events in time and in primal feeling, we were the furthest removed from their grounded, worldly—that is, political, social, historical—meanings. This, I think, is a crucial distinction: that whereas adults who live through violence and atrocity can understand what happens to them as actuality—no matter how awful its terms—the generation after receives its first knowledge of the terrible events with only childish instruments of perception, and as a kind of fable.

It was not that the mythical vision of the world I had put together from scraps of story and imagery was untrue. The mythology, after all, derived from reality. It was just that I knew it *as* mythology and had no way of grasping it as actuality. It would take me a long time to discover and put its real-world components together. But as I was growing up, I had no comprehension of the background to the war or its course, of the circumstances visited upon Poland during the cataclysm, or the contemporaneous situation within which our lives unfolded in postwar Cracow.

In this respect, the postgeneration's trajectory is the opposite of the more general trajectory of response to events. For while the adult world asks first "what happened," and from there follows its uncertain and sometimes resistant route towards the inward meaning of the facts, those who are born after calamity sense its most inward meanings first and have to work their way outwards toward the facts and the worldly shape of events.

Initially, I had no way of knowing that Poland had been, uniquely among European nations, the site of two catastrophes. One was the Nazi war of conquest against the Polish nation and the policy of widespread murder and eventual enslavement of the Poles. The other was the campaign of extermination directed against all Jews of Europe, but executed mostly on Polish territory. Most of the concentration camps were situated on Polish soil, and it has often been assumed that the Germans had placed them there because they counted on the collusion of the Poles in their annihilationist project. This has been repeatedly shown to be untrue. The camps were most probably constructed in Poland because it was a fully conquered country and because that is where the overwhelming majority of European Jews—3.5 million people—resided. And, even in the face of recent revelations about the awful massacres in the towns of Radziłów and Jedwabne, in which Poles, with German permission or perhaps inspiration, murdered their Jewish neighbors, it can still be said that the actions of individual Poles during the cataclysm showed all the variations of human character and behavior. They ranged from the extraordinary heroism it took to save Jewish lives at the risk of one's own, to betrayal and aggression, which amounted to collusion with the Nazis, to indifference which probably characterized most of the population, concerned as it was about its own calamity and survival.

Within Europe, Poland was the country that mounted the largest resistance against the Nazi occupation in the face of the most defeating odds. It was also the country that had been most bitterly betrayed at every step of the conflict: first by the Molotov-Ribbentrop Pact of nonaggression, signed by the Germans and Soviets to enable them to march into Poland from east and west with impunity; then by the Soviet armies, which waited on one side of the Vistula River while the Nazi armies ruthlessly put down the Warsaw Uprising, in which 250,000 people died in the course of six weeks; and finally at Yalta, where the post-

war order was established and Poland was delivered into the Soviet sphere.

Later—much later—these events would become my meaningful history, the history it is urgent to know because it belongs
to one's life, because it shapes ancestral fate and one's own sensibility. But it took me many years to begin discerning the structure of those events; as, indeed, it took a while for the adult
world to learn the full facts, to sort out various kinds of violence
from each other, to put together a comparative picture of conditions and responses to Nazi aggression in various countries
within occupied Europe.

Neither could I be aware, as I was growing up, of the continuing conflicts that consumed Poland in the years immediately
after the war. Those years, with their pan-European turbulence
and chaos, constitute a kind of prehistory of the postwar era,
a quickly forgotten, murky time that is only now being again
historically reconstructed and decoded. In Poland, the short interregnum between 1945 and 1948, which preceded the establishment of the Cold War order and Soviet control, witnessed a
virtual civil war as non-Communist partisans continued to be
killed by the victorious Communists, Poles and Ukrainians continued to murder each other in the east, and in the western territories, horrific acts of collective revenge were perpetrated upon
ethnic Germans even as they were being expelled from Polish
soil.

On the official plane, this was a period of collective punish-
ments, directed at Polish gentry and other "class enemies" (who
were often deported to Siberia); but also, at the non-Communist resistance movement. People who had struggled honorably
against the Nazis were put in prison, and sometimes executed,

in a grotesque perversion of truth and justice. (It is not for nothing that Jan Kott, a brilliant literary critic—himself a Jewish Communist who by the mid–1950s had decided that his faith had been mistaken, or betrayed—was later to write that Poland, as a result of its history, was the central site of the grotesque in the twentieth century.)

Unofficially, there were outbreaks of violence and other kinds of ugliness directed at the small percentage of Polish Jews who had survived the cataclysm. In the small villages to which some of them tried to return, there was rejection, hostility, and worse: expressions of pleasure at their diminished numbers, refusals to return property entrusted to Polish neighbors or seized by them, and, sometimes, murders. In Cracow, in 1945, just a few weeks after my parents' advent there, there were anti-Semitic incidents in which several people were killed. Throughout Poland, more than one thousand Jews were murdered in those lawless years, most infamously at Kielce, where more than forty people coming back from the Soviet territories were brutally attacked by an enraged mob. The Kielce episode, however, was untypical in being politically provoked. Mostly, the murders were spontaneous and committed out of sheer greed, petty vendettas, or pure anti-Semitism—an old prejudice turned vicious through the permissive demoralization of war. For the woebegone remnants who had just lived through torment and loss, the renewal of hatred must have been psychically insupportable, and many Jews left Poland as soon as they could.

How were such events absorbed into Polish consciousness, how was the fate of the Jews—amidst other horrors of the war—understood? This would also later become important knowledge, not only for those of us to whom it was personal but for the world at large. In retrospect, it has become customary to divide the history of public reactions to the Holocaust into several stages, beginning with a period of denial and forgetfulness. But this is not quite accurate: This history has its own prehistory as well. The instances of postwar violence were of course utterly unacceptable. But there was also, initially, discussion, shock, a kind of acknowledgment of what had happened to the Jews under the Nazis' reign. The distinctions between the Holocaust and the wider conflict were not fully intelligible in the chaos of those first postwar years. But neither was a veil drawn over events. After all, everyone in Poland had lived through the war, had seen, heard, or done something in relation to their Jewish neighbors. These things were not yet the subject of memory or forgetting, but of raw emotion, information gathering, and first-level documentary investigation. Before the so-called latency period, before the repressions of the psyche and the active suppressions of Communist censorship, there was, in relation to the Holocaust, as to other aspects of the war, an interval of first, horrified realization, and even some attempts at a reckoning.

Immediately after the war (I learned much later), systematic documentation of what happened to the Jews of Poland was undertaken by both Jewish and non-Jewish institutions. The Central Jewish Historical Committee attempted to register names of all Jewish survivors in Poland (although some chose to retain their assumed "Aryan" names and identities, which had helped them survive, and, they must have hoped, would continue to keep them from lesser kinds of harm). Both Jewish and Polish institutions collected information and personal accounts of Jewish survival and of perishing. The Commission for the Investigation of Nazi Crimes pursued testimony from victims and perpetrators. The amazing project of oral, collective history that eventuated in Yizkor Books (Books of Memory)—humbly written tomes recording communal memories of the Polish shtetls that suddenly were no more—was undertaken shortly after the war. A monument to the Warsaw Ghetto uprising, conceived in a heroic, somber style that was the esthetic of the time, was erected on the ghetto's site in 1948.

In the course of the widespread postwar trials, a number of Nazi perpetrators were transferred to Poland by the Allied powers to be tried by Polish courts. More surprisingly, Polish crimes against Jews were, to some extent, acknowledged and punished by the Polish authorities. There were trials of Poles responsible for informing or perpetrating acts of violence directed against Jews. Twelve of the perpetrators involved in the horrific Jedwabne massacre were tried in 1949 and 1953. Although most verdicts in such trials were relatively lenient, there were some death sentences among them.

At the same time, Polish writers and artists were beginning to grapple with the horror, sometimes with great sensitivity to particular kinds of prejudice and persecution suffered by Jews. Amazingly enough, some of the artistic responses came even as the Holocaust was being executed. Czesław Miłosz, the Nobel laureate who spent the war years in Warsaw, wrote some of his greatest poems after witnessing the destruction of the Warsaw Ghetto. In "A Poor Christian Looks at the Ghetto," Miłosz prophetically imagines "a guardian mole . . . with a small red lamp fastened to his forehead" and "swollen lids like a Patriarch," who, despite the anonymous destruction of bodies, carries on an underground work of identifying the dead, of distinguishing "human ashes by their luminous vapor, / The ashes of each man by a different part of the spectrum."

The poem ends in a cry of impotence and guilt:

What will I tell him, I, a Jew of the New Testament,
Waiting two thousand years for the second coming of Jesus?
My broken body will deliver me to his sight
And he will count me among the helpers of death:
The uncircumcised.

Miłosz's poems are exceptional in their full realization of the Jewish tragedy and in the depth of the poet's reckoning with his own and, by implication, collective Polish (and Christian) conscience. But in most of the creative responses, even the most humane and compassionate, the Holocaust, in those early stages, was not yet perceived as a discrete event, separate from the rest of the war. In her brief, unforgettable book *Medallions* (published in 1946), Zofia Nałkowska, a prominent writer who gathered much of her material from the harrowing testimonies she heard as member of the Commission for the Investigation of Nazi Crimes, places Jewish and non-Jewish stories side by side without comment. At the same time, the ethnic identity of each voice, in her spare, seemingly neutral and nearly unbearable vignettes, is clear; the character of Jewish suffering remarked. This is also true in films such as *The Last Stage,* an account of life in the women's barracks at Auschwitz, made on the site of the camp by two women filmmakers (one of them Jewish, the other most probably not) who had been its inmates. *Last Stage* was made in 1948 and already shows marks of a Sovietizing style and of Communist censorship; but while the heroic figures in the narrative are mostly Communists, there is a tacit acknowledgment in the film that most of those slated for extermination were Jews.

Later, there were other novels, films, poems, and plays, by both Jewish and non-Jewish artists, some of them marked by deep guilt, others by an absurdist nihilism. One need only think of the fiercely bitter stories in *This Way to the Gas, Ladies and Gentlemen* by Tadeusz Borowski (a non-Jewish Pole who was interned in Auschwitz and committed suicide several years after the war), with their uncompromising depictions of life and death in Auschwitz, the belief-defying brutalities and the struggles among the inmates for a piece of bread and an inch up in the camp's ghastly hierarchy. ("The first duty of Auschwitzers is to make clear just what a camp is," Borowski was to write later. "But let them not forget that the reader will unfailingly ask: But how did it happen that you survived? . . . Tell, then, how you bought places in the hospital, easy posts, how you shoved the 'Moslems' [prisoners who had lost the will to live] into the oven, how you bought women, men. . . . Tell about the daily life of the camp, about the hierarchy of fear, about the loneliness of every man.") In retrospect, it seems possible that the struggle to find forms through which to confront the hydra heads of atrocity, to give artistic expression to images and stories from which one wants to, needs to, avert one's mind and eyes, came earlier in Poland than elsewhere. The atrocity, after all, took place right there.

And so the Holocaust was not denied, but it was not yet disentangled from other events, not yet framed as the central horror of the war, a separate category of crime against humanity and a result, above all, of annihilationist anti-Semitism. After

1948, and the consolidation of Communist power, everything changed. The fate of the Jews during the war, and even the existence of a distinct Jewish identity, became taboo subjects in Poland. So did many other issues, including the activities of the non-Communist resistance movement. The reign of repression and censorship had begun, condemning Polish society to a double life of public lies and whispered but doubly cherished truths.

Whatever the vicissitudes of various countries' histories, the chronology of response everywhere seemed to follow a similar pattern. The Holocaust, in the war's immediate aftermath, was not denied or fended off. The world was shocked by the first revelations of the concentration camps. It is perhaps a testimony to our inability to disconnect ourselves from other human beings entirely that some members of the liberating armies who had come upon the concentration camps unawares were affected for life, sometimes to the point of mental disturbance, by what they found there. Photographs, whose power to horrify had not yet been diluted by multiple exposure, were published in widely read magazines. But the expressions of revulsion and horror, although they often took language to its simple limits—to the vocabulary of monstrosity, inhumanity, evil—rarely mentioned the Jews: Concentration camps were seen as a manifestation of Nazi barbarity rather than, specifically, of anti-Semitism.

None of this did I know. I only knew, in my childhood years, that there had been the war. Even so, I sensed something of the distinction between the two kinds of catastrophe. I sensed it in the tone of people's speech, the tenor of the Jewish stories and how they differed from the Polish ones. Jewish speech about "that time" expressed a deeper woundedness, deeper hiding.

The war of the Germans against the Poles was openly acknowledged, even if the Polish politics of that time was, in the public version, distorted. But the non-Communist resistance, while officially banned from memory and discourse, was the kind of secret about which one talked among intimates with proud defiance. The neighbor in our building who had fought in the underground army spoke about it in lowered tones and allusive phrases; but he spoke through gritted teeth with a fervor of fury and pride. I sensed, on the other hand, that what happened to my parents and their Jewish friends was a more obscure matter, the kind of secret one wraps in a cocoon of silence, or protects as one protects an injury.

.   .   .

A consciousness of war, in its most extreme and cruel manifestations, seemed to come with the first stirrings of consciousness itself. And yet I had no direct experience of extremity or collective violence. It was many years before I saw a person close to me die, and more than fifty years before I experienced a historical upheaval *in medias res*.

The paradoxes of indirect knowledge haunt many of us who came after. The formative events of the twentieth century have crucially informed our biographies and psyches, threatening sometimes to overshadow and overwhelm our own lives. But we did not see them, suffer through them, experience their impact directly. Our relationship to them has been defined by our very "post-ness," and by the powerful but mediated forms of knowledge that have followed from it.

It is perhaps simply this that defines us as "the second generation." But while the postwar generation, which is a chronological entity, was here from year zero, the second generation, a more complex concept, did not make its appearance till much later. I first heard the term in the early 1980s, when it was just coming into common usage, over dinner in a restaurant in the middle reaches of Manhattan's Upper West Side. I was speaking to a man of about my age whose family, it emerged in the course of our conversation, also had a Holocaust history. A very different kind from my parents' stories: His mother was one of the few participants in the Warsaw Ghetto uprising to emerge from that particular inferno alive. It was perhaps significant that, although I had talked to my dinner companion on several previous occasions, I did not have an inkling of this part of his biography. We were not yet in a period when one particularly brought up such subjects, or when such a family past was thought to be a mark of interest or distinction. It was in connection with these matters, however, that my acquaintance described a meeting he had attended shortly before of a group consisting of children of survivors, or what he called the "second generation."

I still remember the slight recoil of displeasure on hearing this not very felicitous phrase, especially in a setting so remote from everything the concept implied. How did we, the comfortable children of those who lived through the horror, suddenly become a sociological phenomenon? Was this just another American affectation, a group "identity" conveniently invented at the very moment when everybody was beginning to insist on having one? At the same time, I could not deny that I felt a surge of recognition, curiosity, even excitement. I had mostly thought about the post-Holocaust strand of my biography in solitude, and as something purely private, or at least personal. Indeed, I had hardly identified it as a category of selfhood or experience. But now that it had been so identified, I could quickly see that it could constitute an element of commonality with others.

There are so many ways to conceive of our lives, our identities, our stories—to shape memory and biography. It did not occur to me to think of myself as a "child of Holocaust survivors" for many of my adult years. Other threads of causality, influence, development seemed more important; or at least, I gave them other names. I think this was true for many of us who grew up in post-Holocaust families and for whom this legacy seemed on the one hand simply normal, and on the other, better not dwelt upon.

Identities are malleable and multidimensional, and I am reluctant to fix my own through reifying labels. And yet, we do not only define ourselves; we are also defined by our circumstances, culture, the perceptions of others and—perhaps most of all—the force of an internalized past. However much I wanted to keep the Holocaust history in the shadows, there was no countenancing its presence in my life. I am congenitally not a joiner of groups; but the phrase "second generation" provided a sort of illumination, and a sort of relief. The phrase suggested that there were others for whom a Holocaust inheritance was both meaningful and problematic; that living with it was a palpable enough experience to be overtly recognizable; that it *was* in fact an experience; and that, in some way, it counted.

A certain skepticism still seems to me in order. What kind of grouping is the "second generation," and what is the basis of its claim to coherence? Is it a sociological phenomenon or an existential one, a collectivity or a *mentalité*? If a "generation" is defined by shared historical experience and certain attitudes or beliefs that follow from it, then the "second generation" is surely a very tenuous instance of it. We have grown up, in the postwar Jewish dispersion, in different countries and cultures, under very different circumstances and within different political systems. There have been no great events or public milestones to mark our own histories. The defining event we have in common belongs not to our allotted time on this planet, but to our prehistory.

There's the rub, and the crux of the problem. It is all too easy for us to feel as a consequence that we do not have our own history, that we are secondary not only chronologically but, so to speak, ontologically. And yet, as a growing body of research, literature, and personal testimony makes clear, the "second generation" does constitute a recognizable entity. Perhaps the character of this grouping can best be defined (to use a term borrowed from a certain idea of the nation) as an "imagined community"—that is, a community based not so much on geography or circumstance as on sets of meanings, symbols, and even literary fictions that it has in common and that enable its members to recognize and converse with each other with a sense of mutual belonging. We of the "second generation" do recognize each other across boundaries and languages, and we do have symbolic reference points we can touch on as on common scrolls. The Event that preceded us was fundamental enough to constitute an overwhelming given and a life task. The reference points through which we communicate and recognize each other have to do with our location in the dark topography of the Shoah and with the stages of a long and difficult reckoning—with our parents' past and its deep impact on us; with our obligations to that past, and the conclusions we can derive from it for the present.

II

FROM FABLE TO PSYCHE

The reckoning with the cargo of knowledge carried within the Holocaust legacy has come in different modalities of understanding: psychological, moral, religious, philosophical. For those of us born, as it were, into that legacy, for many children of survivors, the Holocaust, initially, seemed so absolute as to serve for a fable of origins and world-shaping mythos. But it is important to remember: We grew up not with the Holocaust, but with its aftermath; or rather, with that aftermath as it was lived in our parents' psyches. Our first consciousness of the Shoah was transmitted to us through the immediacies and intimacies of the family and through means that were bodily, palpable, densely affective. The first set of meanings to be extricated from our legacy is inevitably personal, subjective, psychological.

How, then, are we to understand those earliest meanings, the contents of what was passed on? At first, it was not rational interpretation, or information, or anything like memories; for even if survivors could recollect their stained spots of time precisely, such things cannot be passed on like some psychogenetic endowment. The attic in my imagination, to give only the most concrete example, probably bore no resemblance to the actual attic in which my parents were hidden. In fact, I had almost no information to go on, nothing that would allow me to put together a real attic in my mind. But what I did sense, as my mother talked about it, was the huddled hiding; the despair, the fear, my father's alertness to danger, my mother's deep resignation. Those were among the molecular elements of my early world, as they were for so many of my background and generation.

In other words, what we children received, with great directness, were the emotional *sequelae* of our elders' experiences, the acid-etched traces of what they had endured. This, perhaps, is always the way in which one generation's legacy is actually passed on to the next—through the imprint of personal and historical experiences as these are traced on individual psyches and sensibilities. But in the aftermath of the Shoah, the traces left on the survivors' psyches were not so much thoughts or images as scars and wounds. The legacy they passed on was not a processed, mastered past, but the splintered signs of acute suffering, of grief and loss.

Such things, in our contemporary parlance, have come to be called trauma. "Trauma" is the contemporary master term in the psychology of suffering, the chief way we understand the personal aftermath of atrocity and abuse. The survivors of such events, we take it for granted, have been traumatized; and Holocaust survivors are the chief exemplars of such damage. "Trauma" is our culture's way of extricating one set of meanings from the Holocaust legacy, and from genocide. But it was not always so, and it is worth pausing to ponder the history of this influential idea and what it may tell us about the conditions of extreme violence and its survival.

Technically, "trauma" means "wound," and in its psychological sense, it is defined as "an emotional shock that creates substantial and lasting damage to the development of the individual" *(Webster's II New College Dictionary)*. But in the first decades after the war, neither the term nor the concept had entered the wider, nonmedical vocabulary, and there was no general awareness that certain kinds of extreme abuse and violence—the violence of genocide, for example—might have an impact that lasts beyond its occasion or wrench the psyche of its target out of its customary position and perceptions.

Neither were the psychiatric or therapeutic professions initially interested in survivors' psychic predicaments. It was only in the mid–1950s, when survivors in large numbers began undergoing psychiatric interviews as part of application procedures for reparation payments, that evidence began to surface and some kind of realization began to dawn: The Holocaust had left internal as well as external traces in its trail. Even so, the realization was slow and reluctant. Those psychiatrists who made a connection between survivors' symptoms and the Shoah were, astonishingly enough, astonished by this discovery. After all, it was several years later; the survivors were the ones who were lucky, and many of them were beginning to rebuild their lives in seemingly successful ways. Other therapeutic workers refused to make the connection at all, or to validate the legitimacy of survivors' claims to reparations. Instead, they ascribed their interviewees' disturbances to constitutional weaknesses or predispositions to "anxiety" and stress.

This almost willful denial of the obvious was in part a function of the period's psychological dogma, which attributed all affective disturbances to early childhood experiences. Adult experiences—even if they were the Holocaust—were not supposed to produce equally deep, psyche-altering effects. In retrospect, however, the disavowal of evidence seems all the more peculiar, since the concept of trauma had not gone undiscovered or undescribed in psychiatric and psychoanalytic theory. The identification of such a condition, initially named "shell-shock," was first made during the First World War, when otherwise brave and diligent soldiers began manifesting unaccountable symptoms of persistent panic, hysterical paralysis, and disabling nightmares. The first attempts to understand such states in psychological terms rather than as signs of contemptible weakness or cowardice, and therefore to treat their symptoms sympathetically rather than through harsh disciplinary measures, were undertaken almost simultaneously in the later stages of the First World War by a number of medical and psychiatric observers, including, most notably, Sigmund Freud and the Scottish doctor W.H.R. Rivers.

One might have thought, then, that the understanding established during the First World War would have been immediately applied, at least by the therapeutic professions, to Holocaust survivors. But the awareness of trauma seems at various times to surface and then subside until it is rediscovered with the next bout of violence and the next wave of sufferers. Perhaps the very idea of trauma, in its strong form, is too disturbing to keep consistently in mind. Or perhaps profound psychic damage is simply not easy to recognize unless one is attuned to its inner workings. Because this is the thing about trauma: Most often, it doesn't show. A traumatized person may look fine, act socially plausible and take care to dress well. A traumatized person is not overtly maimed, or overtly mad. It is only in the family, or among intimates, that the intimate symptoms of psychic injury are evident—and there they are usually understood as modes of behavior, or features of personality, rather than as symptoms of disturbance.

But perhaps, also, the failure of the early psychiatrists to discern deep damage in survivors had to do with political as well as psychological preconceptions, and with the general inability, in those early stages, to distinguish the Holocaust from other aspects of the war, or to differentiate the impact of soldierly battle from the effects of genocidal violence. In the First World War, "shell-shock" was noticed because it was the regular combatants who suffered from its symptoms. After the Second World War, more confusingly, it was civilians, and Jewish civilians at that, who were exhibiting signs of psychic shock. The framework for understanding what had happened to the Holocaust's few surviving remnants may have been simply missing.

Altogether, while we have studied the individual psychology of trauma intensively, we still do not perhaps understand enough about its collective etiology, the external causes that produce it on a large scale. Why do certain kinds of war breed massive trauma and others do not? What are the specific agents in conditions of collective violence, of deep psychic damage? It may seem indecent even to ask such questions, or to look for nuances among modalities of violence. And yet, the questions need to be asked if we are to think about actual forms of human behavior—including war—and about our moral and emotional responses to them. Indeed, the attempt to make distinctions, however troubling, may help us understand something quite important about the relationship between the meanings of human actions—moral, ideological, metaphysical—and their psychic impact.

Anyway, those are the kinds of questions that haunt us in the wake of the Holocaust, that we have to address if we are to distinguish between "just" and "unjust" war, or between war and genocide. They are questions I find absorbing, or necessary, partly because they arise from that early knowledge, even if all war's brutishness is the first thing that needs to be declared. It is interesting, for example, that, in contrast to the First World War, there seemed to be relatively little trauma reported among combatants who fought in the Second World War. This cannot be attributed to differences in physical damage. Even aside from the enormous casualty figures, the Second World War caused untold amounts of injury and physical misery. Why then, were the soldiers on the whole not "traumatized"—why did they not develop neurotic or hysterical symptoms? Is that because they knew what they were fighting for—and against? Did the structure of meanings within which the conflict took place serve to countervail psychic dissolution? Did the soldiers' conviction that they were fighting in a good cause provide emotional aim and orientation? Given that we do not have enough studies of such matters, one can only speculate; but it may well be that, in the midst of war's horrors, having an understanding of the reasons for one's sacrifice and a belief in the justness of one's actions can help keep the mind intact even as the body is shrapneled.

Unfortunately for our moral sense, there is no guarantee that such driving beliefs are necessarily right or based on noble principles. On the contrary, they may be misguided or malignant—

or at least absolutely incompatible with other people's beliefs. The Taliban fighters who tortured people so ruthlessly in Afghanistan believed more ardently than most modern soldiers in the rightness of their cause. That is a proviso that sticks in the craw. And yet, there is no way around it: Conviction helps maintain a sense of dignity and selfhood in the face of adversity, no matter whether it springs from idealistic or destructive sources.

Sudhir Kakar, an Indian psychoanalyst who has tried to study the psychological as well as sociological structure of the violent Muslim-Hindu riots, discovered that fanaticism—even if it is driven by hatred for the Other—is not an indication of a psychotic, or even a neurotic, personality structure. On the contrary, Kakar found that the leaders of those riots, "killers on behalf of their communities," were stable men with considerable self-discipline and self-respect. But then, fanaticism creates emotional conditions that are the opposite of inner conflict. Dogmatic certainty means, among other things, that you know right from wrong, and that whatever wrongness is felt to exist in the world can be expelled from one's own self and projected safely and guiltlessly outwards onto other beliefs, or persons, or tribes. And such clarity of position can, in turn, create a certain internal stability and strength, even if it is not based on sweetness or light of reason.

Perhaps, to translate this into affective terms, it may be surmised that the structure of belief, no matter what its content, may provide a sort of psychic containment for the unruliness of emotional life, for the difficult feelings of helplessness on the one hand, and rage on the other. If this is true, if the moral and ideological framing of action is crucial for psychic resilience, then one can understand why the First World War would have been much more "traumatizing" than the subsequent, larger cataclysm. The First World War was, morally and politically, a much more ambiguous affair, with lines of hostility and causes of violence much less clear. Germany was the aggressor on that occasion, as on the later one, but its ideology at that point was not radically different from the ethos of nations on the Allied side. The enemy was not yet the unequivocally hated, or unambiguously hateful, foe. Initially, the announcement of war induced collective euphoria throughout Europe that seemed to be not so much ideological as strangely Dionysian. But as the fighting took its soul-shattering course, as tidal waves of death submerged combatants struggling literally over inches of ground, the enthusiasm was succeeded by skepticism and a sense of futility. The episodes of British and German soldiers ceasing hostilities for Christmas and coming out of their trenches to sing carols together may have had a certain wistful beauty. But then to have to crawl back into the trenches and kill the very people with whom you have just raised your voices on a snowy night must have produced sensations of extreme confusion and even despair. The distinctions between right and wrong, goodness and badness, must have been ground to a miasma of disillusionment and mental chaos.

But the physical conditions of battle in the First World War were also of a psychologically crushing character. The conditions of trench warfare resembled the circumstances of Holocaust victims more closely than those of ordinary combat. The trenches, for those caught in their imprisoning spaces, were an inferno of claustrophobia and paralysis, and they must have created, in addition to physical horrors, a sense of terrible impotence. Is impotence in the face of horror the traumatic element in trauma? Is it the loss of agency that makes for the crushing of personality, for that deep shame—no matter how irrational—that seems to affect so many survivors of atrocities? After the Great War, many of the soldiers fell silent; many of their near and dear preferred not to listen. There are moving portraits, in English literature, of young men returned from their hell into the normal world and finding that the war had created an invisible, unbridgeable barrier between the two, that they had traveled into regions from which no tales could be brought back and that had condemned them to speechlessness and solitude— that icy isolation which, in the aftermath of violence, is both a feature of deep suffering and an agent of its increase.

War is always utterly deplorable, and the suffering it causes always incalculable. And yet that suffering can come in different valences, different affective tonalities. For all the enormous losses that non-Jewish Poles incurred in the Second World War, and for all the intense cult of memory in that country, the war there is remembered as tragedy rather than trauma. It is interesting in this respect that there is no non-Jewish "second generation" in Poland; that is, no group that conceives of itself as the inheritors of the war's psychological—rather than historical—legacy. But perhaps tragic suffering is more resolvable than the traumatic kind. For tragedy, of course, involves a conflict— agon—between opposing principles and agents. Trauma is produced by persecution of subjects to whom all agency and principle have been denied. Tragic struggle may entail moral agony, but it leaves the sense of identity and dignity intact. Violent abuse can lead to a deeper penetration and fragmentation of the psychic cells, of the victim's self and soul.

The difference between tragedy and trauma is what I think I

heard in the different tonalities of Polish and Jewish speech after the war. For, although this could not be immediately grasped
either by survivors or the witnesses and observers, there is no
question in retrospect that the Holocaust was different from
other aspects of that most cataclysmic of wars, not only in the
number of its victims but in the specific kind of suffering it inflicted and—just as important—intended to inflict.

In her fascinating book *Blood Rites: Origins and History of the
Passions of War*, Barbara Ehrenreich argues that the terrible ap-
peal of war is connected with its ancient, ritualistic origins, and
with the fact that battle summons not only our worst but also
our best passions—the instinct of self-sacrifice, fraternal bond-
ing, altruism. It may be revealing, in connection with this, that
the Latin word for war, *bellum,* comes from the same root as
bellus, or beautiful. But there are no elements of terrible beauty
in genocide, no self-sacrifice in the name of an ideal, nor an ennobling struggle for competing principles. In the unhappy ty-
pology of large-scale violence, genocide is the most uniquely
unredeemed and dehumanizing, so radically repugnant as to tax
the powers of language and of thought. It is the most extreme
form of what Primo Levi called "gratuitous violence"—that is,
violence directed not to the ends of battle or of victory but
purely to the identity and existence of the targeted group. Such
aggression is driven not by self-interest or even greed for power
but by the gratuitous and nihilistic desire to destroy the personhood as well as the lives of a community or tribe, to negate a
group's ethos, tradition, cultural subjectivity. That is why projects of genocide, along the way to extermination, are accompanied by seemingly extraneous and sometimes even costly
practices of sadism and humiliation.

Sadism and humiliation: Those were the distinctive horror marks of the Holocaust. The extravaganzas of cruelty that characterized Nazi behavior towards Jews; the bouts of brutal mockery and loutish laughter that accompanied the free-for-all massacres in Eastern European villages—those, as much as the phantasmagoric statistics of death, gave the Nazi project of annihilation its uniquely grotesque character. The possibility of such behavior leaves a contaminating stain on all our perceptions, on our very idea of human nature. It is no wonder that historians of the second generation, such as Daniel Goldhagen, feel the need to examine the sources of such phenomena yet again, to attempt, at least, to fathom their sources.

There is no injustice like that of racial war. There is no collapse of meaning like that of genocide. But it is yet an added injustice and one of the most maddening ironies of gratuitous violence that not only its physical harm but its symbolic contamination is transferred from the abuser to the abused; that while the perpetrators go on to have a good supper after their day's work, the victims have been in that moment injected with a poison whose infection may last a lifetime. By now, we have come to know that among the most painful elements poured so venomously into the victim's soul is precisely the sense of humiliation—not for having done anything but for having submitted to degrading treatment. The shell-shocked soldiers of the First World War often felt bitterly ashamed of their supposed cowardice and weakness. But the victims of the Holocaust had been forced into a greater passivity, subjected to deeper violations. They were not, after all, engaged in a war, and most of them were not in a position to fight in any way. They were assaulted not for reasons of state, or as enemy combatants, but simply because of who they were. There is no framing of *that* in any meaningful structure, and there was mostly no meaningful action through which they could respond. In order to survive outside concentration camps, they could only hide in attics or under the earth, in peasants' fields or, in the luckiest cases, in locked-up rooms of other people's apartments. They could leap between floorboards of a cattle-car train onto the tracks and run for the nearest forest; or pass through sewers under ghetto walls to the "other side." Again, if they were very lucky and assimilated or acculturated enough to "pass" for gentiles, they could live through the war on "Aryan papers," in which case they had a "good" war, hounded only by fear of discovery rather than by physical torments and indignities.

We have a topography of survival by now, a nearly complete mosaic of collective Holocaust narration. We know the map and the means through which people made it to the end of the war. We also have our readings of the narratives, and we have often tried to convert the torments into heroism, humiliation into a kind of moral grandeur. And, indeed, there was often fearlessness entailed in finding the ways and strategies of survival, or a desperate recklessness, or sheer vitality. There was sometimes shrewdness, a strong orientation to reality, or even wisdom. It took enormous resourcefulness to procure false papers, and strong nerves to enact an assumed identity. It took a kind of incandescent decisiveness to gamble all and make that leap from a moving train. It must have taken—but here, I stop; for I don't know what it took—not to lose the will to live entirely in a concentration camp.

So yes: Sometimes—perhaps often—survival was more than a matter of accident or luck. There was courage in the decision to endure. And yet, the sense of humiliation that followed from its circumstances cannot be quite wished away by our respectful ideas, and it certainly could not be so easily dispelled within survivors' psyches. Sometimes, in order to survive, one had to shed one's humanity for a while, to forget it, put it on hold. There were, in almost every case, details of experience that could not be easily recounted or faced in one's own mind.

I once saw a documentary film in which an elderly Jewish man demonstrated how he and seven others had survived. For eighteen months they were hidden in a primitive ground cavity, dug for this purpose by a Polish peasant in his field. The cavity was under a pigsty, and it held all of them only if they lay side by side without moving. The man lay down on the grassy spot where the hiding place had once been, stiffly, his arms aligned to his body. This is how they lay each day, for eighteen months, he said. In the night, they clawed an opening in the earth above and climbed out to get the food that the peasant brought to them, to stretch and relieve themselves. Then they burrowed back into the hole and squeezed themselves in side by side before covering the aperture above them. I confess that as I looked at the man demonstrating his position, lying stiffly on the ground, I wondered what made this game worth the candle; why he and the seven others would have wished to go on. The paralysis of this situation, the abjection of turning into an underground animal, seemed to me too unbearable, too dehumanizing, to be tolerated. I kept remembering, as I watched the documentary, one of my mother's refrains that had threaded through my childhood, spoken in her wondering, skeptical voice, before I could really understand what she meant: "People just wanted to survive, to live. . . . To live at all costs. Why?

What's so wonderful about this life? And yet, people wanted to live."

Such are the second generation's guilty questions. And if I can ask them—if I can feel a shadow of disapproval; if I want to avert my eyes from the image of eight people squeezed together in the dark under the earth—then what about others, those who had little understanding of that time and who never had to come close to such indignities? Injury, weakness, vulnerability are delicate matters. The first, old instinct is to hide them, to lick our wounds in privacy and in the dark. And it may be that the primitive response to the psychic injury of others is condemnation, or pitying condescension. It takes considerable powers of understanding, or a belief in one's own power, to overcome such atavistic reactions or instincts. When Lyndon B. Johnson famously lifted his shirt to expose his stomach scars, he was exhibiting the potency of his role and a supreme narcissism: Even my scars are lovable, he seemed to be saying—or, in any case, you are obliged to love them. The very fact that I can afford to show them to you demonstrates my power over you and how much reserve force I've got; how exposed I can appear without losing that power.

But those were not the kinds of scars the survivors wore, and they did not feel that their status was going to be enhanced by admission of radical vulnerability. Aside from shame, there was the fear—and the reality—of stigma. The survivors may have spoken of what they had endured among themselves. But among strangers who had not lived through similar things and might not credit those who had, among those who, even if they did credit the stories, might misunderstand or were almost certain to do so, the survivors kept silent. They passed for normal.

This was before the culture of confession, after all; and the environments most survivors came from certainly did not believe in the healthful benefits of telling all or, indeed, in parting the curtains of one's windows too wide.

But even aside from the danger of being misunderstood by others, there was the difficulty, for survivors, of grasping the full extent of what happened to them. The experiences they had lived through were extremely hard to process, to assimilate into a dignified image of themselves; the feelings that followed often too wrenching or too overwhelming for routine acknowledgment. There were in every case things that were hard to make sense of, to bring to the lucid scrutiny of one's own mind, much less to the public light of day. The unspeakable and the unimaginable—those words nowadays so automatically applied to the Shoah—may have initially had to do as much with the literal inadmissibility and inexpressibility of the survivors' anguish as with the nature of the events themselves.

.   .   .

If we do not sufficiently understand the psychological impact of different kinds of war, neither do we have enough cross-cultural studies of reactions to violence. And yet, it seems evident that cultural systems of meaning affect forms of inner pain even as they inform and shape other aspects of emotional life. This may very well extend to suffering of quite an extreme kind. Systematic evidence is hard to come by in this area, but here and there, impressionistic observation or "thick description" can give us revealing glimpses of various systems of response and meaning. For example, in her sensitive and astute book *Night of*

Stone: Death and Memory in Russia, the British historian Catherine Merridale observes with some wonder that the Russians, who have lived for most of the twentieth century with tidal waves of persecutions, famines, Gulag camps, torture, and organized state murder, stalwartly deny any notion of deep psychic damage eventuating from this history. Of course, it is possible that this is simply a semantic misunderstanding and that the terminology of trauma, or neurosis, is foreign to Russian culture in the first place. (Judging by the impishly sardonic views on such matters found in writers ranging from Vladimir Nabokov to Joseph Brodsky, it seems there is something about the psychoanalytic conception of self that strikes the Russian sensibility as either trivial or just comic.) It is also possible that the problem of cultural translation extends itself even further, to behavior as well as vocabulary, and that Russian survivors of terrible events may suffer something we would recognize as trauma were we to examine it closely, but that they express their underlying states in terms or symptoms different from those with which we are familiar—for example, in widespread alcoholism.

But it may also be that the Russians are simply reporting something that is true to their condition. If that is so, then what they are saying should be of great interest to us, for it brings up quite fundamental questions. Why does suffering remain at the level of painful but bearable human experience in some circumstances and turn into something more corrosive and psychologically disabling in others? In the Russian case, could the losses and persecutions be borne because there is a cultural tradition, so to speak, of suffering, an honorable place for it in the complex of moral values, an understanding that it is part of the human condition and man's fate? Catherine Merridale reports that many of her interlocutors, recounting life stories that make the story of Job pale by comparison, speak of the events that have accrued to them precisely in terms of fate, and with a sort of acceptance.

Possibly, if our mental lives are so structured as to accept the power of external circumstances as fate, then perhaps the extra bite of insult added to the injury of persecution, the sense of violation and failure for having to submit to the will of others, is lessened. And, if we perceive pain as an ingredient of the human condition and believe that its action in our lives enlarges rather than diminishes us, then we can perhaps experience through it a strengthening of our own humanity, and of solidarity with the humanity of others. It helps to have Dostoevsky in one's repertory of literary and philosophical references.

It may also have mattered that the Russians went through their national story of Job together. The survivors of the Second World War and of the mind-boggling hardships endured in the sieges of Stalingrad and Leningrad could take pride in having defended their motherland in what was called the Patriotic War. As for the Stalinist persecutions, they were, especially in the early phases, so pervasive that they could perhaps be perceived not as a personal assault on anyone's individuality but as a kind of political fate. There may have been great fear, but there was no dishonor in being Stalin's victim. And it may be that suffering shared, suffering respected, is suffering endurable. Suffering that is misunderstood or dishonored can turn on the self in unendurable pain.

Another, perhaps opposite enigma in the nature of cultural response to atrocity was posed by a group of Cambodian women who had migrated to California after escaping the ravages of the Khmer Rouge and Pol Pot regimes. Through a coincidental correlation of medical data, it was found that about 150 of the refugees, all of whom had lived through truly Holocaustal horrors, suffered from psychosomatic blindness. Their eyes were physiologically functional, but nevertheless they could not see. These were, for the most part, simple women who did not have access to psychological vocabulary and who did not talk about themselves easily. But from the stories they told, it was clear why they might have wanted to stop seeing. What they had witnessed would have made anyone discouraged from looking at the world again.

Still, the doctors, and later the psychiatrists and psychotherapists to whom some of them were sent, found the women's symptoms hard to classify. Were they suffering from hysterical blindness? Surely not, if hysteria is a late and displaced expression of an early, unconscious memory. Were they neurotic, or psychotic? Surely not, if these mental disturbances contain elements of illusion or a distorted perception of reality. These women's blindness did not arise from a skewed vision of the world; on the contrary, it was a symbolically apposite, one could say an appropriate, reaction to their experiences. Their inability to see, it made sense to suppose, was an expression of what we would call traumatic distress. But why did the distress take this form? Was the specific symptom of blindness culturally configured? Why did it not strike Holocaust survivors, who had witnessed horrors of similar magnitude?

But if trauma and its symptoms may be circumstantially or culturally configured, suffering is surely the transcultural bottom line. There is no culture in which people agree to be the objects of cruelty and persecution—although those may be variously defined, and may begin at a different threshold; and there is no culture in which being the target of brutality and injustice does not cause great pain.

It may be that "trauma" is simply our psychological culture's name for extreme suffering, derived from our way of deciphering the self. In recent decades, it has been primarily the language of depth psychology (rather than religion, say, or ethics), through which we have come to interpret the affective aftermath of atrocity. After the initial hiatus, the psychotherapeutic professions undertook the treatment and study of Holocaust survivors on a considerable scale. This does not mean that therapy was the salve of choice for everybody. To many survivors, the very idea of "the talking cure" was as foreign as it might be to the villagers of Cambodia or Rwanda, and they would have considered the whole business of baring your soul to a paid stranger simply an added humiliation on top of all the others they had undergone.

Nor did the majority of survivors think of themselves as "traumatized" or emotionally damaged in unusual ways. Even if the concept had been abroad early on, I doubt that many would have seen it as applying to them. My parents knew they had suffered terrible things, but so had others. They even knew that what they had gone through was much worse than their non-Jewish neighbors; but they did not know that pain could be parsed in different ways. I think this was true of most survivors. Most of them were not psychologically savvy people. They did not come from a psychologically savvy generation, or from psychologically savvy subcultures. The language of depth psychology comes up rarely in survivors' memoirs. Of course, the writers of such memoirs recognize that they were targets of vicious persecution and that they had lived through events on the edges of bearable experience. But few of them engage in probing self-examination, or delve into the inner conflicts or unconscious convolutions that might have followed as a result. Suffering is suffering, no matter how howlingly extreme. It is something you live with; take on; suffer.

And so, many survivors, perhaps most, remained innocent of therapy, and suspicious of it. But for some, therapeutic help made a difference between pain unbearable and bearable. Over the years, particularly in Israel and North America, enough survivors assayed various forms of the "talking cure" to provide hundreds, or maybe thousands, of case studies. By now, the body of psychiatric and psychoanalytic literature that has accumulated on the subject is vast and provides some of the most subtle and elaborated insights we have into survivors' inner lives.

The nature of those insights is not easy to generalize or summarize; but it can be safely stated that the material brought by survivors into their therapies was often excruciating to a degree unfamiliar even to most laborers in the fields of psychic distress; and that the process of unpacking that material, or "working it through," was found to be arduous to an unusual degree. One particularly striking case study (to choose arbitrarily from the many available) is offered by Dinora Pines, a British psychoanalyst who has written movingly about working with Holocaust survivors and their children. Pines tells the story of a patient whom she calls Mrs. M., and who as an adolescent was deported to Auschwitz with her mother and sister. In the concentration camp, Mrs. M. experienced states of extreme hopelessness and psychic death, induced not only by the conditions of that inverted world but also by one horribly charged moment—an encounter, when she first entered Auschwitz, with a handsome man called Dr. Mengele. In that moment, Mrs. M. felt jealous chagrin because Dr. Mengele "chose" her mother and sister for a "select" group from which the young girl was excluded. Her jealousy might have been normal in any other situation; but the group, as she found out all too soon, was slated for Mengele's grotesque medical experiments, in which Mrs. M.'s mother and sister were horribly tortured before their deaths.

Mrs. M.'s entire subsequent development was distorted by the horrible convergence of eroticism with perverted cruelty, which constituted her initiation into sexual feeling as well as into mass death. In her therapeutic work, this patient often reverted to the states of psychic death she had experienced at Auschwitz, and to an intolerable sense of guilt for the moment of attraction to the man who became her mother's and sister's murderer. But she also had to contend with surges of sadistic and cruel feelings—a kind of vengeful eroticism directed via other men at the awful figure of Dr. Mengele. It was only many years after emerging from Auschwitz that she was able to confront these feelings fully, and it was only then that she could come alive enough to mourn her family and her own losses.

The details—the acid-etched details!—of survivors' experiences were, of course, in each case unique, and it is only through a microscopic scrutiny of those details that the acid can be to some extent dissolved. Mrs. M.'s is one story among thousands. Still, certain features of psychic life recur from case to case. Depression, anxiety, psychic numbing, panic attacks. And further, or below these, burning rage and corrosive guilt, an inadmissible shame and a mourning so encompassing that it could surely have no "resolution" within a single lifetime.

Perhaps it could be said, metaphorically, that trauma is suffering in excess of what the psyche can absorb, a suffering that twists the soul until it can no longer straighten itself out, and so piercingly sharp that it fragments the wholeness of the self. Pain at this degree has the ability to arrest time—to freeze it at the moment of violence or threat. The unyielding potency of traumatic memories derives from their all too vivid now-ness. There is plentiful testimony to this. In a sense, such memories are not memories at all, since their content has not been relegated to the past. Indeed, it is the darkness of the past that relegates the present to a dim background. In waking hours or in dream, the moment of horror keeps flooding into the harmless ordinary day. The fear felt so legitimately during the time of atrocity becomes unaccountably attached to mundane interactions taking place in ordinary time. The images of humiliation and physical pain repeating in the mind infect or drown out perceptions of the more benign reality of the normal, peacetime world. The fury at having been persecuted may burst out suddenly in behavior that strikes others as perplexing or unwarranted.

This is another thing about survivors: They are often difficult people, and are found to be so by others. This should come as no surprise in people so extravagantly more sinned against than sinning. But in depth therapy, the causes of difficulty cannot be taken for granted—or at least, they have to be addressed on many levels if the symptoms are not to be left intact. In almost all survivors' therapies, links had to be made, laboriously and sometimes very painfully, between the ways in which people reacted to extremity, and their earlier character, personality, psychic formation. Some have had to face earlier tendencies to passivity, for example, which hampered their ability to react, or act. Others must confront excessive selfishness, or narcissism, which led them to think only, or above all, of themselves. In her analysis, Mrs. M. had to confront unflinchingly her earlier jealousy of her sibling and her desire to be her father's favorite, reawakened so unacceptably by the monstrous Dr. Mengele. This is clearly soul-wrenching material, and it seems that the analyst in this case could not fully maintain her professional composure and detachment. During one session, she cried. It seems also that this was a transformative moment for Mrs. M., whose own unyielding harshness towards herself began to thaw in the salve of another's compassion, so that she could begin to mourn and move on.

.   .   .

Sometime in the 1990s, shortly after both my parents' deaths, I stared at their reparations certificates, containing reports from the psychiatrists who had examined them in the early 1960s, as part of the legal reparations procedure. The reports stated flatly and curtly that my mother and father had, with some variation between the two, suffered from anxiety, depression, attacks of panic, and recurrent nightmares.

All those years later, it was my turn to be taken aback. I had not thought my parents' distress was overt enough to be so clearly visible to a stranger, or that it could be categorized in such bold and standard terms. All those years later, the diagnostic vocabulary fixed their specific personalities into something like a syndrome: It placed them in a framework of a huge historical phenomenon and at the same time reduced them to oddly narrow, or at least impersonal, formulae.

My surprise might itself seem surprising, after everything I had seen and learned, after I had listened throughout my childhood to the minutest nuance of my parents' sighs and speech. But the truth is that clinical insight and vocabulary are neither easily translatable into "ordinary" perceptions, nor, perhaps, "appropriate" outside therapeutic settings. Family knowledge is different from professional knowledge; family relationships offer forms of involvement that, for better and worse, follow principles different from the professional contract of therapy. No matter how psychologically savvy we ourselves became, those of us who lived near survivors did not, perhaps could not, perceive them through the filters of diagnostic concepts or psychoanalytic theory.

The experience—close, phenomenological observation of intimacy; the systematic, theoretical postulates of therapy: These are themselves different modalities of understanding, of intuiting something about another's subjectivity and a victim's pain. In retrospect, it seemed to me that I knew both more and less than the psychiatrists who were initially astonished to discover that they were dealing with deeply scarred people, or even the psychotherapists who later treated survivors. I knew more because I was a close witness to my parents' pain, to the nightmares and rheumatism that were the legacy of their years in hiding, to the sadness and mourning. But I could not begin to grasp the tortuous complexities of the sadness, or inquire into its unconscious causes. I could only stay near the sadness and accompany my parents to some extent within it. I could—at whatever cost to myself—receive it as if it were my own. In a more mature vein, I could speak to my parents about "that" time in ordinary, daily language, and offer them sympathy that

was directed quite precisely at them—the persons I knew—
rather than a congeries of symptoms or sociological abstrac-
tions. Moreover, like others who have lived close to survivors,
and perhaps more vividly than the therapists who worked with
them, I knew that my parents' sadness, although salient, was
only a part of their temperamental texture; and that loss, although central, did not entirely define their lives. I knew that
for all their classic manifestations of posttraumatic stress, they
were often cheerful, amused, and enterprising, that they relished
small foibles of human behavior, despite having witnessed its
eye-opening extremes. To me, they were not "survivors"; they
were only people who had undergone extremity and were now
living another stage of their lives. Their very human condition
did not appear to me as a condition, nor did it seem susceptible
to being parsed into diagnostic categories.

Both kinds of knowledge—the personal and the professional,
the involved and the detached—are useful and salutary. Both
comprise important kinds of recognition; and recognition is the
salutary balm most needed by those who have been targets of
brutality and injustice. It is also perhaps the only redress we can
offer to the victims of great wrongs. Once such wrongs have
been committed, they cannot be undone. The past cannot be
healed or cured. But full and exact acknowledgment—of what
happened, of the wrongs inflicted, of the suffering that continues to wind in the soul—can act as a form of affective, symbolic
justice. It can, crucially, serve to restore for the victim a world of
shared meanings and common assumptions after such a world
has been willfully shattered.

The empathy that arises from being directly affected by others' pain, from taking it in and participating in it, can lessen the

burden of that pain. But it seems that certain kinds of understanding, and of healing, can best be achieved (at least within our cultural framework) in the intimate-impersonal setting of therapy. It is in that setting, after all, that difficult disclosures can be made with the sense of safety provided by confidentiality, and with the security of knowing that the listener will neither reject nor be undone by the revelations. And it is in that setting that the difficult chemistry of the soul can be decoded into its constituent and perhaps more manageable elements.

Even if I could shed tears for my parents, even if I sometimes retreated into my room so as not to distress them further by my distress on their behalf, there were certain kinds of investigation and perception I could not bring to their condition, and it was perhaps only decent I should not. I could not, for example, presume to delve into the half-hidden feelings I sometimes glimpsed in my mother's anguished mourning for her younger sister (jealousy, something like condescension, as well as guilt). Such feelings would have been perfectly normal in an ordinary sibling relationship; but given the way my mother's sister died, they could not be casually exposed. I could not insist on breaking my father's silence. I could only listen to what they were willing to tell me, and absorb its pain. Perhaps, by a kind of inverse homeopathic magic—for I could only take from them a minute dose of what they felt—this alleviated their anguish a little. I hope so. But I could do no more.

.   .   .

Many survivors' children, perhaps most notably the French writer Nadine Fresco, have testified to their strange inability, sometimes persisting even into adult lives, to put together the fragments of their elders' stories, to put together basic facts, or even to grasp them as facts. It was as if information about the Holocaust, or what we could make of it, was too transfixing, too overwhelming, initially, to the ratiocinative capacities, as it induced a kind of trance.

In a context far removed from the Holocaust, Sudhir Kakar, the Indian psychoanalyst, in a book called *The Colors of Violence,* has described his reactions to the family stories he had heard as a child of the sweeping and violent riots accompanying the Indian partition: "It is only now," he writes, "that I can reflect more composedly, even tranquilly, to give a psychological gloss to the stories of the riots. At the time I heard them, their fearful images coursed unimpeded through my mind and reverberated wildly with their narrators' flushes of emotion. There was a frantic tone to the stories, an underlying hysteria I felt as a child but could only name as an adult. After all, my uncles, aunts and cousins had not yet recovered from the trauma of what had befallen them."

The turbulence of survivors' states, the images coursing through the children's minds: In the aftermath of violence, these are intimately interconnected. Reflection, decoding, the psychological gloss—these do not come till much later. But, if we turn the lens on the recipients of those states—the children— then we can see in retrospect that their first imaginings, like their elders' anarchic emotions, held a complex burden of information and emotional meanings. What were those meanings, and how does the passage of such significances, or emotional substances, take place when it happens between soul and soul, mind and mind?

About this, on one level we know quite a bit; or at least can describe much. But much still remains mysterious. What we do know is that we affect each other in ways that are both immediate and invisible, that mental states are communicated, indeed transferred, from one psyche to another not only through rational messages but along unconscious, or at least nonconscious, channels.

In a sense, the possibility of such communications is a hopeful fact of human nature, for clearly we are connected to each other more profoundly and more palpably than we often care to acknowledge. But the hopeful fact has its unhappy side, for pathology and despair can be passed on as efficiently as more salubrious states. There were bonds and transactions between survivor parents and their children that sometimes took lifetimes to unravel. There was a casting of a shadow, a transference of an immensely heavy burden. There were signals conveyed along subterranean passages from survivors to their descendants that injected anxiety into the latter's veins, or exploded like time-delayed bombs in their psyches long after they had been planted.

Where the damage to the parents has been severe enough, such communications, or processes, have come to be referred to as "the transmission of trauma," or, alternatively, "transmission of traumatic memory." As with "trauma," or "second generation" itself, I half balk at the phrases and their implicit reification of tenuous, intricate, and, yes, rich internal experiences. For much of my life, I would have dismissed the underlying notion as well, and with considerable impatience. For who, after all, wants to think of oneself as traumatized by one's very parentage, as having drunk victimhood, so to speak, with one's mother's milk?

And yet, the phrases do refer to real phenomena. For of course, the conditions of survivors' lives, their psychic states and scars, could not but affect or infect those around them, their children most of all. There was a passage of something, by some means. If we cannot yet say exactly what or how, nevertheless, the questions raised by transmission of trauma are an extreme version of more general questions about the transmission of any family legacy. How can the sequelae of catastrophe be passed on across generations? Or, more generally, what features of our parents' personalities enter us and make their deep impact? How do they become preserved or transformed within us, converted into liberating visions, or twisted into paralyzing knots? It is possible that, just as Freud used the study of neurosis to illuminate the structure of the normal psyche, so the close examination of the intergenerational passage of acute psychological states may throw light on more general or "normal" processes through which affective messages are communicated from one psyche to another, and from one generation to the next.

Clearly, the strongest form of such transmission is the earliest. When the passage of subjective states happens between the mind of the adult and the delicate, hyper-receptive psyche of a child, the effects can be profound and formative. Psychoanalysis has long been interested in the inward workings of such transactions. But in recent decades, experimental psychology, and, increasingly, the "harder" sciences of biology and neurology, have undertaken close studies of mothers and infants, and have observed how maternal states are conveyed to the child through body, gesture, ways of holding, gaze. The British psychoanalyst D. W. Winnicott has described how a child's chaotic, inchoate inner states are shaped or left to founder by parental "containment" or its absence. If the mother, or parental figure, can provide some calm, some framing for the confusions of childish sensations, then the child may become calmer, more stable, more confident. If such containment is missing, then internal confusion continues to reign.

Undoubtedly, there were good, bad, and middling mothers and fathers among survivors of the Holocaust. Undoubtedly, most of them meant well—maybe desperately well. And undoubtedly, some of them failed in providing for their children the foundations that happier families may furnish. We may surmise, on that most primal level, that some of the mothers, having undergone so much loss, clung too closely, too insistently to their infants—clung to them for dear life. Others, it seems, were too numbed or too afraid to make much physical contact with their children at all. Afraid, perhaps, of new losses; afraid to pass on what was now inside. Whatever their best desires or intentions, whatever the precise methods of communication, the emotions carried by survivors were often of a radical acuteness, and they were conveyed to their offspring very directly. Judith Kestenberg, a psychoanalyst who was one of the pioneers in second-generation studies, speaks not so much of transmission as of a "transposition" of psychic states. In another formulation, George Halasz, an Australian psychiatrist who is also a child of survivors, describes subtle cycles, or loops, in which maternal states of absence or inner "exile" lead to withdrawals from the infant and the present, in turn driving the child to withdraw in confusion and retreat into his own exile.

What was the impact of such states on the children's psyches? As with survivors themselves, the psychoanalytic literature on the second generation is large. So is the literature, in this instance, of self-investigative testimony. The children of survivors, in contrast to their parents, did belong to a psychologically oriented generation, and have mostly lived in psychologically oriented cultures. Many of them have gone into various kinds of therapy in later lives; a surprising number have entered therapeutic professions themselves. The psychoanalytic literature for this subject is large and often poignantly informative. As with survivors, each case and story is of course different, but there are leitmotifs that recur with sufficient regularity to suggest patterns of feeling, and of family relations.

Over and over again, in second-generation literature, testimony is given to a helpless, automatic identification with parental feelings and their burden of intense despondency. Over and over, the children speak of being permeated by sensations of panic and deadliness, of shame and guilt. And, accompanying the suffusion by parental unhappiness, or absence, there is the need—indeed, the imperative—to perform impossible psychic tasks: to replace dead relatives, or children who have perished; to heal and repair the parents; above all, to rescue the parents. To rescue the parents, and keep rescuing them from their grief and mourning, from death, which has so nearly engulfed them and which has undone so many. To keep undoing the past, again and again. A more than Penelope-like devotion, a more than Sisyphean labor; for this boulder not only keeps rolling down the hill, it can never be rolled up in the first place. A more than Orphic danger, for to look back in this case is to be dragged into Hades yourself. And yet, the children keep trying, are compelled to keep trying: For how can you leave your parents in a state of half-death, how can you not try to bring them out of an inferno?

And the parents so often hoped for rescue. They invested so much in these children, and imbued them with so much yearning. To replace—revive—the dead ones; to undo the losses; to repair the humiliations wrought by the abusers; to provide the redress of unconditional love and protection against deadly danger. There were hopes, no matter how unconscious, that the children could relive all that the parents had lived; and, at the same time, that they could start new and much happier lives.

Unconscious expectations are often paradoxical; the transactions between survivor parents and their progeny sometimes seem nearly magical. Dina Wardi, an Israeli psychotherapist who has worked extensively with groups of second-generation adults, suggests, in her book *Memorial Candles,* that in every survivor's family, one child is chosen as a "memorial candle"— that is, as the instrument of commemoration, devotion, and mourning. Once such a symbolic role is conferred on them, the children rarely have the wherewithal to refuse it. They become votaries on the altar of the Shoah, their own lives and selves dedicated to their hurt parents and to the perished, whether they would or not. In Wardi's groups, the adult "children of survivors" recount, without sentimentality and often with a kind of wonder, dreams that feature scenes and sites of death. The patients discover their deep identification with the parents, but also with lost relatives whom they never knew. Often, those are the very relatives for whom they are named—for almost all of them, it turns out, were named for someone who was murdered. (I think of the moment, at the age of six, when I was told I was named for my two murdered grandmothers; my sister, for my mother's sister. I did not have even the most shadowy images of these grandmothers, nor a sense that I had lost something with their deaths. But I remember my parents' tender sadness as they told me this, and a sense of a somber, though honorific, mantle being draped round my shoulders.)

Sometimes, the identification with the dead has the character of the uncanny. I think, for example, of a young woman, described by Dinora Pines, who came from a newly prospering family of survivors, but who felt compelled to search trash bins for scraps of food at night. It turned out that a perished aunt of hers—whose story she may or may not have literally heard—had been forced to do just that, in another country, in another time. I think of the many case studies that report strange somatic symptoms, especially eczemas and rashes, for the skin is apparently a highly sensitive register of unconscious anxiety. Sometimes, it is precisely the children who express parental fears in these ways, while the parents remain seemingly calm and unbothered; for the adults, in some cases, may have enough wherewithal to "contain" or conceal their worst anxieties, even as the children sense them under or on the skin.

There is a strange fascination in such phenomena, perhaps because we still do not understand sufficiently how they happen, how the mind, or the unconscious, takes in scraps of moods, or psychic states, or half-heard information, and converts them back into eerily apt symbolism. The process can give the impression of an almost literal haunting, a notion that recurs often in writing about the intergenerational transmission of trauma. Something reemerges from the past that we thought had been dead . . . but that has lain dormant in the turrets and caverns of the soul till it returns in the form of specters and shadows.

Such manifestations belong to the world of ghost stories and

the gothic—psychologically speaking, a world of fantasy and inner distortion. For in the second generation, the anxieties, the
symptoms, no matter how genuine in themselves, no longer
correspond to actual experience or external realities. They do
not even correspond to anything that can be called "memory."
In that sense, the guilt, fears, and shames, the mourning and ac-
cidie of survivors' progeny *are* a kind of distortion or exaggeration. And yet, at the same time, this is exactly the crux of the
second generation's difficulty: that it has inherited not experience, but its shadows. The uncanny, in Freud's formulation, is
the sensation of something that is both very alien and deeply
familiar, something that only the unconscious knows. If so,
then the second generation has grown up with the uncanny.
And sometimes, it needs to be said, wrestling with shadows can
be more frightening, or more confusing, than struggling with
solid realities. Like Hamlet's father, the ghosts demand devotion, sacrifice, justice, truth, vengeance.

All too often, the living parents themselves have demanded
vindication and redress. Wardi divides survivor parents into
"fighters" and "victims"—that is, those who took some responsibility for their fate during their ordeals and those who were
forced into a more complete passivity. The "fighters" often
seemed to cope better afterwards, to be enterprising and even
reckless themselves, and to ask from their children a fearless sto-
icism and great achievements. This was sometimes called "not
letting Hitler win," and though the phrase has become something of a stale joke, it is quite telling. Often, the parents
wanted the children to achieve a victory over Hitler.

But of course, no Jewish person was entirely in charge of his
fate during the Shoah, and almost no one escaped great losses. I

think of my father, a fighter if there ever was one, with his intolerance of all frailty, his unreasonable demands of my sister and myself, and his cocoon of fundamental silence. I suppose he was cocooned in silence even in his rages. For he raged and exploded, scattering rancor at those nearest to him. And yet, I felt immense pity for him even then, instead of the anger and resentment with which I could have, perhaps should have, rightfully responded. Somehow, the worm of sorrow worked itself through his silence, as it had worked itself through my mother's speech, and that was what I discerned at the heart of the fury.

Other descendants of survivors speak of an even deeper silence, of homes in which nothing ever happened; of parents sitting vacantly or sleeping; of childhoods spent almost entirely inside those dimmed interiors—for how can you leave parents who are that helpless, that hopeless, in order to consort with your peers? Yet others remember homes in which a façade of forced activity and a willful, artificial de-problematization—a denial of all longings, conflicts, difficulties—camouflaged a flight from all feeling, an emotional anesthesia. Friends tell me about households in which one had to be cheerful, happy, and successful all the time lest what was hidden was allowed a chink through which to surface.

Impossible attachments, impossible enmeshments. If the elements of parental attitudes in these cases are difficult to decode, the ingredients of the children's feelings are even more so. The bonds in survivors' families were often obscure; much about them was not easily admitted. The prohibition on open disclosure, on touching through speech painful or shaming matters, was one of the things that was passed on—or rather included—in the Holocaust legacy. But spoken or not, there was almost always the reparative urge on the children's part, an urge to help, a shared mourning. At the same time, many remember, or later excavate, an intense anger for being yoked to the parents' grief and expectations; for the stifling—through survivors' own desolation—of the ordinary pleasures and carelessness of childhood.

But there were less admirable, less admissible feelings still. There was disdain as well as sympathy for parental vulnerability—for when all is said and done, children and the young want their parents strong. And there was sometimes—to escalate the order of emotional difficulty—contempt for the known or suspected humiliations the parents had suffered, for what they had been subjected to, or forced to do.

Perhaps most paradoxically, there was often, and along with everything else (for the logic of psychological life is more topological than Euclidean), an element of envy. Significance envy, one might call it. Envy has been one of the taboos, or at least untouched areas of second-generation experience, perhaps because it is so hard to fit into any credible scheme of human perception. For how can you envy someone for having gone through hell? But this, too, has to be acknowledged: that aside from its enormity, the Holocaust had enormousness, and that the enormousness was awe inspiring as well as awful. The sojourn in hell and the drama of survival conferred on these parents a kind of existential grandeur that no ordinary experience could match. To have lived through the Shoah was to have faced the ultimate, naked questions of existence, and to have come through.

Moreover, the survivors, for understandable reasons, tended to remember, or at least to recount, those episodes of their wartime years that encapsulated the sense of greatest tension and danger, the seconds when lives hung in the balance and acts of superhuman courage or ingenuity were required for survival. (I remember talking with my sister, when we were in our twenties: "Isn't it amazing what they had done by the time they were our age," my sister said, referring to our parents with admiration—and yes, a kind of wondrous envy. By comparison, we were hardly adults or had anything that counted as adult lives.)

Envy and, with a kind of logical inevitability, a sense of being secondary. The overwhelming power, the incontrovertible significance of survivors' histories—the epics and the odysseys—instilled in many of their children (this is a staple of second-generation testimony) a dogged sense of their own insignificance, a conviction that the ordinary problems and incidents of their own lives could not possibly matter, that their small hurts and fears were so trivial as to be hardly worth mentioning, or indeed feeling.

"You can't know what fear is . . . what hunger is . . . what pain is . . . unless you were there." Such phrases are reported, sometimes bemusedly, sometimes resentfully, throughout second-generation narratives, and probably every child of survivors recognizes them. Such parental pronunciations may have been insensitive and even callous—the survivors did not always calibrate with exactness the effect of their utterances on their children's sensibilities. But the statements were also all too real, and the children, whatever simmers of rebellion they may have been nurturing, tended to accept them with lowered heads and a tacit sense of their own inadequacy, or banality. Their own experience could never measure up to the size and import of their parents' ordeals, to the looming power of the Holocaust. It simply counted for less. ("It's not the Holocaust," I would think in my adolescence as I met with some small but hurtful problem—an awkward social encounter, a summer job interview, a friend's rejection, a rebuke from a teacher.) Not the Holocaust: For many second-generation children, this could all too easily translate itself into a radical sense of their own triviality, smallness, nonpresence; a post-ness that was not only chronological but emotional and existential.

The consequences of this inheritance for later psychic development have also been explored quite extensively, and personal and psychoanalytic literature both point up recurrent patterns and syndromes, shadow imprints of survivors' own malaise: difficulties in forming relationships (for how can one risk genuine attachment if an awareness of deadly loss has preceded an awareness of growth and love, or has come potently mingled with it?); sexual complications deriving from a disturbing commingling of early, Oedipal impulses and the most extreme imagery of violence and death; a need to achieve and overachieve to compensate for parental losses, or sometimes just (in one's mind) in order to survive; a pervasive sense of guilt, no longer corresponding to any specific cause; a hampering insistence on perfectionism and impeccably correct behavior (if one wants to survive, one must make no mistakes!) accompanied by intense fear of punishment for unspecified transgressions; an exacerbated desire to repair all damage in the world, often joined with detonating anger at all manner of wrongs perceptible in that world; an underlying hopelessness about the possibility of achieving authentic satisfaction or happiness, accompanied by a strategic withdrawal from desire and need. As Anne Karpf, in her eloquent book *The War After,* suggests, it is better—starting from such a beleaguered psychic position—to protect oneself against the calamity of new dangers and losses by not wanting, by not feeling, anything at all.

Mind you, this is a catalogue of symptoms that might just be found in any number of groups if they were placed under similar scrutiny. Indeed, some studies of the "second generation" come to just this conclusion: that children of survivors do not suffer from any abnormalities in excess of the normal. Statistically, or observably, the distinctions between second-generation syndromes and the more general pathologies of everyday life do not show up large. For sometimes the vicissitudes of referred trauma can seem barely distinguishable from the more general manifestations of our time, or advanced postmodernity, or life itself. Which is perhaps why "trauma" has so often been used as a metaphor, or an explanation, for ordinary life, or at least ordinary unhappiness.

One should not reify the notion of "transmission" into an explanation writ in stone any more than one should reify trauma itself, or the "second generation" or the "identity" of survivors. And yet, there is no doubt that the intimate legacy of the Shoah was exceptionally dark, that the despair which enveloped so many survivors' families was often of the heaviest, most unrelenting kind. There is no doubt that the whiteness of melancholia also shrouded their offspring's souls, that the gnats of silent anxiety picked at their bodies, that the dead, even if unmentioned and unthought, were present.

The past works its way through the self in powerful and unexpected ways. Although cross-cultural observations of second generations are even less available than those of survivors, it may be that the concept of "transmission of trauma," like that of trauma itself, is our contemporary culture's way of accounting for the continued underground life of the past and the disappeared. Perhaps in some regions, people pursued by dead ancestors would be seen as literally rather than just metaphorically haunted, and would have some kind of exorcism performed on them. Or perhaps, like Maxine Hong Kingston's mother in *Memoirs of a Woman Warrior,* they would struggle with their visiting ghosts through the night in a physical battle and through sheer power of will till the shape-changing monsters are defeated.

It must be said, however, that, whatever its cultural specificity, a psychoanalytic system of explanation seems more obviously congruent with the experience of survivors' children than that of survivors. This is not only because the children are more psychologically minded and understand their own experience in subjective terms; but because their experience belongs to the realm of the psychological, the internal theater of body and mind, rather than to the stage of external events.

In his essay "Mourning and Melancholia," Freud makes the suggestive observation that in order to accomplish the natural process of mourning—to grieve and then move on—you have to know what you have lost. If you do not know what the lost object is, then mourning can turn into a permanent melancholia, or depression, as we would call it today. Freud, who to a large extent altered his theory as a result of witnessing the First World War, did not live to see the Second, and he may not have taken into account the kinds of losses from which it may be impossible to recover—losses, as after the Holocaust, not only of particular persons but of a people and a world. But his observation is particularly evocative for the second generation, whose

entire historical situation has placed it in the "melancholic" position, whose fate it has been to live with a multitude of lost
"objects" that they never had a chance to know. (I think of my
grandparents, whose visages I did not know even from photographs. Again and again, throughout my earlier years, I tried to
grasp that I could have had grandparents, and other relatives,
ought to have had them. That, in some notional way, I had *had*
grandparents who were taken away from me by murder. An incomprehensible loss, the uncanny by another name.) Transferred loss, more than transferred memory, is what children of
survivors inherit; and how do you get over loss that has no concrete shape or face? That way, placeless loss itself, a dimension-
less melancholia, may become the medium in which we live.

Specters *can* be harder to grasp, shadows to wrestle with,
than solid realities. But of course, specters can eventually be dispelled, as realities cannot. Many among the second generation
have gone on to free themselves of their Sisyphean burden.
Many have gone on to live lives free of ghosts. This is not the
same as forgetfulness—indeed, it seems that what is required for
such exorcism is almost the opposite of forgetting. Just as for
some survivors only full remembering could bring about some
catharsis, so for the second generation, only a full imaginative
confrontation with the past—however uncanny, however unknown—can bring the haunting to an end. In Wardi's accounts,
her patients have to encounter head-on not only their own difficult feelings about their parents but the images they have never
witnessed but most dread: scenes of brutality, betrayal, parental
helplessness, and—worst of all—humiliation. It is humiliation
that for them, as for survivors themselves, turns out to be the
most unbearable. Once they become capable of a deeper hon-

esty, many of these descendants of victims admit that what most
troubles the imagination are scenarios of parental indignity, the
possibility that the parents were forced into situations that undermined their integrity, or into acts that involved collusion
with the aggressor.

But whatever their own fears and shames, the children have
to walk up imaginatively to such scenarios (however real or fantasized they may be) in order to dissolve their power. They have
to imagine what they have lost after all, to encounter dead ancestors whom they never met, and regret their loss for themselves. For the children, as for the survivors, the emotional
wisdom is the same: Only the truth shall make you free. In order to get beyond the frightening psychic fable, they need to
face the realities of their inheritance *as* realities. Only then can
they go on to recognize that the awful events in whose spectral
grip they have lived belong to another time; that the past need
no longer live on within their psyches and bodies; that it is indeed the past. The recognition that the past *is* past is sometimes
a considerable psychic achievement. But the recognition is necessary if the descendants of the most awful of historical and familial events are to reclaim, or claim, their own existential
primacy and their lives.

III

FROM PSYCHE TO NARRATIVE

Such, then, were some of the psychic givens many of us came into, to be unwoven, processed, worked through—as is true of all psychic givens—throughout our lives, in deeply individual, often unspoken and invisible ways. Reflection, decoding, historical contextualization, came later. Sometimes much later. For the second generation, after all, the so-called latency period, when the Holocaust seemed to recede from public consciousness, coincided with our own, developmental latency—a period of reprieve, when the problems of one's own psychic past tend to be put on hold, or to go underground.

For me—but perhaps for others as well—there was one large additional factor that complicated dealings with the past and delayed a direct confrontation with the Holocaust inheritance: emigration.

The importance of emigration in the biographies of survivors and their children has been, to my mind, oddly underestimated. Perhaps that is because, in relation to the Holocaust, emigration seemed so much the lesser upheaval, a later, adventitious addition to the main story. The sometimes picaresque vicissitudes of uprooting can be seen as an essentially narrative element—something that just, or merely, happened. And indeed, emigration was a sort of accident of history, a turn of events or a twist of plot, rather than a direct consequence of the Holocaust. But in retrospect, we can see that the turn was taken by so many survivors, especially those from Eastern and Central Europe, and that the twist was so over-determined and determining as to make uprooting an almost intrinsic part of the Holocaust's aftermath.

In retrospect, we can also see the mass migrations of survivors in the context of the immediate postwar period and as part of the tectonic shifts in the world's geopolitical arrangements that followed the main earthquake. The largest Jewish migrations took place between 1945 and approximately 1950, in that uncertain interval that constitutes a largely forgotten prehistory of the postwar era and that is only now being reconstructed by historians and others. Europe after the war witnessed huge population movements of all kinds—mass expulsions and forced repatriations, waves of refugees and tides of fortune-seekers taking advantage of the time's instabilities and widespread lawlessness. Poland itself was in effect moved several hundred miles westward, with massive "repatriations" of Poles in the eastern territories and mass expulsions of Germans, or "Volksdeutsch," in the west, following as a result. My parents' own trek westward from the Ukraine was, as I realized much later, part of those larger migrations, and, in effect, their own first emigration.

The turbulence and the strange vitality of a continent in flux and on the move can be glimpsed in such postwar works as *The Truce,* Primo Levi's wonderfully vivid account of his long trek through Europe as he hustled to survive, having just survived Auschwitz.

Levi, as it happened, was making his way home to Italy; but most survivors, coming out of concentration camps or hiding, were making their treks in the opposite direction, driven for a variety of reasons to leave homes and homelands and seek refuge elsewhere. Some did not want to remain in places associated with their personal tragedies and with mass death. Others were forced to leave by the hostility of local populations, or the resurgence of aggressive and sometimes murderous anti-Semitism. Among those who found themselves in transit camps set up in Germany by the Allied armies, great numbers chose to take advantage of their Displaced Person (DP) status to leave behind their own ravaged regions and relocate to more promising realms. The most promising realm was, of course, North America, followed closely by that other New World—Australia. But many among the DPs chose, often with the encouragement of visiting representatives from Palestine and, soon after, Israel, to join in the great adventure of building a new state. One way or another, the majority of survivors eventually emigrated from the countries of their origin and found themselves in more or less—usually more—unfamiliar climes.

Emigration was, in most cases, the chosen or at least the preferable option, and it seemed, to many survivors, to hold the promise of a new beginning, of improved life conditions, of hope. Certainly, whatever the hardships of that uprooting, they did not compare to, and were indeed largely camouflaged by, the preceding ordeals. Perhaps that is also why the effects of the later event have gone relatively unnoticed, or at least unremarked, in literature about post-Holocaust lives. And yet, emigration is an enormous psychic upheaval under any circumstances. It involves great, wholesale losses: of one's familiar landscapes, friends, professional affiliations; but also of those less palpable but salient substances that constitute, to a large extent, one's psychic home—of language, a webwork of cultural habits, ties with the past. Perhaps even ties with the dead.

Even if it was overtly successful—as it often was—emigration almost always brought with it daily misunderstandings, a distressing diminishment of social mastery and, perhaps most painfully, increased isolation. We roughly know the history of response to those woebegone migrants in the various countries of their destination, the initial indifference that greeted them everywhere, the suspicion and covert contempt. In Israel—the place where survivors should have met with the most spontaneous, an almost familial empathy—they were seen instead as discomfiting illustrations of that old, Diasporic oppression that Israel was trying so hard to purge from the collective national psyche. In a state that was trying to create a "new man"—dynamic, hardy, resolute, able to till the soil and defend himself— the spectacle of woeful victimization was hardly destined to arouse sympathy. The survivors arriving on Israel's shores were suspected of passivity in the face of violence, and possibly worse. Ben Gurion privately thought that those who managed to survive the Holocaust constituted the worst "elements" in Jewish culture, that they were the ones given to corruption and immorality. He formed this opinion after learning about the conditions in the DP camps, where a kind of desperate carpe diem mentality prevailed. But why should decorous restraint be expected of people who had just returned from hell?

In America, even Jewish communities did not always offer

safe havens. Survivors were often met with a grudging welcome from relatives and prickly aloofness from others. One hears all too many stories of American uncles or cousins providing some reluctant minimum for their poor relations at the outset, and throwing out the troublesome guests as soon as possible. One hears of the hosts crudely comparing their own wartime hardships—food rationing, no sugar!—to what their European counterparts had been through. Undoubtedly, there was sheer ignorance as well as rank insensitivity in such behavior. Undoubtedly, many of the hosts were perplexed or even frightened by these disconcerting arrivals. Many years later, a candid acquaintance (an intellectual of some standing) burst out in conversation, "But you must understand! There were hordes of them! How could we know who they were, how could we know if they were to be trusted? They all had these awful stories, but how could we know whether to believe them?"

Well—one can almost understand. Nobody likes to be saddled with inconvenient, needy people, or to be disturbed in the course of daily life by true tales of infernal torment. No less a figure than Marguerite Duras describes, at the end of *The War: A Memoir,* her reaction of disgust and aversion as she watches the wasted body of her lover, recently returned from Buchenwald. The lover happens to be Robert Antelme, who went on to write *The Human Race,* one of the great meditations on the Holocaust. But Duras describes her reactions without any embarrassment, or recoil from herself. And if a person of her sensibility could be capable of such unexamined callousness, then perhaps one should not be too surprised by the callowness of others as they were suddenly confronted with burdensome relations and messengers of terrifying truths.

But for survivors, emerging from the wreckage of the war and hoping to find refuge and some warmth among their more privileged kin, the chilliness of receiving institutions, the coldness of relatives who were supposed to provide a cushioning of hospitality and basic security, were the unkindest cuts of all—unkindest because so unnecessary, where kindness might have been so easy.

It needs to be reiterated that many survivors rode over such difficulties with great panache and made successful adjustments to their new conditions, with or without the help of therapy. But for some of these already shaken refugees, the new rupture, with the new bruises and indignities added to the earlier, harsher ones, delivered a kind of psychic coup de grâce. It constituted what is sometimes rather awkwardly called "retraumatization"—a reopening, through a new blow, of older wounds and memories, a reawakening of pain that can exacerbate the original injuries, rendering them even harder, this time, to heal. Many survivors could not fend off depression, or even despair, brought on by new bouts of helplessness, by disorientation in the face of alien rules and surroundings, the loss of verbal competence, cultural savvy, basic bearings. A permanent sense of defeat seemed to beset some of the post-Holocaust emigrants I knew, no matter how brave and enterprising they were in facing their new circumstances.

Our own emigration came late—in 1959—and was as isolated as any. It happened between larger waves of Jewish migration and took us to Vancouver, Canada—a place then so distant from Cracow along any geographical or cultural coordinate that it might as well have been my native city's earthly antipode. The wealthy Jewish man who sponsored our move to Canada ejected us from his spacious house after three days to fend for ourselves as best we could in our new world, lest we become dependent on his good graces. But he, at least, was not a relative.

As for the more distant Canadians whom we encountered in our comings and goings, to them we must also have seemed to come from an antipodal planet. Insofar as it ever came up in conversations, the history we transported with us—for that cannot be left behind like inconvenient luggage—was a matter either of uneasy embarrassment or eyebrow-raising skepticism. I still remember my mother's acid tone as she reported an encounter with some Canadian acquaintance who had met her allusion to the basic facts of the Holocaust with polite incredulity. This reflected a new level of incomprehension, more fundamental than what my parents had found in Poland. There, they might have met with aggressive anti-Semitism; but no one would have doubted their accounts, or have been unduly surprised by them. There, such accounts were not tales from another planet. But in Canada they were. Indeed, even for the prewar Jewish immigrants, who had managed to get away *before*—the eras of emigration, mentioned always in lowered tones, had the condensed significance of short poems—the whole European catastrophe, the things that happened "over there," often remained remote and vague. One Jewish friend asked my mother, in confidence, whether the concentration camps really had been as bad as all that, or whether people were exaggerating. Soon, my parents, like most other survivors, ceased even to advert to such things except among the small group of Polish Jews who had found their way to Vancouver after the war.

Mind you, there were not many precincts of the globe in the 1950s where emigrants carrying the baggage of atrocity in their souls would have found a different welcome or more companionable understanding. This was the height of the "latency period," which seemed to come upon all regions of the world, as if on cue. After the initial responses of shock and recognition, the Holocaust ceased to be a subject of public discussion or much cultural attention. In Eastern Europe, this happened mainly through the mechanisms of censorship and political repression. But in the West and other parts of the "free world" as well, the early 1950s were a period of forgetfulness, though the reasons for this cultural development are more difficult to diagnose. In recent years, it has been suggested that the seeming suppression of concern was not simply coincident with the imposition of Soviet regimes in Eastern Europe but more causally related to it. Some commentators, most notably Peter Novick in *The Holocaust in American Life,* argue that Cold War policies affected public discourse about the Holocaust even within American Jewish communities. In an enormous U-turn, Germany suddenly became America's new democratic friend, while the Soviet Union was transmogrified from a wartime ally into the archenemy, the locus of totalitarianism, and the future "evil empire." Under the pressures of the new political climate, some Jewish institutions went so far as to draft explicit directives to their memberships, advising them that it was the better part of wisdom to put their hard feelings about Germany aside. It was suddenly not in anyone's interest to dwell on the vileness of the recent German regime.

That may be part of the story; but it is difficult to know what the broader "latency" consisted of—forgetting or more forceful denial, repression or simple indifference. Probably all of them, though it is possible that the shift from the first, horrified confrontation to a kind of deletion of the Shoah from the forefront of concern was also propelled by a natural, or at least understandable, impulse to turn away from the spectacle of carnage and towards the future. In Western Europe, this was a time of recovery and expansion; in the United States, of great optimism and economic boom. It might well have seemed to many citizens of the globe's more privileged zones that the world had at last become a better, safer, more civilized and progressive place; and that the atrocious devices of gas chambers and killing camps were an irrelevant atavism belonging to another, more primitive epoch. Surely, they did not belong to the second half of the twentieth century, to the yet-again modern, progressive world! So the Holocaust, the whole wretched, shameful, unspeakable business, went underground—except of course in the families of survivors, where its knowledge, however articulated or unexpressed, continued to percolate through everyone's psyche and the family systems.

All of this sharpened the incongruities and widened the gulfs of incomprehension between post-Holocaust emigrants and their new cultures—and, by further reverberation, between survivor parents and their children. From conversation with many of my peers, from various second-generation testimonies, I have learned that this was true even if the parental emigrations came early, and before the children's onset of consciousness; or even if, as was true probably in the majority of cases, the children were born in the countries of arrival. For, of course, the parents' perceived and real marginality, the cold spaces between the Holocaust families and their environments, affected the children as well as their elders—and affected the relations between them. The parents became a problem for the children—the kind of problem they might not have been had they stayed in their cultures of origin. The cultures of home and the outside world became not so much incompatible as non-compatible and non-congruent, pulling desire, perception, ego-ideals and aspirations in sharply different directions. This is a theme that comes up in any number of second-generation writings, from *The War After* by Anne Karpf, whose parents were refugees in England, to such memoirs as *Losing the Dead* by Lisa Appignanesi, whose emigration brought her family to France and Canada, or *All My Mothers and Fathers* by Michael Blumenthal; or the deeply felt novels by the Israeli writer David Grossman; or the informal reminiscences of European Jews who underwent the initiation into sabra life in Israel, or into the culture of positive thinking in North America in the 1950s and 1960s.

We are constructed by our contexts. Families that might have remained normal, or normally unhappy, had they stayed in their own worlds, become suspect or dysfunctional in their new ones. This is partly because of how they are read in their new surroundings. But the changes are also internal, for emigration confuses the patterns and sequences of family life, and the basic transactions and balances between the generations. Immigrant children assimilate into their new cultures faster and more easily than the parents. Sometimes, they gain a premature and anxiety-provoking authority, or advance more quickly than their elders, or leave their families behind, rejecting the "old ways," and causing, in those left behind, complex knots of admiration and resentment.

Such things are known from studies of emigration undertaken in many non-Holocaust contexts, and from the many accounts of second-generation lives—those vaster immigrant second generations. It is also known that transplantation from places of family origin makes it more difficult for the children to understand their parents, to know where they literally and figuratively come from, and therefore to make sense of their beliefs, habits, attitudes towards their offspring, their very personalities. For the post-Holocaust children, there was, in addition to the cultural incongruities, the gulf between past and present. The radical rupture in time created by the Holocaust removed survivor parents even more definitively than most emigrants from any intelligible social or cultural framework. Some of the attitudes, the mental traits, that the children growing up in America found so galling in their parents reflected not only personal quirks but the general values of the disappeared cultures and communities the elders came from. The disregard of privacy, the indifference to the advantages of individual freedom, the tribal closeness—such attitudes were natural to those Eastern European shtetls from which, perhaps, the majority of survivors hailed. The patriarchal or familial authoritarianism, the assumption that the elders have natural rights over the young and deserve their unquestioning respect, were characteristic of Central European Jewish milieus (and the non-Jewish bourgeois cultures as well). At the same time, an often fearful regard for hierarchy and figures of authority, the suspicion of "others," the secretiveness, the mistrust of the public sphere and its institutions—those were also shtetl traits, developed by the virtue of centuries' separateness from the surrounding world, and through that world's prejudices. But for the children growing up in their more optimistic and open climes, it was nearly impossible to intuit the character of the communities their parents came from, or where the parents had fit into the close-knit but hierarchical social fabric, or how unlikely it would have been for anyone living within those communities to knock on the door of a family member's room before entering. Even for those of us who had grown up at least near the parents' original culture, it was often difficult to unravel various threads of cause and effect. What, in my mother's timidity towards the larger, urban world, was the shtetl and what emigration? What of my father's anger was personality and what the Holocaust—and therefore, how much should I accept, tolerate, forgive?

What to forgive: Perhaps most centrally, among all the other problems, there was, for this particular second generation, the problem of reckoning with, accounting for, the dimensions and weight of parental victimization and pain. It is part of every generation's developmental trajectory to move from received ideas and sentiments to independent understanding, to evolve from childhood fantasies, excessive fears, and unrealistic hopes to a more considered apprehension of reality. But for children emerging from overwhelming histories, the negotiations with the past and the parents are particularly poignant and charged. Insofar as it requires a certain degree of separation from one's original family and a certain detachment from the previous generation's vision of the world, the trajectory towards maturation, for inheritors of catastrophic pasts, is often fraught and arduous. With the onset of consciousness, the internalized past begins to be understood, to some extent, as real; and for the post-Holocaust adolescents, the huge fact of the Shoah, the historical legitimacy, so to speak, of the parents' suffering and difficulties, upped the ante in all adolescent conflicts, including the conflicts between parental and peer cultures.

Moreover, as it happened, our post-Holocaust adolescence came just as the generation gap was being discovered, or invented, at a time when the governing principles of American adolescent culture in particular came to require a wholesale rejection of the adult, parental world. There was undoubtedly much to rebel against in middle-class, suburban 1950s United States—the stifling work ethic, the conformism of suburbia, the narrow frame of reference, and the routine bigotries. But for children of people who had emerged from *that* history, who had themselves been persecuted, rebellion was rarely a simple or insouciant matter. How to abandon parents who had been so abandoned, how to reject those who were already isolated? And how to explain to parents who were already disoriented the new rules obtaining in the New World, and one's own newly acquired rights to the pursuit of fun, if not yet adult happiness?

There was probably no gulf wider than that between the ethos of postwar youth culture in America and the mental world of most survivors. The tensions between what were in effect two human cultures often boomeranged right back into survivors' households, increasing frictions between the generations, the mutual incomprehension, reproaches, remorse. Survivors' homes were often stormy places. Some of the children found the disjunctions between parental demands and what they had come to understand as their inalienable rights and privileges too wrenching or too unacceptable. Some did rebel, with a thoroughness proportionate to their sense of oppression, lashing out against the parents and all they stood for, or abandoning homes in which shtetl closeness and the shadows of the Shoah came to seem too heavy, too constricting. Others kept shuttling between their two worlds, getting caught, or lost, in the disjunctions, the disparate sets of norms, gestures, mentalities, expectations.

Because our emigration came so late, I was unusual among children of survivors in having reached early adolescence in the country of origin, and in undergoing the quake of emigration quite consciously. I also went through it to a large extent with my parents. I understood all too well what they felt and thought in those first stages of dislocation, the thousand unnatural shocks they were undergoing. Indeed, emigration increased my protectiveness towards them—and, it seemed, their need for protection. They were, in the early stages of their uprooting, more vulnerable than they had been in Poland, their social situation more precarious. Like so many other immigrant children, I was called on to mediate between them and their surroundings. Sometimes, the reversal of roles was dramatic. There was, for example, the occasion I came to dub in my mind (probably to deflect its insult) "A Day in the Life of an Immigrant Family," when I was called on to serve in court as my mother's character witness. The incident that led up to this improbable occurrence involved one of those small Kafkaesque misunderstandings that plague immigrant lives. My mother had been accused of trying to take something from the local grocery shop and, a few months into our emigration, was incapable of explaining what actually happened. She was summoned to court. I was summoned as her sole witness. I was just fourteen. Courts, in the Communist Poland we had just left, were not places where you wanted to find yourself. As to the proceedings, I hardly understood them at all, not to speak of the legal system in whose workings I was so suddenly and so perplexingly participating. The very notion that I could vouch for my mother's character in such circumstances was disconcerting enough. Even more crushing was my sense that I had no idea how to do it.

The judge, luckily enough, seemed to understand something; my mother was cleared of the absurd charges. But what was most upsetting was my father's reaction when we came home that afternoon. He hadn't gone to the court with us; but the incident, for him, seemed to revive some sense of profound, baseline danger—surely dating from That Time, and now returning with a literally breathtaking power. He who had been so fearless was now stricken with fear—of deportation, prison, not ever being able to work again.

In retrospect, I see that the whole sorry episode may indeed have been, for my father, the specific moment of "retraumatization": a reversion to a time of radical helplessness. Whatever one calls it, the incident, so trivial in itself, seemed to trigger great alarms. Anxieties that had been hitherto suppressed or contained now broke through such scar tissue as my father had built up. But at the time, I could only see that my father, usually so strong and resourceful, was now reduced to a kind of panic. He was suddenly the one who seemed to need reassurance, and that in itself was a revolution in the order of things, a violation of family image, self-image, identity.

Nor was there any place where I could take such episodes or concerns, no holding place, so to speak, for the past that seemed to be returning so bafflingly from its repression. For my Canadian contemporaries, including most Jewish teenagers, the concerns would have seemed too peculiar, or embarrassing, for mention. The war, the Holocaust—such things were, to my new peers, simply not of interest, although lack of interest does not fully convey the extent of the general incuriosity. This was not yet the time of an interconnected globe; Europe was very far away, and Eastern Europe even farther; and I doubt that many high school teachers, in that phase of "latency," had talked to their students about that appalling part of the continent's twentieth-century history.

Not that I myself knew at that stage what I might have wanted to convey to my new friends on this forbidding subject. My parents' biographies were acquiring an overt reality; the horrors they had lived through were something to which I was beginning to bring conscious reflection. But the word "Holocaust" had not yet entered the language, and I did not have a grasp of the historical outlines, never mind the details, of the events that were soon thus designated. Nor did I wish to inflict burdensome instruction on others. Who wanted to be a prig, after all, perpetually talking about something awful that had happened far away, or "defending" one's elders against the misunderstandings or the indifference of one's peers? If I wanted to pass—or at least try to—for a regular, North American teenager, I had to pretend at least to shed some of my odd filial loyalties, some of my cumbersome sense of responsibility. And I did want to pass. I wanted my teenage fun, and my youth.

And so I stifled my unmentionable sympathies and pushed the past to some sequestered place so that it wouldn't slip out in public. It seems that others were doing the same. Much later, I learned that a boy whom I thought I had known well in my Vancouver years had parents who had also endured the Holocaust in Poland and lost many relatives. The boy was born in Canada and was in every perceptible way a regular Canadian teenager. I had met his parents and knew that they came from Poland at some vague earlier time; but the subject of their wartime history never came up between us. In a moment of candor, my friend confided in me how much he resented, or was embarrassed by, his parents' low status, which pursued them despite their newly gained prosperity. But I had no inkling of anything else—not of his mother's breakdowns, or illnesses, or other aspects of a troubled family life.

Neither did I confide anything to him about my family history. The lack of a wider framework for such matters would have made it hard to know how to talk about them; in fact, it rendered the broader subject nonexistent.

I do not want to exaggerate. The Holocaust was not on my mind most of the time, and the general indifference about its occurrence—its almost entire evacuation from wider consciousness—did not often give me pause, or seem politically suspect, or radicalize me in some pro-memory cause. For me, it was emigration itself that was the seismic quake, occluding the delayed reverberations from the greater cataclysm. Emigration, after all, happened to me, the losses it brought me were of things I had actually known.

And yet, the deeper past was one of the dimensions, the axes of meaning, along which alienation traveled. Perhaps oddly, I felt the absence of war in the atmosphere, in people's consciousness, as a kind of lack. This was a difference that carried with it layers of implication, for attitudes towards grief, loss, suffering—the very shape of human destiny. Even if I did not yet know the Holocaust as history, it was part of my psychic formation, my bones. It was also—no matter how obscurely, or darkly—a source of meaning. In a strange way, I used to value my parents' sadness, for it seemed to put me in touch with basic human experience. Now, the sadness and all it derived from became an encumbrance, an awkwardness, a vaguely unseemly imposition on the sanguine and sanitized atmosphere prevailing in North American suburbia. What meaning could my family's awful history have in this large, expansive, cheerful New World? And why should it intrude on my peers' ordinary, mundane activities and their well-justified optimism?

But the general silence on the subject, the lack of interest, meant that in many families, the secret past became even more of a secret, that the different kind of silence prevailing among survivors became reinforced, that the children, as they were growing up, were thrown into greater confusion and emotional isolation. The latency period burrowed right back into families and minds, reinforcing the psychology of suppression, delaying the reckoning with the past and its aftereffects.

If the parents felt they had to conceal the facts of their past, the children had to hide their identification with that past. And while superficially it might seem that this would force, or encourage, a quicker separation, the result of such denials can of course be just the opposite. In an ideal scenario, the early attachments resolve themselves through a gradual distancing from the parents, and a more considered balance between criticism and sympathy, attachment and autonomy. Instead, for many second-generation children, the conflicts grew acute and sometimes bitter, the contradictory imperatives making for sharper splits, the urge to protect clashing head-on with the need to protect oneself.

.   .   .

In "normal" adolescent development and drive to autonomy (at least as devised in recent decades in Western cultures), the rules and the aspirations are clear: The entire effort of the adolescent—an effort, moreover, congruent with the broader values of the cohort group and endorsed by the culture at large—is to get away, to gain maximum freedom, to start constructing, as soon as possible, an independent life.

But for children of people who have been vulnerable and persecuted, there is no such congruence between aspiration and emotional urge. The ideal of autonomy is undercut by claims of loyalty and compassion that cannot be easily dismissed or gainsaid. The need to stay acquires the force of an imperative; the need to get away becomes freighted with the risk of betrayal and perhaps justified guilt. Perhaps justified: There's the rub.

On one level, the quandaries involved in relations between survivor parents and second-generation children are affective and familial; but as the children reach fuller consciousness, and as their sympathetic capacities enlarge beyond their own needs, the conflicts acquire a moral valence. In its progress to adulthood, the second-generation story blends with the story of the larger postwar generation. College, marriage, children, professional life: How children of survivors negotiate such milestones is on the one hand in each case individual, on the other, not all that distinguishable from the experiences of their peers.

But if, for many children of survivors, relations with their parents have involved an internal agon of an intensity beyond the normal battles and conflicts, that is because in the aftermath of atrocity, the weight of history places tremendous pressure on personal story; the claims of historically legitimated suffering charge ordinary decisions with the force of ethical demand. What are the responsibilities of the young—on whom, through no fault of their own, part of the past's burden has fallen—to parents who have been victims of awful histories? What can be demanded of people who have been persecuted and wounded in their relations with others? What power does each hold, and what powerlessness?

The choices children of survivors have had to make have been, most often, not between rights and wrongs, but between equally legitimate claims and imperatives. And, as we know, it is conflicts between right and right that are the most wrenching and that sometimes, if the stakes and consequences are significant enough, earn the name of tragedy. And sometimes, the dilemmas arising out of the Holocaust legacy did lead to quiet personal tragedies of a kind. In the most extreme cases, the children, overwhelmed by the weight of their responsibility, subjugate their own needs to those of the parents, taking care of them, making their elders' continued survival their first task and mission, existing through them and for them in life-sapping reversals of normal parent-child scenarios, in self-renouncing submission. I have occasionally come across such poignant pairings, fathers and daughters, mothers and sons, in which the initial losses are perpetuated, however quietly, in a kind of continuing sacrifice.

Others, in an attempt to slay the dragon of excessive empathy, arm themselves with anger or cold detachment. They assert their own rights over those of their elders, no matter how hurtful the consequences. Or they develop disdain for their parents' vulnerability and contempt for weakness altogether. This, too, is an understandable human response—a self-preserving defense against the dangers of subjugation, even to the putatively powerless. And yet, this seemingly more liberating, or at least self-preserving, alternative does not come cost-free either. One cannot cut oneself off from an intimate spectacle of vulnerability or pain with impunity or without an eventual hardening of one's sympathetic arteries.

I suspect that, in our progress to adulthood, most children of survivors were caught on their private see-saws, oscillating between the demands of autonomy and attachment, self-sacrifice and self-interest. On every overt level, I left as completely as a person could (for Texas, New York, London; college, graduate school, professional life). And yet, like many, I kept coming back, literally and figuratively, sometimes descending into my parents' underworld. Not because I wanted to or chose to, exactly. Rationally, I knew that I could not succeed in bringing them out or relieving them of their memories, and that there was a risk of being dragged into the undertow of those memories myself. But not to come back at all, to declare myself aloof and unconcerned, would have required a cooler distance than I would have chosen. (Or perhaps than I was capable of. For it is worth noting, if only because such intricacies come up so often in more reflective second-generation conversations, that just as there are moral implications to impulses and desires, so there can be elements of unexamined emotion in ethical choices. It is possible [just for one example] that I exaggerated my parents' vulnerabilities, as did others with theirs; that there was a conversion of our own vulnerabilities, or even envy, into what the therapists would call "omnipotence"—an excessive conviction of one's efficacy and power. It is possible, in other words, that there were more questionable elements in the seemingly laudable sense of obligation, duty, need to rescue. But that, as the narrator of Fitzgerald's *The Great Gatsby* might have said, is finally only personal.)

Nor were the parents, in such scenarios, always perfectly self-knowing or perfectly considerate, or incapable of their own authoritarianism and mundane cruelties. Many second-generation memoirs testify to this. (For a particularly stark instance, read Michael Blumenthal's *All My Mothers and Fathers*, a tale of baby-swapping, rejection, and almost parodic stinginess visited by survivor parents on their affection-starved son.) Other survivors were not above resorting to a more or less conscious co-optation through history, to feeling, or suggesting, that their earlier sufferings entitled them to unquestioning self-sacrifice from their offspring. Partly, survivors were transporting habits of earlier life into new milieus; but sometimes, the demands from hurt parents to their supposedly stronger children can amount to a kind of psychic exploitation.

But even with the best all around intentions, the quandaries posed by relations between persecuted parents and their progeny are not ones that admit of easy resolution. Of course, in an ideal scenario, one would—one must—make distinctions between bonds and bondage, goodness and guilt, sympathy and symbiosis. But in intimacy, such fine distinctions are not easy to draw. In purely moral terms, the obligation of compassion, of extra altruism, for the second generation is genuine. But the obligation surely cannot extend to adding new deprivation to the earlier losses, or carrying selflessness to the point of self-abnegation.

In microcosm, such quandaries are an instance of an issue that has become central to our time: how to treat individual victims of persecution and groups that have been victimized by historical events. The private and the public realms are hardly commensurate, nor governed by the same principles; and yet, private knowledge can perhaps be instructive for broader attitudes as well. For what children of persecuted parents learn with great immediacy is that "victimhood" is neither an essential quality or condition nor a guarantee of moral purity. Even those greatly sinned against are capable of greatly sinning. Nor is it possible, or desirable, to reprieve even those who have been greatly persecuted from the normal responsibilities of life. In the realm of personal relations, to offer such reprieve is not an act of empathy but of condescension. I could not treat my parents exclusively as people who had been hurt—could not stop making ordinary demands of them, or react in anger when I was treated unfairly—without reducing them to powerlessness, or nonsignificance. As anyone who grew up in such families knows, survivors were rarely so diminished as to become quintessential "victims." Nor were they so purified as to become quintessentially virtuous. Aside from having suffered great losses, those who survived retained, or regained, reserves of strength, and also their ordinary personalities, their weaknesses, foibles, and abilities, their greater or lesser capacity for love. To reduce anyone to the rigid identity of "the persecuted," or to treat them as if they were incapable of sympathies and generosities of their own, would be to abandon them to their deadly realm in another way, to eject them from the networks and bonds of authentic and lively relationships.

In these complex relations, cultural dislocation further twisted the knots and confused, or dramatized, the terms in intergenerational conflicts and struggles. For me, emigration for a while masked the Holocaust strand of my history, and pushed many other concerns and aspects of identity into the background. En route from that first, fairy-tale knowledge to a more conscious confrontation with the Holocaust past, the attic of my parents' hiding for a while receded into the background, seemingly out of thought, out of mind. But it was there, it was there. Eventually, I would have to return to it via another route, and in another vein.

IV

FROM NARRATIVE TO MORALITY

The story of the second generation is, above all, a strong example of an internalized past, of the way in which atrocity literally reverberates through the minds and lives of subsequent generations. That is the way the story is usually told: as personal, affective, intricately psychological. But the Holocaust past, aside from being a profound personal legacy, is also a task. It demands something from us, an understanding that is larger than just ourselves, that moves beyond the private vicissitudes of the inner life. The second generation after every calamity is the hinge generation, in which the meanings of awful events can remain arrested and fixed at the point of trauma; or in which they can be transformed into new sets of relations with the world, and new understanding. How we interpret the implications of our primary narrative, how we translate psychic information into information about the world, matters for more than ourselves.

How such a transposition happens is always difficult to pinpoint. When did conscious confrontation with the Holocaust past begin to supplant simmering awareness? For a long time, those relations were subliminal; at some point, however, a kind of reckoning had to take place. Undoubtedly, the growing, or returning, cultural awareness of the Shoah (the books, films, widely watched television shows that began to appear with regularity in the 1970s) informed my own awareness and willingness to address this theme—for our understanding of ourselves always takes place in a context of broader understandings, and in a dialectic with them.

It must be said that I still do not think about the Holocaust every day. It is still not always the foreground problem in my mind, or the main parameter of my "identity." And yet, there is no doubt (as I think about it in retrospect) that much of my moral and intellectual development has been informed by the first knowledge I had come into. The issues that matter to me are often the ones that grow out of the war and the Holocaust; much of my elaborated vision of the world was forged from the bleakly dramatic post-Holocaust topography.

Clearly, one set of questions posed by atrocity is fundamentally moral in nature. Who did what to whom (the question that, some skeptical Eastern Europeans declare, points to the heart of all morality): how the evil was perpetrated and why; and further, the very nature of evil—and of good—are the first, and surely the most profound, problems that strike us in the aftermath of gratuitous violence. Indeed, at a time when moral categories, at a certain level of intellectual discourse, are generally seen as suspect or outmoded (no basic values, please!), the arena of collective violence—especially the violence of genocide—is the one place where our ethical instincts cannot be denied, and the moral response cannot be gainsaid.

The moral problems posed by the Holocaust have been the object of anguished inquiry ever since the event took place. In that respect, the chronology of second-generation response is different from that of the world at large, for moral awareness requires mature, or at least a maturing, consciousness. But of course, such awareness is not primarily a matter of chronology. A set of moral meanings is inevitably nested within the Holocaust legacy, especially for those of us who came into that legacy via intimate transmission. Indeed, it is part of the second-generation condition—but also its opportunity—that our inherited past brings with it such fundamental questions; and that, through our transactions with that past, we have to grapple with these quandaries not only notionally or in the abstract, but through close engagement, and in the smithy of the soul.

Any morality worth its name begins in passion, or at least in subjectivity; and, in order to become an ethics, it needs to be extricated, sometimes painfully, from the messy undergrowth of feeling and internal conflict. It also begins with specifics. That suffering was to be pitied; and that cruelty, or "the Germans," were to be hated: Those were the two germinal motifs of my own early morality, and insofar as I am a moral subject (as we all necessarily are), my views in this arena had to be forged out of, and tested against, these potent early notions. Our moral intuitions probably always begin with various kinds of human figures presented to our imagination, and in the case of the second generation, our moral education has begun with the most dramatic examples imaginable of "us" and "them," of persecutors and the persecuted.

The first part of that education, I believe, is constituted by the relations between children of survivors and their persecuted parents. The close witness of suffering, the intimate coexistence with those who have been hurt, is a great and perhaps not always an entirely "fair" challenge; but it is also part of that transformative process whereby that first, psychically imbibed knowledge is converted into a more conscious ethics and vision of the world.

If close encounters with victims are the first part of our ethical task, the other, contrapuntal challenge involves relations between descendants of survivors and those of the perpetrators; between ourselves and that most charged other—the other who has been the absolute enemy. The task of defining relations with real and figurative perpetrators is one that every second generation, coming out of every calamity, has to face; and if the task is so arduous, that is because it, too, revolves not only around abstract convictions but deep-seated feelings; because it often involves a conflict between the summons of our best ideas and the compelling pull of our first knowledge and primary, morally charged imagery.

.   .   .

The perpetrators. The Germans. All children of survivors have their odd and inchoate feelings on this subject, their anecdotes of first trips to Germany (a kind of loss of virginity, a crossing of a line), their accounts of contacts with young Germans and older Germans, their reactions to the German language. Some feel extra discomfort about being there (dogs in Germany mean something different from dogs elsewhere; efficiency has ominous connotations). Others discover an odd at-homeness (their parents spoke German at home, a few grew up in DP camps located in Germany). Simultaneously, there are very few members of the second-generation tribe who believe today's Germany should be blamed for Nazi crimes, or who would admit to anything as firm as a prejudice towards this country. Many have friends or professional contacts there, have met in groups or engaged in projects with second-generation Germans, follow German literature, love Berlin. Most aver a perfect friendliness towards contemporary Germany; but a perfect neutrality, in this generation, is still hard to achieve.

My first stay in Germany did not take place. In the summer of 1968, after I finished college, I made my first journey to Europe since leaving Poland—a standard student trip, with various countries visited at whirlwind speed, and various friends met in front of American Express offices in a succession of unfamiliar cities. It was during one leg of this journey, as I was traveling by train from Prague to Paris, where I had an appointment with a friend in front of just such an office, that I discovered the route I had taken required me to disembark and spend a night in Frankfurt. I quickly consulted with myself and found that I simply could not do it. It was not exactly fear, but something deeper that made a stop in a German city impossible: a sense of nearly absolute taboo. At the risk of losing track of my friend altogether and causing him considerable anxiety, I stayed on the train and went (as I recollect) to Amsterdam instead. I arrived in Paris some twenty-four hours late.

It was therefore not until some years later, well into my adult life, that I met my first German contemporary. The meeting took place at a house in Fiesole, a fragrant suburb of Florence that, as it happened, had once belonged to one of Thomas Mann's children and was now inhabited by American academics. The setting was, admittedly, evocative; but I don't think that is why I remember the encounter so vividly. It was odd, I suppose, that I had not come across any actual Germans before; but in America, in those less mobile years, such meetings did not occur often in the natural course of events. And so, although this is now difficult to reconstruct, until that meeting, I had only my frightening childhood specters, and the mediated iconography of literature and film, to serve for my conception of "the Germans." Now, here I was, over an ordinary dinner, face to face with the most fraught Other, the figure of my most troubled imaginings; and here he was, in the guise of an academic lawyer, a person I quickly recognized as someone of my generation and similar intellectual formation, someone for whom I might ordinarily feel an unforced cultural affinity. As we quickly discovered, he was exactly my age and therefore also born soon after the war. His father had been a Nazi judge and was briefly imprisoned in the process of de-Nazification. He himself decided to study law, he said, partly as a way of repairing the damage that people like his father had wrought, not only to individuals but also to the very system and ideals of justice. In his late twenties, he went through a period of extreme, radical rebellion, in which he tried both to repeat his father's fate—to get himself jailed—and to repudiate it. I recognized in this an eerie counterpoint of a familiar psychic complex: the desire to repeat a terrible parental fate, and to escape it. As the conversation went on, the young German told me he had been brought up on the love and mystique of the forest. As I remember, this was not only because of the Germanic mythology of the forest but because his father had attended hunting weekends in the Black Forest and in the great forests of Eastern Poland as well. The Nazi elite, he said, loved that untouched wilderness, and the cathedral-like, gothic rise of trees. I suspected a quiver of nostalgia in his voice as he told me this. I told him that the forest is also important in Polish iconography and imagination; the two countries, after all, are geographically very close to each other. I, too, loved forests as a child. But the forest, I said to him, was where my parents had hidden during the war, where they spent fearful nights in their bunker as they tried to elude the Nazi hunters. His father's hunting lodge, I thought; my parents' attic.

At this, we looked at each other with a kind of flummoxed resignation. For what could we do except acknowledge both the utter disparity and the strange symmetry of our histories? He could have expressed compassion, I suppose, if it had been "appropriate," or pity for my family's fate. I could have delivered some high-minded diatribe, had that been in the least called for. It wasn't. There was a historical horror between us; but we were distinctly not enemies. Indeed, we were looking at the horror from a similar point of view—if from opposite ends of the telescope.

That is the way it often is, with meetings between second-generation Jews and Germans, driven as they are by a potent mix of fascination and dread, resistance and a strange sort of recognition. Such encounters, in structured or informal forms, have come to constitute another rite of passage, or at least a recognizable feature of that morally dense and intense post-Holocaust terrain.

I am sometimes impatient with the terrain itself, with the intellectual melodrama of general prejudice and general stereotype, with the moral coloration of every position we are called upon to take, with the overdetermined meanings of our erratic opinions, with the demand to speak from our "sitings" and our "identities." And yet, it has to be acknowledged that Germany is not for me only one spot on the globe among many. The idea of Germany, if not the country itself, is indeed part of my deeper landscape, of that internal theater where dramas of encounter with significant Others, even if those Others are collective entities, are staged. Germany, for Jews of my generation, has significance perforce, whether we will or not. There is a task to be accomplished in relation to it, of self-examination at least: of understanding where our preconceptions of Germanness come from, and how they square with present realities; of deciding what our feelings about this part of the world are, and what we might want them ideally—that is, if we hold ourselves to our own best standards—to be.

As in transactions between children of survivors and their parents, here, too, ethics and deep affect are closely intertwined. Here, too, in order to arrive at examined attitudes, it may be necessary first to acknowledge the grip of deeply ingrained images and emotions. I do not disavow my early refusal to spend a night in Germany, nor my initial opposition to automatic sympathy. The sinister associations that extended to all things German in my childhood were not derived from real-world knowledge; but neither were they spun out of whole cloth. If the imperative to hate the aggressor was so powerfully entrenched, that was because, like the imperative of loyalty to the victim, it had a legitimate moral component. Germany—with collective assent—had brought into being a regime of surpassing moral ugliness. Germans—many Germans—had done the most odiously reprehensible things. Specific, though unknown, Germans were responsible for the destruction of lives close to me, and for damage to the lives of almost everyone I knew in the course of my growing up.

I do not think one should love one's enemy too readily or easily, or else such affection may be meaningless. I was not beguiled by the young Jews of my generation who took up a putatively "unprejudiced" affirmation of all things German as a way of flirting with political transgression. There were undoubtedly a lot of unreconstructed prejudices towards Germany floating around in the postwar decades, and these needed to be reexamined. But nevertheless, I thought that an instinct of caution towards a country that had wreaked so much atrocity was not indecent, and that, if one was going to get over that instinct, one should do so not by the dint of radical chic rebellion but via some more genuine or more reflective route.

But by the time I met my German contemporary, the question of course was: Who, or what, constituted the enemy? It was surely no longer he, or those numerous Germans born after the war who were grappling with the appalling history bequeathed to them. I could not, in good conscience or calm rationality, hold them responsible for the sins of their fathers or mothers any more than I want to be held hostage to ancestral beliefs, or even to the Holocaust inheritance, forever.

.   .   .

In the immediate aftermath of atrocity, in the generation of direct participants, the gulf—moral, political, affective—between the victim and the perpetrator is nearly absolute. The gulf is created in the first place by the perpetrator's utter failure to recognize the humanity of the victim; it is reinforced by the in-

justice of the deed itself; and it is sealed, most often, by the failure of most perpetrators to feel remorse for the deeds they have
performed.

There are exceptions to this, of course; but for the most part,
it seems that the engineers of collective crimes, while undoubtedly regretting the loss of their power, and sometimes living
with the fear of retribution, rarely suffer pangs of conscience or
undue psychic discomfort. Indeed, they often remain convinced
of the rightness of their cause, and therefore of the necessity of
deeds perpetrated in its service.

This much we have learned, although the observation, it
seems to me, does not astonish us enough. But it is one of the
added injustices in the wake of so much injustice that the burden of brutality is carried, not only in its occurrence but in its
aftermath, not by the abuser but by the abused; that the bitterness of the contamination penetrates most of all the hearts of
those who are subjected to it, leaving the perpetrators for the
most part remorseless and guilt-free.

This seems apparent from accounts and observations of the
actors in the all too numerous collective crimes we have witnessed in the twentieth century: the close studies of high-ranking
Nazis by such writers as Gitta Sereny or Kazimierz Moczarski;
formal or informal statements made by the culprits in South
Africa's ugly apartheid regime; from conversations with deposed
dictators such as Idi Amin or Mengistu; from the few disclosures made by perpetrators of Rwanda's genocide; or, for that
matter, from public testimonies of such world-class villains as
Slobodan Milosevic, and the brazen remorselessness he evinced
during his trial at the International Court at the Hague.

But why this should be so is one of the more troubling puzzles of human nature, and one that can bear further examination. For one thing, we do not have enough psychological studies of such figures. Tyrants and torturers go into therapy much less frequently than their victims, and don't often leave behind soul-searching testimonies.

What we do know is that people recruited to commit systematic acts of brutality receive a kind of training in sadism, via a gradual habituation to escalating levels of violence, and an indoctrination in extreme contempt for its targets. The SS groups that executed the first massacres of Jews in Eastern Europe came to their task already convinced that they were dealing with subhumans. Even so, some of the men assigned to the job found it onerous at first, though the killings got easier quite quickly till they turned into a routine, or even an exhilarating activity. The torturers of the Argentinian junta were conditioned, step by step, to disregard the expressions of pain emanating from the objects of their work and to take pleasure in the precision of their own procedures. In other settings, for example in the recent Yugoslav wars, the less reliable soldiers of mercilessness were plied with vodka or even drugs to deaden whatever inklings of compassion they may still have harbored. Such methods constitute an education in inhumanity, in an absolute objectification of the Other.

The information, from that dark other side, still keeps coming out. In a recent book called *Interrogations: The Nazi Elite in Allied Hands, 1945,* the historian Richard Overy has gathered hitherto unpublished transcripts of court interviews conducted with a group of high-ranking Nazi prisoners who were awaiting trial at Nuremberg. Here is one fragment of such a transcript, in which Otto Ohlendorf, a leader of one of the Einsatzgruppen, is explaining why he issued orders to forbid individual executions:

QUESTION: Why?
  ANSWER: Because this type of execution caused a serious emotion, not only on the part of those who were carrying out the executions, but also on the part of those who were shot [resulting in] serious mistreatments . . .
QUESTION: Such as?
  ANSWER: Namely, that such a person lost any feeling and respect for human life and when those people who had to be shot were emotionally affected or excited, then beatings would result as a matter of course.

Ohlendorf therefore opted for mass executions, which were apparently better for his troops' moral health. This is surely an extreme form of what Zygmunt Bauman, in his brilliant meditation on the sources of genocide, *Modernity and the Holocaust*, has called "the production of distance"—a process that permits a radical detachment and denial of empathy, or even a minimal recognition of the other as human. And perhaps it is this cut in the soul, the cauterization of all ordinary sensitivity and fellow feeling, that later persists as a calcification of conscience and an imperviousness to guilt. Still, we do not have enough insight into the inner dynamics of such psychic hardening, the processes through which the normal confusion and ambivalence felt by most mortals is reduced into a monomaniac rigidity of hatred, or of the defensive strategies through which a sense of inadequacy, say, is converted into a compensatory sense of grandiosity or racial superiority.

Germany's collective humiliation after its defeat in the First World War has often been cited as one of the causes of its turn to Nazism, and the story of Hitler's early failures is well known. But in general, the henchmen of disaster are not satisfied people, and the ranks of terror are not usually drawn from successful strata of society. The vicious secret police service in Romania, the Securitate, recruited its minions from orphanages and other hopeless places, so that they would be, as one member of the service told me, "faithful as dogs."

And perhaps, once such faithfulness is adopted, there is no stepping back from it, and no stepping out of one's calcified skin. The Nazis interviewed at Nuremberg were, almost to a man, guiltless and unrepentant. But for "the fraction tortured by a genuine sense of guilt," Overy notes, the consequence was a smoldering depression. "Why don't you just shoot us?" was a question posed by one of those exceptional prisoners.

Well, one can see how a man in whom some embers of humanity were still alive might feel like that—and why most might want to avoid such a state. Possibly, the only alternative to fanatical rigidity is utter disintegration. Possibly (one wants to hope) the calcification of soul is somewhere—in the depth of the unconscious, or in the realms of poetic or a heavenly justice—its own punishment.

It is one of the features of the second-generation condition that such matters come up in conversations all the time, and on quite innocent occasions. This is, after all, the moral territory within which we grew up, and its details continue to surface in the imagination and to nag the mind. Just recently, a friend

happened to tell me about the death of an old Gestapo man in
an English old people's home. My friend was visiting his father,
who had once been a prisoner in Buchenwald; and it was probably for that reason that a young nurse talked to him about the
old Nazi's death. The nurse was well used to people dying; but
that death was terrible. The Gestapo man, she said, realized that
there were two alternatives: Either there was an afterlife, or there
wasn't. And for him, it was not clear which was worse. He was
apparently struggling with his conscience at his ultimate moment, and he suffered. My friend was impressed by the nurse's
resources of compassion; but what I find reassuring about this
fragment of a story is its suggestion that the moral sense is not,
after all, completely eradicable from the human soul; and that,
when defenses break down sufficiently to leave even an old
genocide warrior vulnerable, then we recognize evil *as* evil, and
find its dark glamour turned to pure horror.

. . .

But mostly, remorse, in the perpetrators of the Holocaust,
seemed to be absent. There are, of course, exceptions to the general patterns on both sides: perpetrators who are capable of
some transformation of consciousness and conscience; victims
who have the largeness of spirit, if not to forgive—for sometimes, forgiveness itself would be indecent—then at least to
avoid wholesale condemnation or the impulse of indiscriminate
hatred. But in most cases, it could be said that the perpetrators
placed themselves outside the pale of tolerance, or sympathy.
The limits of tolerance are also imposed by a kind of recognition: If we are to recognize the agency, intentionality, motives of

genocide's executioners, then, in an ethical world, we must acknowledge that they deserve our condemnation.

In the immediate aftermath of atrocity, the first need is to recognize wrongs as wrongs. How that is done, what mechanisms of justice are brought to bear in an imperfect world, is another matter. But in the wake of the Holocaust—an event of that magnitude of moral horror—no systematic "dialogue" between victims and perpetrators was possible or called for.

But in the second generation, the situation changes fundamentally. There is the obvious fact that the children of perpetrators are not themselves guilty of crimes; but there are also—at least in the German case—the changes wrought by their own intricate negotiations with a terrible past.

I suppose it is in that gap, between the first and second generation, and in the necessity of acknowledging it, of bringing my consciousness in line with new realities, that my German education has taken place. A few years after the meeting in Fiesole, I was asked to discuss a memoir by a young German woman, Sabina Reichel, on a television talk show. The memoir, expressively called *What Did You Do in the War, Daddy?* was an account of growing up in postwar Germany, with a father who had been a mildly involved Nazi (Reichel's father was a musician who entertained the German troops). I read this text with great curiosity and, initially, great skepticism. I continued to read with increasing, if reluctant, identification, for the parallels between Sabina's and my own childhood were striking: We both grew up in countries of ruined cities, in straitened circumstances, in families with a distinctly patriarchal ethos. But ought I to feel about ruined German cities as I felt about Polish ones? Was I obliged to pity little Sabina for her childhood of material deprivation as I had pitied the orphaned children I had known in Cracow? Could I possibly sympathize with Sabina Reichel's exquisite discomforts and belated pangs of conscience for her father's—for her father's generation's—actions? I wasn't sure I should even be asked to do so. And yet, after some reflection, and almost to my own surprise, the answer came quite clearly: Yes, I could. I could see the difficulties of having even a minor Nazi for a father. I could imagine the dismay of learning you are the inheritor of a tainted, an abhorrent history. If I had failed to admit this, I thought, I would be guilty of a willful failure of the imagination, or, rather, a dogmatic refusal to alter my ideas in the light of what I could newly imagine.

I cannot view German history from within. I cannot pretend to enter fully into—have intuitive empathy for—the dilemmas of the postwar generation, or follow the turns of the dialectic in German discussions of the Second World War. For all the mirror-image analogies, the German experience begins from a fundamentally different point of departure, and I cannot easily penetrate its felt content or subsequent transformations. And yet, the impetus to find out about it has been strong. Germany, whether I would or not, is part of my significant history. The Germans born after the war, I began gradually to realize, are my true historical counterpoint. We have had to struggle, from our antithetical positions, with the very same past. This was an avenue to interest and even fascination. And the more I discovered about it, the more I came to feel that the psychic predicament of that contrapuntal "second generation" was something to be reckoned with; that, in some ways, it seemed more soul-splitting than the psychoethical quandaries of the Jewish "side."

So I felt as I read the interviews with children of high-ranking Nazis collected by Peter Sichrovsky, an Austrian journalist, in his book *Born Guilty*—interviews breathing fire and fury at the parents and describing impossible family scenarios. So I sensed as I watched the German film *Nasty Girl*, based on a real story of a young woman who almost by happenstance begins to uncover her small town's wartime past—and who becomes the target of the most vicious opprobrium and harassment from her good German neighbors. So I thought much later as I read *The Reader* by Bernhard Schlink, a novel about a young boy's romance with an older woman who turns out to have been a concentration camp guard implicated in the most awful cruelties.

Schlink's narrative, in its attempt to absolve the older woman of real responsibility for heinous actions, is problematic; but it gives insight into what may be the crucial dilemma of the German second generation. While the conflict for children of victims is between the imperative of compassion and the need for freedom, the quandary for the children of Nazis—perhaps for children of perpetrators everywhere—is caused by the imperative to hate those whom they love. That is surely a proposition to impale one on pincers of emotional contradiction. For how can you ever come to terms with the knowledge that your parents, your relatives, the very people for whom you have felt a natural, a necessary affection, are actually worthy of moral disgust? That the relative who was fond of you, or a neighbor who treated you nicely, or indeed your mother or father, may have performed ghastly deeds? Or that the whole previous generation, which has served as your first model of adulthood, is tainted by complicity with such deeds?

Like Jewish second-generation accounts, the German writings on such themes indicate certain recurring patterns of response, a sort of collective psychobiography in the aftermath of historical crime. Nearly all the stories of postwar childhoods tell of growing up in homes where a heavy atmosphere of secrecy reigned; of parents who were perceived as chilly and distant; of subjects that were untouchable, and of gradual or sudden realizations that something had been recently and deeply rotten in the state in which the children were growing up.

The quality of silence described in the German accounts seems different from that of the victims'. This was silence not of pain or mourning, but of sullen grievance. Many former Nazis thought themselves unjustly punished in the war's aftermath, and their cause unjustly condemned. In the public realm, too, a tacit silence prevailed in the first postwar decades on this worst of all subjects. In Germany, more than elsewhere, there were compelling reasons to "turn over a new leaf" after the war, and the Holocaust was the object, if not exactly of censorship, then of a widely endorsed amnesia. This part of German history was not bruited about in the media, nor taught in schools until the mid–1960s.

The delay in disclosure, however, meant that by the time the postwar generation of Germans began to learn the full and lurid facts of their country's conduct in the war, the discoveries came as a very rude shock. As it happened, the revelations also coincided with that generation's adolescence and added volatile fuel to ready rebelliousness. For some families, especially those whose members had actively participated in genocidal crimes, the effects were explosive. There are descriptions, in German literature on the subject, of violent confrontations as the children presented the parents with newly discovered facts; of demands for confession and contrition and, most often, the elders' refusal to offer either; of the chilling of affection and the death of respect; and sometimes, a cessation of all contact.

On the political level, the postgeneration's indignation expressed itself in such radical phenomena as the Baader-Meinhof gang and outbreaks of terrorist acts. The forms of action were themselves surely unjustifiable and often misplaced in their targets; but the problem was that the rage had an element of ethical justification. Not only had German society colluded with the most heinous of crimes, it was still permeated, at every level, by the perpetrators of those crimes. If you were young, idealistic, or at all morally sensitive, this must have made for a maddening political climate.

In its overt manifestations, the anger with which the young Germans lashed out at their parents and their society seemed just the opposite of the involuted mourning, the renunciations and self-abnegation that often characterized the children of survivors. And yet, in the psychoanalytic studies of second-generation Germans, there are descriptions of phenomena that eerily echo the symptoms and syndromes found on the other side of the equation. For the perpetrators' progeny, too, there were unnamed fears and unspoken guilt, strange hauntings and soul-damaging identifications. One case study, recounted by Gabriele Rosenthal and Dan Bar-On (to cite an arbitrary example out of the many available), describes the history of a German woman whose parents had been involved in the Nazi euthanasia program. Specifically, the parents worked in a department under whose mandate children judged "deficient" were put to death. In her childhood, this patient somehow learned, either through overheard fragments of conversation or through more uncanny or underground means, about the murders of children at her parents' hands. Being herself a vulnerable child, the girl identified entirely with the victims in this gruesome scenario. She became possessed by the fear that, if she made mistakes, if her own imperfections were discerned, she, too, would be put to death by her own parents. The parents, as it happened, were among those who after the war adopted a sullen, defensive silence; their behavior towards their daughter was characterized by a lack of tenderness or overt affection. In later years, for reasons one can easily imagine, this woman came to hate her parents with a cold, or rather an iron, determination. But this, in turn, led her to stifle any stirrings of inner life that might endanger her psychic armor and to assume a posture of permanent, if false, toughness. In her psychoanalysis, in order to emerge from her position of frozen rage, this patient not only had to unearth her terrifying childhood fantasies but to acknowledge—wrenchingly enough—that she not only hated but also loved her parents. She somehow had to disentangle their monstrous deeds from what she knew of their humanity.

Not an enviable task. In psychoethical terms, the predicament in which this German woman, and many others like her, found themselves places them in a no-win position; for to remain fixed in hatred and fear of one's parents, one's first objects of love, is to risk emotional stultification, or even death. But to give in to impulses of attachment and affection, when they are directed towards parents who have committed horrific crimes, and who have done so not out of passion but from conviction and belief—to accept this is surely to give up a part of one's own moral being.

Such untenable choices can sometimes lead to even more contorted forms of feeling. The patient whose parents had participated in the euthanasia program developed, along with the hatred of all things German, a kind of pseudo-identification with Jewish victims. She felt she was like them; she wanted to know Jews and feel close to them. This, too, is a theme that surfaces in German second-generation literature, and it is a delicate and a troubling one. Sympathy for the victim and a reparative urge are the decent responses in genocide's wake. But the desire to impersonate or appropriate the identity of the other in order to disburden oneself of one's own carries with it the risk of inauthenticity and the seeds of bad faith. Still, it is perhaps in stories like this patient's that we can find clues as to the roots of that wider identification with the victim that has been such a prominent feature of postwar German politics.

The deep parallels between Jewish and German childhoods suggested by the psychoanalytic literature are intriguing, and perhaps less puzzling than they might seem. For after all, a child growing up against the background of horror does not yet have the imagination of cause or consequence. It does not know on what side of the historical abyss it finds itself, or who did what to whom. It only knows the weight of secrecy and silence, the frightening imaginings that fill the gap, and the intimations of a consummately dark, consummately threatening universe. Perhaps the dread was all the worse for the German children because, even without historical knowledge, they might have sensed that it was associated with the parents, embodied in them.

But there the psychological parallels probably end. For while the characteristic difficulty, for the Jewish second generation as it came into consciousness and young adulthood, was an anguished and sometimes excessive identification with the parental past, the defining gesture for the young Germans was of violent counteridentification. That movement was undoubtedly helped by postwar Germany's official political mood, which was (in West Germany at least) determinedly democratic, tolerant, and dedicated—from the 1960s onwards—to openness and self-scrutiny.

On all these grounds, the public climate in which the younger Germans grew up was diametrically opposed to the belief system of their parents. Indeed, Peter Sichrovsky interestingly suggests that the contradictions between what he calls a "fascist family structure" and the postwar democratic ethos both increased the tensions between the generations and ultimately enabled the young to rebel against the parents and break the bonds that tied them to the past.

. . .

It is that postwar trajectory and the tenor of West German politics that have provided the context for contemporary encounters between Germans and Jews, and for the interfaith dialogues, thematic conferences, therapeutic workshops, and other kinds of structured conversation that have been taking place over the last decades, often to powerful effect, in Israel, Germany, the United States, and elsewhere. The period of conscience searching and self-examination in West Germany, the prevailing ideological tenor of the postwar German generation, have assured that such meetings take place in a framework of relative psychological safety, that they begin not from argument but from consensus. For, in the second generation of Holocaust's heirs, the German and Jewish interpretations of events

have to a large extent converged. There is no fundamental dis-
agreement between the parties to this discussion about the
causes of the Holocaust, the attribution of responsibility, or the
character of the villainy.

Those are the normative views. They count, and they need to
be honored. They also make dialogue possible. But if our imaginative transactions with figurative perpetrators remain so am-
bivalent, if the working out of attitudes in this area is still such
a demanding task and test, that is because this part of the topography too is rooted in the early dark impressions and landscape of feeling; because our ideas on such matters inescapably
arise out of that potent first knowledge. The substratum of
childhood fears, phantasms, preconceptions, is not easily extracted from the soul. The stereotypes, the imagery that each
group has received about the other are of the most disturbing
kind. The brutal faces, the shouting dogs; the sight of Germans
approaching the attic, who to my parents meant certain death:
I can never entirely delete such pictures from my inner storehouse. I do not know what images of sadism and humiliation,
aggression or contempt, were transmitted by their parents to
postwar Germans; but judging by my own experience, *those*
traces of the past are not easily dissolved.

The Holocaust history, in the second generation, still courses
in the veins; it is still a felt past. It is the fuel of that legacy that
lends encounters between the two groups their continuing tensions, and their heuristic potential. The disjunctions between
the perpetrators and their descendants, between our best intentions and the substratum of "incorrect" feeling, cannot be resolved through sheer good will. But the good will and the
consensus of views among the two groups make dialogue and

disclosure of difficult feelings possible. In meetings with postwar Germans, the children of survivors encounter the most fraught aspect of our history through its human representatives. It is through this that we can confront the most troubling aspects of our legacy—and the demonic part of our mythos—in their embodied immediacy.

Of course, neither the psychological force of such exchanges nor our moral rights in the second generation are as strong as they would be in the first. It is not my role or right, at this late stage, to forgive the perpetrators themselves. If some among survivors find it in themselves to arrive at this most transcendent of ethical resolutions, then they cannot be gainsaid. But I, who have not been the direct object of persecution, am not entitled to dispense reprieve on behalf of those who were. Nor am I entitled to ask for responses from my German interlocutors that are not freely given. While we might hope that some genuine reparative remorse arises from a lived connection to the past, we have neither the right to ask for it nor the power to absolve anyone from it. The role-playing exercises that are sometimes enacted in second-generation groups, whereby the descendants of the perpetrators take on the "identity" of the victim, and vice versa, strike me as possibly being too easy by half, even if their lesson is well taken. Yes, we all have the potential to be both victim and perpetrator. But of course, it is not so difficult to admit this if you are not in danger of becoming one or the other.

Still, by all accounts, second-generation encounters can be both cathartic and instructive. It is in such exchanges that disturbing feelings can be at last brought to their symbolic addressee. On the Jewish side, the need may be to give vent to anger and reproach and thus, perhaps, to soften rage into reconciliation. On the German part, the impulse may be to express remorse or give belated recognition to the representative of victims to compensate in some small measure for its earlier lack.

But it is also through encounters with the once-hated Other that we come up most concretely against broader questions arising out of our history: issues of national responsibility and collective identity (in what sense are these Germans like our parents' "Germans"?); questions about continuities or discontinuities in cultural "character" and the relationship between political ideologies and deeper cultural belief. And it is through such dialogue that our ideas about such matters may undergo a genuine shift, not through a facile reaching for "correct" views, but through a deeper alteration of perception and feeling.

That is for the sake of ethical thought, and improved relations. But there are also the rights and needs of the imagination. Our childhood iconography was made up of inhuman forces. It is hard, in the wake of the Holocaust, to get beyond the sense of diffuse danger, of a darkness that cannot be encompassed or given finite shape. But the forces were, of course, human, and they behaved according to human laws of motive and result. If we can confront the demons of our first knowledge through the figures of its symbolic representatives, that will not diminish the horror of our history; but it might help us to understand that history in its proper terms and distinguish between actual threats and imaginary monsters.

·   ·   ·

I have now visited Germany several times, mostly for professional reasons. I have talked to numerous people whose views

EVA HOFFMAN

are very close to mine. I feel perfectly comfortable in its prosperous, conveniently arranged cities, so far removed from those first infernal landscapes. Yet there is always a remainder, a reminder of something, in these visits, in these polite and civilized conversations. Perhaps by now, a reminder only of significance. We know what each other knows, and how terrible that knowledge is. My hosts tend to be solicitous about "how it feels" to be in Germany; I keep wishing not to be an object of such solicitousness. They want to make some gesture, however small, that is reparative, compensatory. I would prefer to be treated as a perfectly normal person with whom one can have a conversation on any subject, including German and Jewish issues, without assuming anything or speaking from particular "sites" or "positions." In other words, I want to be seen as a free agent rather than a "child of Holocaust survivors." And I would prefer to see the people I meet as free agents rather than figurative or literal children of murderers. But this, within our generation, is not yet easy. The Shadow falls on our psyches too darkly still and it would be another kind of falseness to pretend it isn't there. I cannot come to Germany with a tabula rasa, cannot erase the tremor of suspicion about older Germans or delete the slight recoil from the sound of certain German words ("Achtung" or "Arbeit" will never be neutral syllables for me). I cannot eliminate the subtle strain that attends my visits and that, in order to carry on as normal, I have to overcome.

I do not know what comparable associations I evoke in my German acquaintances, what sensations of guilt or images of humiliation, impulses of hidden sadism or urges of reparative compassion, are prompted when they meet a Jewish person. I cannot know, and I have no right to inquire. There are privacies

128

of the soul we are all entitled to, in such areas, too; and it is my civilized obligation to take my interlocutors at the level of ostensible utterance and intention. On that ostensible level, it is by now only the gestures of overcoming that mark even the friendliest and open exchanges between Jews and Germans, and that are the mark of our still living, still singeing relationship to the past. Overcoming what? Prejudice, counterprejudice, unspoken assumptions we make about each other's assumptions, a too eager need to communicate the propriety of those assumptions, a too eager rush to good will. And sometimes, more complicated twists of attitude still. In a recent conversation, a German intellectual I had just met worried that the younger, "third" generation of Germans is refusing to take on that burden of guilt which was assumed by people like him willingly, and as an unquestioned moral duty. Trying to speak from some perfectly free, "impartial" position, I replied that I could understand why these very young people would balk against injunctions to historical guilt. Why, after all, should they take any responsibility—even that of a bad conscience—for events from which they are as temporally remote as I am from the First World War? I believe my German companion looked uneasy, or even unhappy, at my saying this—though whether that was because I was depriving him of the comforts of familiar discomforts, or because I was taking the liberty of having unexpected views about *his* history, I do not know. However that may be, it seemed that in my overcoming I had gone a step too far.

But truth to tell, I was not, in my attempt to be entirely "objective," entirely honest either. For would I want to reprieve the new generation of Germans of all moral answerability—or at least embarrassment—for their country's history quite so easily?

In this question lies the whole delicate quandary of our connection to the past, of how much we owe to it or are shaped by it. On the one hand, it is possible to understand the young Germans who refuse to take on the mantle of an awful history, or assume a notional guilt for deeds their grandparents committed in a crazed world long ago. What is Hitler to them or they to Hitler? I can see how the "third generation" of Germans might want to shrug off such questions as irrelevant, and declare, as many younger German writers do, that they are interested in questions of personal happiness instead. We all, eventually, want to be free enough to think about questions of happiness. In the second generation, the sense of responsibility for the past is created through a still lived bond, an intravenous transmission. But in the third, the link becomes almost metaphysical. In what sense are third-generation Germans "German" as their grandparents had been German?

Generally, on such themes we tend to speak with forked tongues, perhaps because the problems themselves really are multi-layered and complex. In contemporary discourse, we are very aware of the ways in which culture constructs our identities; but at the same time, we energetically disavow any notions of national character. And indeed, subtle distinctions are called for. Certainly, the idea of intrinsic and permanent national "character" or permanent psycho-national traits has been repeatedly shown to be an untenable shibboleth. "Nation" itself is a recent construct, and the behavior of specific nations highly circumstantial. But culture—understood, in its broadest sense, as a system of meanings through which we perceive the world— is an undeniable, if pliant shaping force. Culture *does* mold our subcutaneous perceptions, as well our overt beliefs; it influences

forms of feeling and even the very structure of desire. It sometimes also shapes ideology and political phenomena. It is possible, mind you—this is a caveat that must be added from the
perspective of this moment—that in our much more mobile
and intermingled world, formative power of particular cultures
is lessening, that the speed of criss-crossing influences is making
us all more similar. But for now, we still recognize each other as
French, or American, or German. Our cultural past is not shed
so easily. And so there are still questions emanating from the
past for the younger Germans to ask, or be alert to. The inter-
section of deeper values and more fluctuating political beliefs
still bears examination. What, for example, are the links between the ideas fueling Nazism of the 1930s and the bitter
ressentiment evident in neo-Nazi ideology and rhetoric today?
What has happened to the structures of conformity and authoritarianism that the older generation had rebelled against?
And are there undercurrents of continuity between the *longue
durée*—as opposed to immediately political—sources of chau-
vinism or xenophobia in Germany that had permitted a lethal
outbreak of virulent anti-Semitism in the 1930s and the outbreaks of racism today?

In East Germany, no less than in other Soviet-bloc countries,
the politics of memory during the Cold War dictated massive
suppressions and falsifications of history. Improbably enough,
the story of the Nazi period there was told as a narrative of
Communist resistance to Fascism. In those precincts of the
newly united Germany, the history of Fascism has just begun to
be addressed, and there is still a need for basic education about
the actual course of events, and for open examination of East
Germans' participation in the Holocaust, which was no less

widespread or culpable than that of their Western counterparts.

An event as cataclysmic as the Second World War has a long afterlife, and its unfolding in German consciousness can still be observed today. In the last few years, by some riddling movement of the Zeitgeist—perhaps it is simply that enough time has elapsed to allow for the return of the most ambiguous and disturbing specters from repression—the memory of violence visited upon the Germans at the end of the Second World War has begun to resurface in German consciousness. The indiscriminate bombing of cities by the Allies, the mass rapes of women by Soviet soldiers, the subsequent suicides, the attacks on ships carrying cargoes of children—these events have become the subject of widespread discussion, scholarship, literary excavation, sometimes accompanied by the suggestion that ordinary civilian Germans should be counted among the war's victims.

I feel a knot of ambivalence when I read about such events, the horribly vivid descriptions offered by W. G. Sebald, the bard of German memory and amnesia, of the fire-bombings of Hamburg, in which tens of thousands of civilians were incinerated in a burning inferno. More horrors to add to the catalogue, more images one doesn't want to image. And more moral problems to confront, of the kind that have no answer. The vindictiveness of the Allied retributions was extravagant, and it is surely right that this part of history too should be recovered from a long forgetfulness or self-censorship, that it should be incorporated into young Germans' picture of their history. Indeed, in his book on the subject, *On the Natural History of Destruction,* Sebald makes the interesting suggestion that the silence in Germany about losses incurred in the retributions had been, so to speak, the foundational act of postwar denial; and that this stifling of reaction contributed to the Germans inability to mourn for the unspeakable losses they inflicted on others. And, almost six decades later, as the memories of *this* consequence of war resurface, and as we keep trying to draw some lessons from the past for administering justice after ever new conflagrations, it is important to distinguish wild revenge from just retaliation. Still, I balk at the idea of moral equivalence between the two kinds of violence, or at the conclusion that "Germans were victims too," which some commentators have been tempted to draw. Sebald, with all his imaginative capacity to envision Hamburg's inferno, nevertheless energetically refuses that idea, and does not let us or his countrymen forget that Nazi acts were, in effect, the first cause of the hellish fires.

But who indeed—to come back to that awkward exchange— am I to pronounce on such things, or suggest to my German interlocutor how he should reckon with his history? What rights do I have altogether in the German-Jewish dialogue, what can I legitimately ask of my German peers on the ostensible level of utterance and avowed ideas? No more, I suppose, than reflection and vigilance. Vigilance about those remainders of Nazi ideology that, according to some observers (for example, Anna Rosmus, writing about her researches to her Bavarian town's past—and present), still circulate within the German republic. Vigilance, perhaps, about the reverberations of the past in the present.

I cannot enter German history from within. I cannot always judge how much danger certain phenomena pose, or what hidden trends within the society they reflect. And yet, Germany's history has been fatefully connected with my own. Possibly, it is right for me—possibly I am within my rights—to declare my interest in this past and how it is dealt with. In its normative expressions, the West German story has been not of blind reenactment, but indeed of vigilance—of conscientious confrontation with the past. But finally, it is up to those who live on the ground where the crime was committed to decide how to reckon with the past and its instantiations in the present; when special watchfulness is no longer called for, or when the time is ripe for self-forgiveness, or forgetting.

·   ·   ·

"They were the worst. If it hadn't been for them, how would the Germans have known who was Jewish? It was they who gave us away! Do you know how many lives could have been saved if they had wanted to help?"

The man is in a fury, and I feel all my moral faculties constricting, tangling into an impossible knot. He is old, and he has his grievous story. A Pole had informed on one of his relatives, thus causing his death. Of course, I understand his rage, and his right to it. And yet, I cannot help but feel, his pure anger leaves out too much.

"Why do they hate us so much? Why are they so hard? They wanted us to love them. They didn't care about us one bit, but they wanted us to risk our lives for them. We would have had to risk everything to save them! It's not just, what they say about us."

The woman is speaking in urgent tones. She is old, and she wants to impress on me that she's speaking the truth as she perceived it. And the terrible thing is that I can—almost—see what she means. The other terrible thing is that she leaves out so much.

I have been in these conversations before, public and private, have felt the brunt of fierce anger on both sides. And yet, the fervor and fury of these debates continue to astonish me, and to wrench me between what are, after all, two parts of my own cultural identity: Polish and Jewish.

No context of safety, or of shared assumptions, such as has framed the German-Jewish exchanges has been present in encounters between the postgeneration of Jews, and that other significant Other of the Jewish imagination—the Poles. Poland, in the minds of many children of survivors, remains a sinister and forbidden landscape; the place where one would not set foot, the imaginative locus of the most primitive and barbaric anti-Semitism. It is also a place towards which one can nurture a pure enmity—as one would not allow oneself to do in relation to Germany.

Attitudes towards collective Others are for us what attitudes towards sexuality were for the Victorians. Our public morality—indeed, our very idea of what it means to be a moral subject—is defined these days by our views on cultural difference, on groups that are not ourselves. But such positions, much more than private ethics, are malleable by quite abstract forces and pressures—of public opinion, climate of ideas, political structures. The contrast in the prevailing views held in the postgeneration about Poland and Germany has been for me a matter of fascination and, sometimes, perplexity. But it is also an interesting study in the formation of attitudes towards various Others, in the relationship between broader political contexts and personal response, and in the different valences of "memory" we bring to painful pasts.

For me, the question of Poland is hardly abstract, nor are Poles an unfamiliar Other. But "the question of Poland" matters to all postwar Jews because the Holocaust was executed largely on Polish soil. In the minds of many, this has come to mean that Poland was responsible for that event, or at least that the Nazis placed concentration camps on its territory because they counted on the collusion of the natives in executing the Final Solution. Both contentions have been shown to be entirely untrue; but the imaginative associations remain. For Jews who had survived the Holocaust, Poland was the site of their tragedy and greatest losses—a site of something to which many of them never wished to return.

But for many centuries before, Poland was home to the largest Jewish minority in any country (between 13 and 15 percent at its height, in contrast to less than 2 percent in Germany), and the largest Jewish population in terms of absolute numbers—more than 3 million people at the outset of the war. It was a population, moreover, that, in contrast to Western European Jewry, retained its distinct, mostly Orthodox identity and traditions; a visible, socially striated, sometimes highly successful and hardly powerless minority. The history of this minority, and of Polish-Jewish relations over the centuries' long period of coexistence, is, not surprisingly, rich, varied, and complex. It has included periods of conflict as well as relative harmony, episodes of violence as well as long intervals of mutual laissez-faire. But for several hundred years, it was Poland, or "Poyln," more than any other country, that, for the vast majority of Jews in Diaspora, was home.

But since the Second World War, proximity and familiarity were replaced by a nearly total suppression of contact and knowledge. The barriers created by the Iron Curtain meant that for most Americans and Westerners, for the numerous descendants of Jewish emigrants, Poland and all of Eastern Europe became the Other Europe—a region tinged with gloomy connotations of totalitarianism and a screen for large and vague projections. Even while Germany came to be understood as "one of us," a progressive, democratic country, Poland became fixed in the Jewish imagination as the land of unreconstructed anti-Semitism. Germany had been seen to undertake a very public process of conscience searching about the past; nothing like that had been done, in the Cold War decades, in Poland. At the same time, to younger Poles, born after the war and brought up under the system of Communist censorship, Jews and Jewishness—once so much a part of their country and culture—were becoming an unknown continent surrounded by fogs of fantasy, superstition, and atavistic prejudice.

A comparison between the attitudes towards Germany and Poland in the second generation is also a study in the effects of distance on perspective. In relation to Poland, I stand at a very different distance than I do from Germany. My subjective images of Poland are based on landscapes I have actually seen and lived in. Polish people are to me neither stereotypes, nor archetypes, but people I have known. My sense of Poland can never be as stark, or even lurid, as my images of Germany had once been. The intricacies of Polish-Jewish relations are something I sensed through my own experience; the Polish-Jewish past is what I have turned to in my quest to deepen understanding of Jewish history. It is that past that has everything to do with me, and that it has therefore been important to grasp *as* history.

But this is the inverse of the relation to these two countries observed by most of my Jewish contemporaries. While Germany, in the last decades, has become a familiar entity to most Western Jews, Poland has remained a terra incognita, an imaginary entity made up of received ideas and fierce opinions, scraps of family anecdotes and almost entire absence of information.

The distance is mutual, as most younger Poles have never met a Jewish person and were not likely to learn anything about the vanished world of Polish Jews in the course of their Communist-sponsored education. The official taboo on the subject of Jewishness meant that until recently—until 1989, to be exact—there had been almost no public discussion in Poland of the Holocaust or the longer Jewish history, no revision of received narratives or rhetoric, no pressure to correct stale stereotypes or face the challenge of opposing opinion. Poles and Jews are each other's significant Other; but they are just emerging from a period of almost total severance.

Projections are easier to maintain from a distance, and so are rigid and oversimplified positions. It is by gauging the strength of my own earlier preconceptions about Germany that I can begin to appreciate the stubborn strength of prejudices still prevalent in Polish-Jewish relations. Indeed, insofar as the contemporary attitudes of Poles towards Jews and Jews towards Poles have been formed in an almost pure vacuum of knowledge, they constitute a pure illustration of the sheer power of projections: the strength of their hold upon the imagination, the urge to cling to them—indeed, the pleasure of retaining them in their original form; the difficulty—indeed, the seeming danger—of modifying them in the light of new information.

But then, within the broader political arrangements of a Cold War world, there was no broader context within which to test such projections against realities, no pressure on either group to reexamine its ideas of the other, to learn more about their fascinating common history or moderate the language in which one speaks on this subject, as we are careful to do with other nationalities and groups. Within Poland, there was positive discouragement of such a process; but on the Jewish side, too, there was something of the permitted prejudice that could be sensed in commonplace attitudes towards Poland—a prejudice one needn't examine or bother to conceal. Prejudices, too, come in different valences, and there is something of a familial coloring in the freely pejorative opinions Poles and Jews hold about each other—a trace of that former familiarity that sometimes breeds affection and sometimes contempt. Certainly, the familial derogation was there in the long centuries of Polish-Jewish coexistence, along with other tonalities of feeling and opinion. But in the postwar generation, in the absence of actual contact, former familiarity could become thinned down to a few starkly reduced formulae. On both sides, fragments of folk wisdom, insinuations, half-remembered proverbs. On both sides, the sense that this is an Other whom one can denigrate freely, the way one denigrates someone whom one doesn't need to respect, without the dignity of explanation or the restraint of political etiquette.

But beyond this, beyond intimacy and ignorance and a sort of pre-political rudeness, as I listen to people on both "sides" of this conversation, as I try to understand the desperate defensiveness and bitterness of the mutual accusations, it seems to me that I begin to hear a deeper reason for the stubbornness of this contestation—one that can be found in a head-on clash of two martyrological memories.

For both Poles and Jews, the Second World War was a time of tragedy. Both think of themselves, with justification, as innocent victims of that event. The Poles, in addition, have thought of themselves, also not without reason, as heroically self-sacrificing in their battle. They suffered great losses (3 million non-Jewish Poles were killed in the war), and put up the most concerted resistance to the Nazis of any European country, in the face of just about hopeless odds. It therefore comes as a great shock to their self-conception to be perceived, or to have to see themselves, as sometimes having been on the wrong side of this history, as aggressors rather than victims. The discovery that in some cases Poles aided and abetted the Nazis in the assault on the Jews comes into direct conflict with a vision of history on which postwar Polish generations were nurtured, with the memory, maintained unofficially and at great risk, of a heroic and noble Polish resistance. The shift of view, the overturning of sanctities and self-image, is so wrenching—I have come to understand—as to be nearly unacceptable.

As for the role of Jews in this unhappy history, insofar as they were targets of Nazi annihilationist policies, they were of course wholly innocent objects of overpowering violence. This does not mean, however, that everyone caught up in the cataclysm behaved with utmost rectitude—how could they?—or that Jews did not sometimes take positions that were in conflict with Polish loyalties and interests. The fairly widespread welcome extended by Jews in Eastern Poland to the occupying Red Army was entirely understandable from their point of view; but from the Polish perspective, it was tantamount to collusion with the enemy. For younger Jews, however, especially those who grew up in America and have barely heard of the Soviet occupation, the Polish charges of Jewish disloyalty, when Jews were under such threat, seem either pathologically anti-Semitic or just plain fanciful. Inversely, the bitterest Jewish reproaches—"Why did you not save us?"—strike Polish interlocutors as springing from a special animus, or a wholesale misunderstanding of their own wartime situation and the threat they were facing, of national extinction.

The clash of martyrological memories: Morally, affectively, this is the most painful of all kinds of collective disputes. For both groups, the very possibility of detaching themselves from the myths and memories they grew up with can be felt as a form of betrayal, a deferred disloyalty to what has become a sacrosanct version of the past, a memory of great suffering.

As for the real behavior of the Poles during the Holocaust, it ranged from terrible acts of violence—the recent revelations about a massacre in the town of Jedwabne indicating the degree of brutality at one end of the spectrum—to acts of heroic rescue in which people risked their own lives to save Jewish ones. It included, in the great middle, a large majority who were indifferent to the Jewish tragedy or fate as they attended to dangers of their own. Comparative statistics, which are beginning to be gathered in this area, show that the ratio of rescuers to informers was approximately the same in Warsaw as in Amsterdam. The degree of danger for Poles who would help Jews was much greater than for the Dutch. But nevertheless, for so many Jews who were living in Poland, and whose losses were therefore the most massive, the Germans were seen as an almost abstract evil;

whereas the acts of informing and violence by Poles were felt as intimate betrayals—perhaps the most wounding of all.

This is a much more murky set of propositions than that encountered in the German-Jewish dialogue. Just as the unequivocal horror of Nazi behavior enforces a clarity of judgment and interpretation, so the ambiguities of Polish history continue to make it a fiercely contested past. In the German-Jewish conversations, aside from the rightist neo-Nazi fringe, or some elderly former Nazis still nursing closet dreams of Third Reich glory, everyone involved in the conversation is firmly agreed on who the victims were and who the villains, on the nature of the wrong and its causes. In the Polish-Jewish transactions, a shared interpretation has yet to be achieved. Both parties are still vying for basic recognition of their perspective, and their respective exceedingly difficult pasts. Each has felt itself to be unequivocally on the side of the angels, and for both, a questioning of their purity threatens not only their *amour propre,* but the very fundaments on which their sense of collective identity has been built. To both groups, the accusations leveled by the other—often indeed inflated or inaccurate—appear not only as a difference of views, but as a mockery of their own tragedy, and a travesty of their moral truth. For both, the leap from suspicion to trust carries the danger of betraying the stern gods of tribal solidarity and fidelity to suffering.

There is something, in this refusal to alter one's views in this charged arena of suffering, of the childhood prohibition on tampering with received versions of family stories. The ethical imperative, in this case, seems to call for stasis. But as with the errors of childish memory, the very idea of literalist loyalty may be based on a misapprehension. The ancestral memories to

which we ostensibly remain faithful were probably, in their original incarnation, much more textured, nuanced, and manifold
than what has been passed on, or left of them, across the long
lacunae of the Holocaust, and of intergenerational transmission.
A second-generation friend recently told me that she cannot
bring herself to go to Poland (a common sentiment among
quite a few postwar Jews). "I'm afraid of the Poles," she said.
"Of course, that's not true of my mother. She grew up there, she
knows the place. But I only got all those awful stories from her."

This simple anecdote encapsulates much about the passage,
and the ambiguous nature, of intergenerational memory. In a
sense, in the second generation—in relation to Eastern Europe
perhaps more than elsewhere—we need to perform a considerable labor in order to arrive at the experience of the previous
generation; to reconstruct, through knowledge and imagination, the colors and complexities of variegated cultures. But in
addition, we might want to take a further step and use our own
generational vantage point, as well as the accrued knowledge of
the last few decades, to re-view a history whose interpretations
have all too often been frozen at the point of greatest trauma.
The benefits of our experience come from its globalization and
almost instinctive interculturalism. We could usefully bring a
cross-cultural, comparative vision to Polish-Jewish history, and
Jewish history altogether: to the study of behavior towards Jews
in various countries during the Holocaust; to an examination of
Jewish fate in the light of histories of other minorities; to a study
of minority attitudes towards majorities, as well as vice versa.

It is ambiguity, not certainty, that poses a threat to our convictions and forces us into harder positions. But it is ambiguity
that can—or should be—a provocation to thought. It is in rela-

tion to the vexed, thorny, contested questions of the Polish-Jewish past that there is still a demanding task left for the postwar generation: the task of unfreezing myths that have been left intact on both sides, and of unpacking stereotypes so sharply engraved on our minds as to seemingly stand for acceptable truths; of addressing aspects of our own histories that have been so untouchable as to have the force of intellectual taboos; and of admitting the prohibited perspective of the other into the area of permissible thought.

In a sense, as we progress to adult knowledge of the Holocaust, we may need to attain in the moral and intellectual sphere that separation from unquestioning tribal attachments and received ideas that originally had to be worked through in the psyche, and in relation to family narratives—a separation that is so necessary if we are to gain some freedom not from, but in relation to, overwhelming pasts.

Paradoxically enough, the steps towards such reconsiderations may be easier to take for those who are on the historically powerful or culpable side of the conflict. From that position, it is clear what to do: Examine your historical guilt, face up to your own prejudices, make such amends as are possible, apologize. It is much harder, it turns out, to relinquish grievance—in which there is so much genuine pity and legitimate grief—from the position of the symbolically victimized or less powerful side. It is much harder to know, from that bitterly wronged vantage point, when it is right to do so without dishonoring the past or betraying one's own.

And clearly, the onus, in confrontations with contested pasts, is on the more "powerful" side to take the first steps in the process of self-examination, to look at its own history critically and acknowledge responsibility for its dark episodes. Such a process has begun in Poland, where a broad discussion of the most difficult issues in Polish-Jewish relations—Polish behavior during the war, the longer history of folk and ideological anti-Semitism, and the contemporary manifestations of this prejudice, still too rampant in some quarters—has been taking place in the last few years in the media, political institutions, and other public forums.

And yet, especially in relation to pasts as complex as those that united and divided Poles and Jews, there is something that needs to be done from the minoritarian, the more injured side as well. At some point, that most risky gamble of giving the benefit of a doubt to the other—even if that other is symbolically figured as the more powerful—has to be taken.

It is in observing attitudes of my Jewish peers to Poland and Polishness that I am most aware of just how difficult this moral or psychological gesture is to achieve. For the generic skeptics, there is no Polish position, act, or view that can be construed as legitimate. Amnesia about Polish involvement in the Holocaust is justifiably seen as unacceptable; but so is the phenomenon of curiosity, evinced by many younger Poles, about their country's Jewish past—a sentiment interpreted by many Jewish observers as exploitative nostalgia or bad faith. So are the attempts to grapple with the genuine ambiguities of the Polish-Jewish past. These, coming from the Polish side, tend to be perceived as a kind of self-exculpation by complication, or simple whitewash.

Fortunately, the climate of opinion, of collective imagination, has been changing in this arena since 1989. The possibility of travel between East and West has had its beneficial effects. The monolithic pictures of each other are breaking down. And both sides—or at least their more curious members—are beginning to understand that before the Holocaust there was, for eight long centuries, a vital Jewish polity in Poland, with rich traditions, flourishing culture, politics, institutions of learning. Within Poland, there is a new cadre of historians, or just ordinary young people, who are studying that polity as an intrinsic part of their own country's past.

Indeed, in the Polish-Jewish case, the stories of the two peoples are so interbraided that it is impossible to understand our own history without taking into account the history of the other. The extremity of Nazi behavior can yield only moral disgust and unequivocal condemnation. It is the more intricate history of the Polish-Jewish relationship that can lead us to thorny but fruitful questions about cross-ethnic coexistence: about circumstances and structures that permit groups to get along amicably and those that encourage hostility; about responsibilities of majorities and minorities towards each other; about choices that the Jewish polity made during its Polish centuries and the range of human motive and behavior under pressure of extremity.

In a sense, there is not much at stake in Polish-Jewish relations except the past. But this is a past within which intense moral sentiments, and our very sense of identity, are deeply implicated. There is much to be gained from exploring it strenuously, and from admitting into our consciousness the fate and perspective of an Other with whom our own fates have been intertwined. On both sides of the Polish-Jewish complex, it may be time to step back from purely loyalist positions and move towards a greater recognition of the Other—to do each other a more generous justice.

There is much that remains to be done on the Polish side in combating the realities and the rhetoric of anti-Semitism, in fighting general xenophobia and developing an idea of "Polishness" that is not dependent on the fervors of beleaguered patriotism. But if we as Jews demand strenuous self-examination and full disclosure from the Other, then we also have to start looking at our role in a complex past, not only as victims but as actors. Perhaps most saliently, we have to be able to distinguish bad faith in others from authentic ambiguity. We cannot hold others to standards of conscience or honesty higher than those we demand from ourselves. In order for second-generation dialogue to achieve its reparative work, the recognition, when offered, needs to be recognized. That, too, requires a certain courage and a certain trust; that, too, is part of the moral test and task.

V

FROM MORALITY TO MEMORY

During a recent trip to Poland, I had occasion to visit the concentration camp of Majdanek, near the city of Lublin—one of the well-marked sites in the closely charted, late post-Holocaust geography. I went there specifically to see an exhibit, put together by an interesting group of young Poles, called "Grodzka Gate" (after the gate that used to lead from the Polish to the Jewish neighborhoods of Lublin), and based on materials recently rediscovered in Majdanek's archives and elsewhere. Some of the archives contained accounts of daily life in this labor camp turned death factory, documents left behind by its child inmates, or collected later from people who had been children there.

The exhibit is somber and dignified. In a small entrance space, a Polish children's song, its tune ballad-like and wistful, is continuously played. This was the melody that a nine-year-old girl named Elżunia (a diminutive of Elizabeth), had specified for a verse she had written in Majdanek. The verse (in my own, approximate translation) is this:

There was once little Elżunia,
She's dying all alone now.
For her daddy's in Majdanek,
Her mummy in Auschwitz-Birkenau.

I believe this is the most piercing single verse I've ever heard and after all I have read, learned, and absorbed about the Shoah, the fragment strikes me with a wholly penetrating, unprepared sense of pity and sorrow. Maybe it is that I am now far enough away from my own childhood to feel, aside from everything else, the heart-tearing grievousness of a child being forced into such a situation and such a consciousness of death. Perhaps I am adult enough to feel, simultaneously, the heart-tearing help-lessness of adults who had to witness a child in that condition. Or maybe I have traveled far enough from the Holocaust as the basis and norm to understand the perversion of all human norms—the crazy-making cruelty—inherent in a child's intern-ment in a concentration camp. Others, pausing to listen and read the translations of the four-line verse, are similarly pierced. Among other things, this small, rhymed lamentation puts paid yet again to the idea that no poetry was possible after Ausch-witz. Poetry existed in Auschwitz as well as Majdanek, and was written in the Warsaw Ghetto; and for some, it was almost as important as bread and water. It was important to little Elżunia, who hid a scrap of paper with her verse under the sole of a shoe, with directions as to the melody to which she wanted it sung. This nine-year-old girl wanted to give voice to her ordeal. She wanted the ordeal to be known and witnessed. We must, for this moment, pause to ponder it.

The main barracks room into which we move from the entrance space is lined with circular wooden structures, from which taped voices emanate, as if from deep wells, reading the archival transcripts. Groups of Polish, Israelis and American visitors walk through quietly, listening to the plain, bleak descriptions of ordinary days in Majdanek. But in the center of the barrack, in front of a large central well, a young woman kneels, and begins to wail. We walk around her gingerly, giving her a wide berth. She continues to wail, in her kneeling position, her knapsack on her back, and doesn't stop. Nor makes an effort to stop. I pause for a moment to decide whether she is in need of help. It does not appear to me that she is. It appears to me that she is bringing attention to her extraordinary, her altogether extravagant powers of empathy. It seems to me that she may be luxuriating in her extremely commendable emotion. Certainly, her presentation, or exhibition of it, is distracting, or distancing other visitors from the exhibit. It occurs to me that maybe something unpleasant has happened to her on her trip and she is taking this perfect occasion to express her unhappiness. Or that she is a dissatisfied young woman, and that this is a perfect place in which to endow her dissatisfaction with a tragic tinge and blend it with something indubitably significant. It also occurs to me that perhaps I am being very unjust to her. But I don't know. And I guess I'll never know.

.   .   .

Sixty years after the events took place, our relationship to the Holocaust is at a delicate point. We view the events that constituted the Event from a very long distance—temporal, cultural, geographical. At the same time, our collective curiosity, fascination, preoccupation with the Shoah has reached a new pitch of intensity. In the last years of the twentieth century, the seeming amnesia of the earlier decades has been succeeded, in America especially, by eruptions of near-obsessive interest: a constant stream of newspaper stories on subjects related to the Shoah; an unprecedented proliferation of survivors' memoirs, films, literary exhibits; the building of Holocaust centers or museums throughout the United States; the inclusion of courses on the Holocaust in university and high school curricula; and the huge amassing of documentary testimony.

After years when social allusions to the Holocaust were greeted with embarrassed silence or sternly nipped in the bud, every dinner party for a while seems to revert to this somber subject, as if it were an irresistible, darkly compelling magnet. Survivors, so shunned in earlier decades, are sent to suburban high schools, interviewed, begged for their tales from hell. Their children, after having for the most part succeeded in blending indistinguishably with their peer culture, become an object of respectful interest. We had been close to the real thing. Our parents had those kinds of stories. We had been touched by horror, by hardship, by history.

There are understandable reasons, of course, for this quickening of interest, and sometimes of concern. As survivors are reaching the end of their natural life span, as our line to living memory becomes severed, the urge to preserve testimony, to listen to the last direct voices from the heart of darkness, grows more pressing. Perhaps there is an impulse, amidst all else, to offer—aside from such practical amends as can still be made— some belated moral reparations to those survivors, some compensation for the earlier indifference. It is as if we remembered, at this late moment, that we had forgotten them.

At the same time, the postwar generation is reaching its later middle age—the phase of life at which we begin, as if pulled by some strange evolutionary logic, to feel the palpable need to understand our own patch of the historical past. For the postgeneration as a whole, the Second World War is the great event of that relevant past, the central point of reference, the referent, indeed, for the very idea of "history." The Holocaust is the most harrowing and philosophically pivotal heart of that cataclysm, the part of our larger past with which we have to struggle if we are to grasp something about our twentieth-century legacy, whoever we are.

But the question is: How should we think about the Shoah from our lengthening distance? What meanings does it continue to hold for us, what kinds of understanding can we bring to it or garner from it as it recedes from looming view and actual memory into the more remote realm of the past and history?

.   .   .

The world's understanding of terrible events begins with discovery, astonishment, moral shock. The first response, as we learn about atrocity from close up or afar (and increasingly, we find ourselves in a paradoxical position of witnessing distant events with seeming immediacy), is basically one of moral emotion—of outrage, grief, need for justice. The first things we want to know are who was responsible for crimes, and how the guilty should be punished. In the immediate aftermath of the Holocaust, in the period of first shock and discovery, the rhetoric of reaction was mostly moral. It was man's inhumanity to man that was lamented, and the Nazi capacity for evil that was reviled.

But in recent years, discourse about the Holocaust has moved from the vocabulary of morality to the tropes and slogans of what is called, in a more or less metaphorical shorthand, "memory." On one level, the Holocaust has entered public consciousness and the public sphere through the extensive and growing culture of commemoration. Holocaust memorials and museums are ever more a part of post-Holocaust topography. Holocaust anniversaries, especially the Holocaust Memorial Day, are often observed by non-Jews as well as Jews. The United States Holocaust Memorial Museum in Washington, D.C., is attended by more people than any other museum in the United States. Politicians who would assume the mantle of moral gravitas repeat the injunctions to "remember," or "never forget," as if they were religious mantras.

In another domain, books about memory and its processes—on how cultures "remember" and inscribe the "memory" of the Holocaust into their national consciousness; on the shaping of traumatic memory in survivors' narratives and the problems of witnessing such memories; on representations of the Shoah in art and memorial monuments, and forms of commemorative rituals—have supplanted writing on the Shoah itself. Indeed, in the higher reaches of intellectual culture, the very notion of "memory"—usually understood as referring to tragic or traumatic events—has become a governing term of discourse and explanation, supplanting such previous candidates as "class," "gender," "deconstruction," or "culture" itself. (Too numerous to count have been the conferences held under every disciplinary umbrella in the last decade with some combination of the terms "Memory," "Narrative," and "Identity" in the titles.) In this vein of contemporary thought, "memory" itself is treated as a source of value and virtue—perhaps the one virtue we can affirm, in our ironic and skeptical time, without cynicism or denigration. The Holocaust, for this body of thought, is the central pillar and paradigm of tragic and exalted "memory." Indeed, it has become the model for thinking about traumatic memory and history all together.

In turn, this body of thought and the phenomenon sometimes all too smoothly referred to as "memory of the Holocaust" has inspired a body of secondary or even tertiary critique, in which it is the responses to the Holocaust (or its "memory") that are the subject of disputation. In all of this, the Holocaust itself—the Event—can seem very far away, an increasingly abstract point of reference, a pretext for strangely gratifying emotional gestures or curiously abstruse theoretical debates.

In other words, in our increasing preoccupation with it, the Holocaust has become a cultural phenomenon ("the Shoah business"), as well as a historical event. Like any such phenomenon, this one is many-sided, multisymptomatic, and diffuse. Its quality, causes, and consequences for actual understanding of the Shoah are hard to gauge. For, on one level, it is simply inevitable that the Holocaust is becoming the object of retrospection rather than immediate reaction, a receding past rather than a still circulating present. But it is also true that from our perceptual distance, response can get attenuated, deflected, convoluted. The combination of fascination and partial knowledge, reverence and naivete, can lead to odd distortions of perspective and excesses of sentiment. Of course, these dangers extend to us in the literal second generation as well. In a way, it has become too easy rather than too difficult to feel right, righteous, correct, and compassionate about the Holocaust. It is easy to mistake keening for ourselves for keening for the Shoah.

The Holocaust is too large a theme for facile positioning, our attitudes to it too impalpable or too subjective for easy judgment. I do not know whether in my own reactions to the girl at Majdanek I was bringing excessive second-generation severity to bear on the moment, whether I was being too austere on behalf of a history that to me has most serious meanings. But there *are* problems to be aware of as we enter the era of memory; there are forms of response to guard against if we do not want, even in our ostensible piety, to violate the meanings of the past.

. . .

At a garden party in London last summer, I met a man from Rwanda, a survivor of *that* horror. It is perhaps a feature of second-generation sensibility that we note such encounters, or even, in some way, court them. Anyway, it seemed to me there was something I recognized in this man: the quiet presence of pain, perhaps, an absorption of it into the personality so that it could be alluded to in normal tones and carried within oneself with entire dignity. I have seen this look in the eyes, the faces, of so many survivors. Also, the quiet, smoldering indignation at the injustices that have followed the carnage in his country. The Rwandans are not having a good atrocity aftermath. The United Nations is apparently making a botch of attempts to bring at least some of the perpetrators to justice; indeed, there are perpetrators, this man says, among the appointed judges.

The Tutsis, who were the victims, have to live in close inter-mingling with the Hutus who executed the ghastly massacres; and the perpetrators, he tells me, appear entirely remorseless. The French, who most egregiously incited the massacres by funding the radio station that acted as a sort of central command for their execution, have now, cynically in his view, offered to host a truth-and-reconciliation commission.

The carnage in Rwanda was bestial, the subsequent injustices an infuriating insult added to the injuries, and I feel the rise of that old helpless rage at it all, and a welling up of need to console and compensate somehow, anyhow. Then a recoil from this, almost a sense of shame: It is too tempting for me to become a receptacle for this kind of pain. Who knows what vicarious impulses my sympathy holds in relation to this distant disaster? And then, the next oscillation still: Why should I not acknowledge this—the reparative urge—as something significant in itself?

Such are the turns of the second-generation inner dialectic, or perhaps every thoughtful person's emotional uncertainties in relation to other people's horrors. We encounter evidence of these every day, often in the most unlikely settings. What do we do with the evidence, how do we respond?

The Rwandan was also concerned with something that was of immediate interest to me—how the genocide will be remembered. He spoke, with great sadness, about the instant erasure of material evidence—and therefore, potentially, of memory—from the scene of the Rwandan genocide. The bleak witness of murder, machetes, axes, human bones (the Rwandan genocide was a very low-tech affair); but also objects left behind in people's huts, photographs, humble mementos—all these have been instantly eliminated, he said, through deliberate intent, or the speed of flight, or the inability to think about such things amidst the horror itself. The signs, the traces of people's deaths, but also of their lives, are vanished, gone.

He is worried about this. The survivors of the Rwandan genocide are made desolate in so many ways; among them, by the loss of family members and communities with whom to mourn. The rituals of mourning are communal, he told me, and members of the tribe are needed to accomplish it properly. He thought that the emptying of the physical scene of mass murder, the elimination of objects, of objective correlatives for memory, would make the task of remembering and of mourning even harder, that the crushing dimensions of loss will be compounded by this later erasure.

This survivor was studying in a graduate program at an American university, and he told me that he has benefited from his studies of the Holocaust, and how its memory has been maintained. But he also mentioned with some bafflement that he has read and heard critiques of that "memory" from Jewish people, from those who should be most concerned about it themselves. "Perhaps there are issues that Jewish people have," he says. "Something different from us."

Well, yes, I wanted to say. There are issues. Strange issues, they must seem, from his perspective, from his submergence, and just yesterday's reemergence from horror.

Memory, too, has not only its processes and pathologies but its phases and stages. In its essential first impetus, remembrance is a form of recognition, and of honoring. It is a quintessentially moral act, partly because it is gratuitous. Perhaps remembering the dead is the very opposite of gratuitous violence—a gratuitous retrieval of meaning from oblivion. The dead do not profit from it, and neither do we. But the meaning of being human would be diminished if we could not hold those who have died in our minds, if we could not sustain a symbolic relationship to them. Memory is the act of contemplating others through the significance of their lives rather than through their concrete presence, or the uses we can make of them. And, in the case of those who died unjustly, through the significance of their deaths.

On the collective as on the individual plane, the need for recognition through memory, for shared mourning and common commemoration, is intense. Without these palliating responses, it is exceedingly difficult for individuals and groups to put the past behind them, to move on.

The importance of shared memory can be gauged from the instances in which it has been lacking—for example, in the case of Armenian genocide, in which as many as a million helpless civilians were slaughtered by Turkish armies in 1915. For intricate and not very pleasant political reasons, the enormity of that event has never been properly acknowledged by the world at large. While the Holocaust has loomed ever larger in our cultural consciousness, the Armenian genocide receded for many decades into the realm of remote and forgotten events. This is all the more ironic since that atrocity was, in its intent, brazenness, and totality, a clear precursor of the Holocaust; and since the world's early indifference to it apparently gave Hitler perverse comfort as he contemplated his own project of exterminating the Jews. Cautioned that such an undertaking might give him a bad name in history, he reportedly said, "Who now remembers the Armenians?" Chilling words. But the persistent discounting of their tragedy in the world's eyes means that nearly a century on, the Armenians are put in the position of Ancient Mariners, trying to buttonhole all and sundry in the hope that their tale will find its true listeners and that the tellers can thereby obtain some relief. This is the stage before recognition comes, a stage in which collective, no less than individual identity, is helplessly locked in the moment of trauma, in which we remain fixated backwards like Lot's wife on the scene of destruction.

In order to turn our gaze away from horror, we need, collectively as well as individually, to perform the labor of remembering and mourning, a labor assisted by the *therapia*—the healing power—of sympathy and understanding. The attempts to mark and remember the Holocaust in the first place, to absorb it into collective consciousness, had, for a while, an urgent point and purpose. For those who had suffered earlier indifference, the recognition of their tragedy brought relief and, perhaps, a reprieve from too heavy a burden—the responsibility not only to bear witness but to battle the resistance to knowing. For us children of survivors, the broader cultural recognition of events was also important. In some cases, it enabled parents and children to talk more openly. In others, it meant that the Shoah's impact on our lives could be confronted more directly.

The process of reckoning with the Holocaust has led to some strenuous and profound reflection. Aside from the enormous body of historical and other scholarship, the fictional and reflective literature about the Holocaust has grown vast, and it includes some of the important, and some of the great, writing of our time—works ranging from the poetry of Charlotte Delbo and Paul Celan to the stories of Ida Fink and the novels of Aharon Appelfeld, or the hybrid texts by W. G. Sebald, to mention an arbitrary selection. The Holocaust is a formidable subject for imaginative writing, not only because of its immensity but because it is so difficult to retrieve from it a framing structure of meanings, and, therefore, of form. One had better approach this theme with utmost intelligence and a sense of imaginative responsibility. But where art does find the structures—the felt form—through which to encompass aspects of the Holocaust, it is a true use for "memory,"—a conduit to the Shoah, which allows us to imagine and ponder the stark questions and situations posed by that event.

The oral and written testimonies of survivors have also been invaluable in conveying the human textures of an event that might otherwise have remained too abstract. The most immediate impact of atrocity is on the cosmos of each individual self; and it is that impact we need to grasp first if we are to understand something of the nature of such events and their consequences. The literature of testimony also includes some of the central works of the twentieth century, ranging from memoirs of Elie Wiesel and Primo Levi to those of Anne Frank and Etty Hillesum, both written during the atrocity itself. But the memoirs of less famous survivors have also given us indelible glimpses of responses to extremity, of great fear and great courage, of selfishness and sacrifice, of the imprint of dehumanizing circumstances on individual sensibility and the efforts to sustain spiritual as well as physical selfhood. Without such chronicles and testaments, our understanding of the Holocaust, our capacity to imagine what it is like to live through horror of such magnitude would have been impoverished.

The sheer cultural concentration on the Holocaust, the attention and resources brought to it by survivors and others, have also resulted in important educational institutions, foremost among them the United States Holocaust Memorial Museum in Washington. The museum itself was a subject of concerted and highly politicized debates at its inception, and has come under criticism since then. And one can undoubtedly question the selection of exhibits presented in the museum, indeed, the very idea of a museum to atrocity. One can wonder, as many have done, why this most devastating of buildings stands in the place of honor in the capital's Mall, as if the Holocaust were an event in American history. But when all is said and done, the great merit of the museum is that it offers a meticulously researched, densely detailed history lesson of great documentary and pedagogic value. Within its walls, the Holocaust does have its somber and sober history—a record that cannot be gainsaid, denied, or canceled from our imaginative landscape.

Indeed, as one contemplates the vast body of work created in response to the Holocaust—work undertaken not only by those on whom the events had a direct bearing but by others as well—this in itself can be felt as an act, or enactment, of reparation and consolation. The balm of recognition has been applied to this most injurious, wounding rupture. And, if the Holocaust has become the sometimes abstract paradigm of all atrocity, it has also served as a template for the study of analogous events and certain fundamental problems. It was oddly consoling to me that the Rwandan to whom I talked found the meditations on memory and trauma emerging from the Holocaust helpful for his own thinking and coming to terms with his catastrophe. If that was so, I felt when I talked to him, then the labor of reflection, and, indeed, of mourning undertaken in response to the Holocaust, has not been in vain.

. . .

But what happens when we focus on "memory" itself rather than its object, on the rituals of remembrance rather than their content? For something like that seems to have happened on the way from the era of "latency" to that of "memory," from forgetfulness to fascination.

"Memory" in all its guises is the most slippery and Protean of human faculties. Even for survivors, for those who lived through terrible events, it is a fluid process rather than a fixed entity. The acuteness of some recollections may subside with the passage of time; others resurface with redoubled force from thickets of carefully erected defenses or camouflage. Still, even if interpretation of personal experience changes under the pressure of internal reworking or re-viewing, surely the substance of survivors' memories—of memories that powerful—is indelible and irrevocable. Their content cannot be extracted from their minds, or decisively altered.

But as the age of living memory comes to an end, as the human conduit to the Shoah becomes attenuated, we are all entering the era of virtual memory. The way in which such impersonal, mediated memory is usually understood is through the concept of "collective memory"—a term that was first devised in the 1930s by the French sociologist Maurice Halbwachs, and that refers to the kind of shared "memory" in which we hold certain aspects of the past as cultural property in common and "remember" them together. "Collective memory" has enjoyed somewhat of a revival lately, but it is itself a concept of some virtuality, veering between a useful and a misleading fiction. For within such "memory," there is no subject who remembers, no process of remembering, no link between reflection and experience. That is not to say that the concept is meaningless. All tribes, nations, groups, even institutions, have points of reference in the past through which they define themselves, and that contribute to their sense of cohesion or at least commonality. We partly know that we are French, or Czech, or English through allusions to symbolic moments in our collective past—the French Revolution, or the White Mountain Massacre, or D-Day. All nations mark such milestones with commemorative rituals, and encapsulate their significance in monuments and solid form.

But the severance between experience and retrospection does mean that "collective memory" is simultaneously so Protean as to slip through our fingers if we try to grasp it, and so potentially rigid as to be purely formulaic. Impersonal memory, much more than embodied, personal remembering, is malleable in the extreme, and highly susceptible to deliberate shaping or exploitation—to propaganda and censorship, to tendentious selectivity and willful emphasis. It is, in other words, an instrument not so much of subjective reflection or understanding as of cultural agendas, or ideological purposes. The uses of group "memory" are various, and so are its transactions with actual history. To anyone growing up in Eastern Europe after the war, for example, it was clear that in Communist regimes, unofficial, dissident "memory" actually functioned as an antidote to official lies, and as a repository of authentic history. A very different use for national "memory" was found in the Yugoslav wars of the 1990s, in which allusions to long-ago battles and defeats were relentlessly conjured up by the Serbian leadership to drum up militant antagonism towards Bosnian Muslims.

Certainly, the Shoah has become the object of collective memory—a past that is no longer actually remembered by many, but that is relevant to us together, and that has affected our cultural consciousness. But what kind of "collective memory" is it, what are the reasons and the possibly hidden purposes of our preoccupation with such a terrible event?

In his seminal work *Zakhor* (the Hebrew word for "memory"), the historian Joseph Yerushalmi has written of a relationship to the past that was central to Jewish consciousness throughout much Jewish history. In this form of "collective memory," a vision of the past based on the biblical narrative had powerful moral primacy, and important occurrences in the life of a people were seen as a repetition of foundational events and interpreted through their prism. Throughout much Jewish history, Yerushalmi notes, history was seen as a form of eternal recurrence in which the expulsion from Spain, for example, was seen as a repetition of the expulsion from Egypt; the massacres during the Crusades as a new instance of the persecutions in Roman times.

For some religious Jews, and perhaps for others as well, remembrance of the Holocaust carries such sacred resonances. The Shoah is yet another recurrence in the formidable lexicon of Jewish suffering and martyrdom; its memory is a memory in the service of collective, ritual mourning.

But for most of us, in our contemporary world, the meanings of events—even of the most tragic kind—are seen in more secular terms; and it is in such terms that the vicissitudes of Holocaust "memory" are usually interpreted. In one prominent strand of critical commentary, the uses of "Holocaust memory" are analyzed in the classical categories of politics and ideological agendas. For example, Peter Novick, in his important book *The Holocaust in American Life,* has suggested convincingly that attitudes towards the Holocaust were shaped within American Jewish organizations to suit various communal needs and wider political mood. In the early stages after the war, concern with the Shoah was suppressed, so as to minimize anti-German feeling at a time when Germany became an important new ally. Later, as Novick has shown, the Holocaust was quite knowingly promoted as the centerpiece of American Jewish identity, meant to salvage a sense of belonging to a Jewish community at a time when both religious and ethnic bonds were subsiding.

In another strain of analysis, it has become an article of faith that the Shoah has been quite willfully recruited in the service of Zionism and conservative Israeli nationalism, its painful memory invoked to justify Israel's right to aggression and, more latterly, occupation. And it is undoubtedly true that, after a long period of latency and denial in Israel, of efforts to purge the image of Jewish passivity and victimization from the brand-new national consciousness, the legacy of the Holocaust was brought into the foreground for a time. There is no doubt that, for a time, memories of near-annihilation were invoked as a "legitimating narrative" used to justify Israel's actions, to bolster the citizenry's resolve in fighting the country's difficult wars, and to underwrite the right to occupation.

And yet, when all is said and done, the Holocaust does not lend itself easily to patriotic politics. In Israel, the discontinuities between Diasporic and national history and the fact that large portions of the population do not share the Holocaust past have meant that the Holocaust could not become a collective cornerstone in the national mythos, or a strong instrument of propaganda, for long. And perhaps, after all, genocide is too horrific, too spiritually devastating, to be used as a foundation for national identity.

But while the nature of the Shoah may not be suited to ideologies of patriotism, it is very congruent—as has been noted by many observers—with a more postmodern form of political discourse: the politics of identity, and of trauma. In that sense, the sudden foregrounding of the Holocaust in cultural consciousness can be seen as part of a broader preoccupation, regnant especially in America, with traumatic memories and catastrophic histories. In the last interval of the twentieth century, in a great swing of the cultural pendulum, the victimized or oppressed position began to be seen as a more noble and morally credible location for "identity" than the position of power and privilege; and both individuals and groups rushed in to lay claim to histories of calamity and victimization. On the individual level, obsessions with "trauma," "abuse," "recovered memory," and "false memory" succeeded each other at great pitch and speed as the ethos of positive thinking—which had left out so much—met its nemesis in the culture of complaint. In the domain of ethnic politics, episodes of collective suffering or catastrophic defeats— the Nanking massacre for the Chinese Americans, the great famine for the Irish Americans—were "rediscovered" and adopted as the defining events in various groups' histories, moments whose "memory" could be taken as a guarantee of significance, identity, and collective virtue.

In this "victimological Olympics," as Novick has rudely dubbed it, the Holocaust has no contenders, and an entitlement to its inheritance seemed, for a while, to guarantee—by a neat flip of previous attitudes—an exalted moral status. An association with the Holocaust made one, in a sense, untouchable. For Jews, it became advantageous, preferable, fashionable to claim moral rights by association with that event.

But for others as well, the "memory" of various historical catastrophes could provide an objective correlative for private anxieties and failures; the "identification" with history's noble victims could be a way of ennobling, and enlarging, one's own concerns. In this more elusive psychocultural phenomenon, the Holocaust has served as a paradigm of historical horror par excellence, the grandest projection screen on which to exercise a fascination with trauma or "identifications" with history's most persecuted people.

For most commentators writing about the "uses" of the Holocaust, what is at stake are the *kinds* of uses to which the Holocaust is suborned—the particular stripe of ideology that is being promoted with its assistance, or the state of the culture revealed thereby. In other words, the Holocaust, in such interpretations, is seen as currency of exchange within contemporary debates. (Is it good for the left, or the right?) I am, perhaps naively, dismayed by the very idea of deliberate use, of drawing on the legacy of the Shoah as coinage to be exploited in the service of our psychological needs or narrow partisan interests. The Shoah, above all, involved profound suffering; and it seems to me a violation of that suffering to recruit that past to our own purposes. If we are to "remember" the Holocaust, surely we should do so not through the lens of ideological positioning, but through somber and sober reflection; surely, what is at stake are not our necessarily evanescent political "issues," but a regard for the human realities of an awful event, and for the past itself.

.　　.　　.

Beyond specific and willful recruitments of the past, as the Holocaust burgeons into a cultural phenomenon, it becomes, like any such phenomenon, susceptible to trivialization and dilution of meaning. The sheer quantity of productions around this atrocity, the familiarization of horror through the reiteration of images and formulaic phrases, makes it available for increasingly glib perceptions and representations. The Lucite models of Treblinka sold in some Holocaust museums, some of the art works produced in response to the Shoah—for example, an installation in which the tyranny of brand names is compared to the tyranny of concentration camp uniforms—suggest a phase of the "memory" cult in which expression begins to degenerate into mere estheticization of horror, or into kitsch.

Our contemporary culture sweeps up difficult ideas with great ease and churns them into something smooth and palatable. It serves up models of response that can then be brought to almost any occasion in conveniently prefabricated form. For the millions of visitors wending their way each year through sites of calamity—the Holocaust museums, the concentration camps, the former slave quarters—the possibilities for easy sentiment are all too readily available. It is all too possible to view the pitiful exhibits on view in concentration camps for their frisson of dread or schadenfreude (this happened to Them, and not to us). It is possible to feel that we have seen such things already (all that reproduction of imagery, even the most extreme kind), that we are not as horrified as we would like to be. On the other hand, it is perhaps all too easy to mistake a kind of facile "identification" with the victims of atrocity for serious imaginative engagement, to familiarize the Holocaust's meanings by absorbing them into the framework of our own mundane miseries.

As for the actual survivors of the Holocaust, those who did live through extremity, their current elevation from yesterday's untouchables to the Brahmins of the trauma elites is surely better than former neglect; but such idealization also holds the hazards of turning horror to fashion, of an improbable popularization. ("My friend was in Buchenwald," a guest was overheard to say to another at a recent party. "Oh," retorted the other rather smugly, "Our friend was in Auschwitz.") Survivors of the Holocaust rarely thought of themselves as "survivors" until the term became routine, and an honorific. Of course, having such a term may be salutary, may help people crystallize their experiences and honor them. But the pressures on survivors to become professional witnesses, to repeat their tales again and again, may result in an odd distancing from their own experience. (I have heard survivors tell stories that left me shaken and in tears, even as the narrators remained dry-voiced and dry-eyed. But I have also heard tales so polished and smooth-edged that the teller might as well have been referring to somebody else's experiences. Confession, if it is routinized enough, can turn into a form of repression, or self-alienation.)

Testimony, like memory, has its stages. The encounters between survivors and students that have become yet another feature of the late post-Holocaust landscape have, in many cases, had genuinely educational effects. Many young people have received their most vivid sense of the Holocaust's reality from such visitors. But the impact of oral testimony on their recipients, no less than the effects of visual evidence, can also be blunted by overfamiliarization.

"These days, we hear all these stories about the Holocaust, and we are fascinated," a student of mine (in a class having nothing to do with the Holocaust) said recently, speaking with warmth. "We love them."

"Do you really love these stories?" I asked her. "Is that the word?" "Yes," she said, with innocent enthusiasm. "Because they're so dramatic. And we need to remember what happened." Here, combined with our time's moral formula, was "witnessing" made easy, and testimony, after a number of cultural permutations, presenting itself as fairy-tale and true-life adventure again—but this time devoid, apparently, of its dread and pain. Narrative—much as we believe in its curative powers these days—isn't always salvational. Making a "story" out of extremity—or wanting such a story—sometimes offers false and facile consolations.

One particularly vivid illustration of how close a pseudoidentification with victims can come to their betrayal was provided by the publication of *Fragments,* a false memoir about a Holocaust childhood by a Swiss writer calling himself Benjamin Wilkomirski. It is unclear whether Wilkomirski, who had his own private story of childhood unhappiness—he was given away by his mother, and adopted—actually mistook himself for a child who had survived inhuman torments in a concentration camp, or whether he was using this "identification" in a more deliberately opportunistic way. What is clear is that he saw the possession of such an identity and story as advantageous, ennobling, desirable. Possibly, the act of imagining—or pretending—that he had a Holocaust history was a way of aggrandizing even for himself his own less historically significant trauma. But what Wilkomirski's imposture makes dramatically clear is how

smoothly pseudoempathy can glide into unseemly vicarious-
ness; how imperceptibly "identification with the victim" can
turn into exploitation and the violation of the one thing that
ought never be thus used: the pain and death of others.

·   ·   ·

While on the one hand our understanding of the Holocaust
has become susceptible to trivialization and diminishment, on
the other—at that far end of the spectrum where opposites
meet—it is threatened by the kind of inflation of rhetoric
within which specific, or actual, meanings also tend to thin
down or dissolve into nebulous fogs of abstraction. On one
level, the Holocaust in recent years has been transposed from an
event in Jewish history into a sort of pan-memory, a global (or
at least Western) heritage. In the United States, its incorporation
into national consciousness is signaled in many ways. Outside
the United States, to give one example of the past's absorption
into a universalizing narrative, at an international forum on the
Holocaust held in Stockholm in 2000, political and govern-
mental leaders from forty-six countries (according to one informed commentator, Ruth Ellen Gruber) in effect "officially
acknowledged the Holocaust as part of their countries' national
histories."

To some extent, this is only right. The Shoah does belong to
us all. Many countries were implicated in the Holocaust as it
happened; in its aftermath, it has altered everyone's consciousness of history, of the most extreme possibilities of human nature and our common existential condition.

But memory, too, can be "thick" or "thin," to use a distinction Avishai Margalit makes (after the anthropologist Clifford Geertz) in *The Ethics of Memory*. Without the force of specific associations, and from our ever-growing remove, the Holocaust is in danger of becoming an empty if universal symbol, not so much the model as an allegory of historical horror.

Indeed, it sometimes seems that in our simultaneous inflation of "memory" into something both sacred and impalpable, and our remoteness from the events themselves, the sense of history as fable with which some of us began, resurfaces again, this time as cultural discourse and mode of interpretation. The rhetoric of the "unfathomable" and the "unspeakable," so hypnotically repeated, echoes a childhood sense of an incomprehensible cosmos, of sacred or demonic forces. And, just as we as children were overwhelmed by the enormousness of the Event hovering over us, so now we behold its enormity with a kind of interpretative awe, and sometimes helplessness. Moreover—to carry the speculation further—there may be, in this adult awe too, an element of that strange envy we felt towards our survivor parents. Authenticity of experience, in our period, is often conflated with catastrophe, with those traumatic histories with which we are so eager to identify. The Holocaust, above all events, has historical reality. While artistic artifacts, political strategies, and our psyches can be deconstructed nearly out of existence, the Holocaust cannot. It stands beyond our intellectual strategies and our capacities to dissolve all ideas and realities with the acid of our skepticism. The Holocaust cannot, in all decency, be dispelled into something "constructed" or "invented" or imagined. It is the limiting case for such concepts, an event almost reassuringly beyond our sophistication, or sophistries.

To put it another way, it sometimes seems to me that the preoccupation with the "memory of the Holocaust" has come to reflect the postgeneration's proximate but mediated relationship to the great events that preceded its arrival in the world—and its own sense of being, in relation to this history, subsidiary; secondary.

Mind you, it is sometimes hard to avoid a sense of awe as we try to grasp the dimensions of the Holocaust as a whole and contemplate its night-dark landscape. It is hard to avoid feeling that we are touching on something not quite human, or rather, on that place where human behavior reaches a stratum of the bestial and demonic, where the human itself changes into something else. The spectacle of such will to destruction, such vast fields of death, can overwhelm us with its almost ontological darkness, an almost metaphysical malediction.

But, of course, the Holocaust was a humanly engineered event; and without a framework of very particular belief (for the significance of the Shoah is a matter of profound discord among religious Jews as well), the exaltation of "memory" and the rhetoric of awe can turn into the idealization of horror, into an unintentional sacralization of something that was vile. The vocabulary of immensity can turn into merely formulaic piety. The injunctions to "remember," repeated frequently and hypnotically enough, can become precisely a summons not to make the effort of thought, not to consider what we are remembering or how difficult such a feat really is.

I sometimes think that in our secular sacralization of the Shoah, we are doing the opposite of what Freud called disavowal—that we are practicing a kind of avowal. Disavowal is the strategy whereby one denies, or sometimes literally does not see, something that may be right in front of one's eyes but that is too disturbing to acknowledge. In our strategy of avowal, we declare that we remember, identify with, defend, and idealize something extremely disturbing that we have not experienced. We avow, or vow ourselves to be faithful to a *terribilitas* that we simultaneously declare to be unimaginable.

This is collective memory turning into a kind of hypermemory, which itself can function as a secondary amnesia—the kind of amnesia in which the Shoah is in danger not so much of vanishing into forgetfulness as expanding into an increasingly empty referent, a *symbol* of historical horror, an allegory of the Real, the familiar catastrophe and a stand-in for authenticity and for history.

.   .   .

Stand too close to horror, and you get fixation, paralysis, engulfment; stand too far, and you get voyeurism or forgetting. Distance matters.

Our need to reckon with the Holocaust should not be underestimated or diminished, as is sometimes done in the more "tough-minded" critiques of the Holocaust "cult." But the question and the challenge at this moment is how to find the right tone of response, and measure of expression, in relation to this event. Aharon Appelfeld, the Israeli writer and himself a child survivor, suggested, in a series of lectures on the subject, that survivors should think about their experiences in ordinary, daily language; that they should incorporate those most painful and dramatic shards of memory into the stream of larger life-memory, of accessible feeling and humble, concrete words.

But those who have not lived through the Shoah receive its

knowledge, at this late date, through mediations—sometimes several layers of them. We view it no longer directly, but through memorials, artistic representations, literature, film. We also view it through the filter of our own ideas, capacities of feeling, emotional and intellectual interests.

The difficulty of regarding the Holocaust past from our distance is a template for—or an instance of—the problems inherent in, to use Susan Sontag's phrase, "regarding the pain of others." We live, in our world, with a constant spectacle of other people's suffering. Images of exceeding horror are brought to us, courtesy of instant communications, from far away, but right up close—or at least with the illusion of such closeness. It is hard, in such conflations, to find an adequate valence of reaction. On the one hand, a costless sympathy is easy, from the safety of our living-rooms, to express—or even, for a moment, to feel; on the other, perception becomes numbed by overfamiliarization as we begin to be able to look unflinchingly at images that, several decades ago, we could hardly bear to regard. Compassion fatigue sets in as we begin to accept the unacceptable—this time through too much rather than not enough knowledge—with relative calm.

The habituation to horror doubles back on our perceptions of the Holocaust's iconography. In addition to everything else, we now view this past through the filter of subsequent events— Rwanda, Cambodia, Vietnam. Certainly, the idea that the Holocaust was "unique" is no longer possible to sustain, even if the Shoah remains the most total project of extermination, and the most vilely, deliberately, and thoroughly executed. But the "uniqueness" debate was never very useful, except within the competitive politics of trauma; and somehow the very notion of comparison, when it comes to events of such horror and scale, begins to seem indecent. Still, our imaginative capacities are not limitless; and the later genocides of the twentieth century add to a kind of routinization of atrocity and a numbing of our capacities for what might be called a first-order, direct response.

But again: The Holocaust, and people's responses to it, are not a matter for positioning, or for facile irony. It is hard to know what goes on in people's hearts or minds when they resort to the rhetorical tropes elaborated around the Holocaust, or enter a small Holocaust museum in a province otherwise innocent of this history. I had a glimpse of the difficulty—of the ambivalences attendant on such encounters—in my conversation with the man from Rwanda. Every emotion short of specific, personal sympathy becomes, in such encounters, suspect. But at the same time, we do have such emotions, and perhaps, by small increments, we can learn from them. Perhaps, it is sometimes possible to also react more powerfully, more freshly, to events that do not carry the baggage of one's own associations—that stand apart from oneself, there to be seen. Perhaps it is possible to be moved into sudden awareness by something unexpected—as I think most visitors to Majdanek were jolted and shaken by Elźunia's song. I do not know what happens in George Bush's internal configuration when he visits Auschwitz in the early morning during a state visit to Poland and pauses to pose for photographs. In this case, it is certain that the gesture was on one level opportunistic and purely formal. But perhaps even through such ritualized or rote gestures some movement of reflection, of recognition, can occur.

I suppose the best that we can ask for, as we contemplate the Shoah from our lengthening distance, is that we distinguish au-

thentic from inauthentic response, genuine perception from va-
rieties of bad faith. Perhaps sometimes it is better to admit that
until we can speak genuinely, we should remain silent. Unless
we want to engage with this past with imaginative integrity, we
should not force ourselves to "imagine" or "identify." The victims of the Holocaust also need their privacy. In a sense, we
need to acknowledge the distance at which we stand from
events—and from which we have to start if we want to further
the reach of our knowledge and sympathies. This is a matter of
what could be called moral esthetics, and it is important both
for our own and the past's sake.

.   .   .

Within the larger culture of response, the literal children of
survivors stand in a particular relationship to events. The Holocaust, for us, will never be psychically distant; it is part of our
interior landscape and mental theater, not so much a "collective
memory" as (to use a phrase coined by the cultural critic Mari-
anne Hirsch) a "post-memory"—a memory not of theoretical
abstraction or ideological strategies, but of proximity charged
with feeling. In a sense, the very question of memory is moot
for me, and perhaps others like myself. I have never "forgotten"
the Holocaust, nor is it for me an object of virtuous "memory."
Perhaps that is why the broader turn from the discourse of event
to that of memory seems to me so abrupt. In the psyche, time
moves slowly, if at all, and "the Holocaust," or at least the portion of it that is personal to me, is part of my psychic formation.
This is true even if I do not "remember" the Holocaust in the
literal sense, or even make the gestures of "remembering," in the

sense of turning my mind towards this event very often. I suppose the Holocaust for me, as for every child of survivors, is, if not an embodied internal presence, then at least a deeply embedded one. After all, in the second generation, the transmission of knowledge was very direct. We had grown up with survivors and their accounts; and if what had been conveyed to us was not memory, it was nevertheless something memorable and concrete. The imprint of family speech—or silence—was, for better or worse, and with whatever reactions followed, potent and profound.

But the literal second generation too is reaching the age of retrospective reflection. For us, the doubling back of memory involves a double process: a reckoning not only with the Shoah, but with our relationship to those who had lived through it, to our parents and elders. It is our first knowledge of the Holocaust and the method of its transmission that is now becoming the object of memory, a past to be processed, interpreted, understood. At the same time, the dilemmas bequeathed by our family legacies continue to circulate through our minds and psyches. Problems that we thought were resolved—of autonomy, or anger, or residual fears and phobias—turn out not to be.

In recent years, in North America and elsewhere, there has been an outcropping of cross-generational groups in which survivor parents and their children encounter each other in therapeutic settings, with the intention of confronting together the impact of the Shoah on their lives and their relationship to each other. (My sister, who for many years seemed exempt from the burden of the past, has conducted one such group in Vancouver. The Holocaust inheritance is not one that can be easily circumvented or evaded.) In such settings, where truth is supposed to emerge, where it can be spoken to the powerless—a task perhaps more difficult than speaking it to power—the two generations face each other, all too often, across barriers of painful misunderstandings. The children reproach the parents for their silence, their secrecy, for enfolding them too closely in the family embrace, or for being excessively aloof and severe; for not passing on to their offspring enough "identity," or pushing them too hard to succeed and achieve. The parents are often flummoxed by such revelations, and sometimes deeply hurt. If they stayed silent, they thought, it was precisely to protect their children; if they were enfolding, that was because they loved the children so much. If they were distant, it was because they didn't want to infect their offspring with their sadness. But the last thing they wanted was to make the children unhappy; indeed, what they wanted most of all was for them to be happy.

The children in such groups often find the parents maddening—and maddeningly resilient. This is a motif that comes up in informal conversations often, as children of survivors reach their own middle age. The grown-up children note, half with wonder, half with resentment, that the parents, after having gone through so much, with all their histories of formidable persecution behind them, nevertheless sometimes seem to be able to cope with life better than the children themselves, that they get less depressed, anxious, afraid. It is that they passed on the damage to us, the children sometimes speculate, with wry irony. Or, more tentatively—for how can you even conjecture that the survivors in some way might have been more fortunate than those who came after—that they had lives before the Holocaust. Both may well be true. The difference between coming into the world imbued with the Holocaust and having experienced a more normal world before turns out to be significant.

But from the parents' point of view, this must be extremely difficult to comprehend. I suspect that sometimes, after discovering the extent of their offsprings' plaint, the survivors suspect the children of self-indulgence, or plain wimpishness. What had they gone through, after all, what do they have to complain of, in their comfortable lives? Why are they so fragile, so full of complexes? I confess that occasionally I have nurtured this suspicion, too. I sometimes think, impatiently, that the therapeutic groups themselves reconstruct the misunderstandings between the very different ethos of the two generations, that they represent an Americanization of the problem, and of the post-Holocaust map. How long can one blame the parents for the inadequacies of one's precious identity, how late demand of them that they repair the deficiencies?

But often, in the later phases of the life cycle, there is an enlargement of sympathies between the generations and an easing. In the observations of psychoanalysts such as Dan Bar-On and Dina Wardi, it seems that the end of life, for survivors, sometimes brings a yielding of carefully preserved defenses. Parents who were incapable of physical intimacy with their children become capable of it now. As frailty sets in, as the discipline of repression weakens, there is sometimes an opening of spaces, and of memories, that have been hermetically shut. This can be poignant in the extreme to witness, as survivors' old fears—of showers, of a knock on the door, of Them—are revived. But in Dina Wardi's accounts, the communications that emerge, no matter how painful or disturbing, are, for the children who have had no access to the shut spaces, precious.

I certainly found this to be so when, in his eighties, my father began to speak about his brothers, whom, until then, he hardly ever mentioned. A lava of long-suppressed love and guilt erupted in a lament that moved me all the more because I knew how long it had been stifled. My father was in many ways a hard man; but it turned out that all those decades, he had missed his brothers terribly, that all that time he had lived with a rankling self-reproach for having made a "wrong" decision that, in his mind, led to their death. The fateful "mistake" was made at the very end of the war, during the last salvos of cross-fire between the retreating German troops and the advancing Soviet ones. After the brothers decided to leave the peasant's house where they were all huddled during this endgame, they were killed—accidentally, and not at that point because they were Jews—in the indiscriminate shooting. Surely, the decision to leave and seek what might have been safer circumstances was theirs as much as my father's, and surely, it had its own rationale. But it was my father who survived, and in his mind, it was he who was responsible for their terribly ironic and gratuitous death—at the end, at the very end, when they might so easily have lived. More than fifty years later, my father cried out his protest and remorse; and although this was poignant in the extreme, it was also, for me, a deepening of a bond.

Sometimes for the children too, after our own "latency period," there is a deferred mourning—for those perished relatives, for our parents' hard lives, perhaps for ourselves and the inchoate sense of loss we were bequeathed. For some children of survivors, the fears of transferring their own early anxieties to their children, of excessive protectiveness towards such perishable humans, become a new quandary. The trail of our first knowledge will probably continue to trace and wind, or unwind itself, throughout our lives.

It seems that the impact of the family legacy continues unto the third generation. The grandchildren of survivors are still deeply affected by their elders' experiences, memories, accounts. Indeed, there is moving evidence (for example, in intergenerational studies conducted by the Israeli psychoanalysts Dan Bar-On and Gabriele Rosenthal, or case studies reported by Dina Wardi) that for the aging survivors, relationships with the third generation can be deeply solacing and liberating. Many of them, it appears, find it easier to speak about what they endured during the Holocaust to the grandchildren than their own children. Perhaps there is less danger, from the greater generational distance, that the fraught cargo of guilt, fear, and sorrow will be transferred directly into the listener's psyche. Perhaps, without that fraught cargo, the grandchildren can offer freer compassion. Or perhaps, as Dina Wardi suggests, the restoration of an affirmative order and sequences of life brings reassurance to the survivors so that losses that were unbearable can now be faced.

Even as I felt the grief of my parents' deaths—and a wrenching sense of regret for losing, in them, my last direct thread to a whole world and sensibility—I, too, was oddly consoled, and in a sense astonished, that both my mother and father had lived out a whole life span. A belief in a natural order of life is for us, the children of survivors, also very hard to attain.

The deep effects of catastrophe, the kind that are passed on from psyche to psyche and mind to mind, continue to reverberate unto the third generation. But after the third, or in rare cases the fourth generation, the thread of direct memory will be severed. The experiences of the Holocaust, even if they continue to be part of family narratives, will not be conveyed to further descendants with the authority of actual witness and vividness of an embodied voice.

.   .   .

What, then, from our vantage point and moment in time, shall we do about the Holocaust?

Some years ago, after my first book was published, I was contacted by a stranger who told me he was a Holocaust survivor and had something important to tell me. I had no doubt that I would go; the sense of obligation was instant and not up for question. I met him in a gloomy New York restaurant, an aging, small man, and listened as he unfolded a long chronicle of his survival, detailed and horrific, filled with those improbable twists of plot, twists of fate, that stretch credulity and should induce astonishment. I kept waiting for a specific point to emerge, for some request to be made that would explain his summons. But none came. He ended, and we left the restaurant. It turned out that he wanted nothing except to tell his story—and to tell it, specifically, to me. This happens to people like myself, children of survivors now become adults, especially those who have put pen to paper. We are the ideal recipients of such narratives, their designated carriers. And I could see, with some poignancy, why the aging survivor wished someone to know his part of the Event, why he didn't want it to disappear entirely from the human record. After you had lived through something like that, shouldn't it be redeemed at least by being set down somewhere, inscribed as one tiny gene in our collective cultural DNA, remembered? I believe I listened attentively, and well. I knew the place names he referred to, understood the real geography of his escapes, and the human geography as well—the kinds of people he met, the probable motives for their decisions. And yet how could I really absorb the ins and outs of another horrific tale, and what was I going to do with it—how make it meaningful? What should we do with transmitted memories and narratives of the Holocaust, how shall we mold them before passing them on?

The legacy of the Shoah is being passed on to us—the post-generation as a whole, and the literal second generation in particular. The inheritance, whether we would or not, is being placed in our hands, perhaps in our trust. Like many of my peers, I have balked at the very idea of trusteeship. Why should I accept the burden of this heaviest of pasts, why continue to carry it within myself, or assume any responsibility for what had happened to others long ago? And of course there is no binding obligation to do so, no duty to pick up the wand, or accept the inheritance. And yet, I do not know of many who entirely escape it, who do not, in their adult lives, look around or look back and find they have to come to terms with the Holocaust not only as intimate heritage but as a broader concern or a subject. In one way or another, the Shoah pursues us and demands something from us. It ambushes us, as a friend recently said, even when we thought we were done with it. It is, after all, our past.

The legacy was transmitted to us first of all in the family, and as personal disclosure, in the form of encapsulated sagas and condensed feeling. In trying to understand the past retrospectively, this is the trail we have had first of all to follow. As we accumulate our own experiences, and indeed memories, we have had to decode our own position vis-à-vis our family narratives, to excavate our own struggles from under the shadow that sometimes made them seem so insignificant, to discover the shape of our own lives. In a way, we have needed to separate our voices from the spellbinding, significance-laden voices of the survivors, to stop being ventriloquists for our parents.

Many have done so through the self-examination afforded by psychoanalysis or therapy. But the urge to give voice to our own experience has also given rise to a considerable body of writing and of art, emerging out of the specific experience of "second-generationness." The literature is large enough to warrant an anthology, with the suggestive title *Nothing Makes You Free*. As with the vast corpus of work produced by survivors, much of the second-generation's writing is personal and autobiographical, but the contrasts between the two bodies of literature are instructive. It could be said that survivors' memoirs are written *from* memory, and take the veracity of that faculty, the correspondence of recall to real experience, for granted. It is the realities of that experience that are the brunt of survivors' mostly realistic narratives. The second-generation texts are often *about* memory. They foreground precisely the uncertainties of recollection, and the difficulties of knowing the past. In the literature by children of survivors, intimate history is not so much given as searched for; the processes of overcoming amnesia and uncovering family secrets, of reconstructing broken stories or constructing one's identity, are often the driving concerns and the predominant themes.

In the hands of talented writers, the quest for a hidden past or the reckoning with the scars and wounds left in the wake of the Holocaust can produce powerful and suggestive works, such as the autobiographical *After Long Silence* by Helen Fremont, or *Losing the Dead* by Lisa Appignanesi. But writers of the second generation cannot count on the primary power or persuasiveness of their material, on which survivors' memoirs often rely. Sometimes, it must be said, the texts that emerge from their more elusive themes run the risk of self-indulgence, or sentimentality, or moral preciousness. It is possible, when reckoning with the deflected past, to attribute too many of one's minute miseries and neuroses to the Holocaust, thereby conferring unearned significance on problems that really are purely individual.

Self-indulgence is an issue in the second generation, a subject that comes up in conversations and a category of critique. Children of survivors tend to suspect each other of complaining, or even whining. ("He thinks he didn't get into Princeton because of the Holocaust. She thinks she has social anxiety because her father was in Treblinka.") And self-indulgence among sometimes indulged children of survivors is a danger. Seeing yourself as a victim of victims, as damaged by calamities that had been visited on somebody else, is not a sympathetic position. If you don't get the proportions right, if you bring the formidable weight of the Holocaust to bear on commonplace problems of everyday life, then you may end up not so much illuminating the past as turning the searchlight on your own narcissism.

But much of the second-generation writing is complex, robust, and tough-minded. Many of the personal texts unflinchingly show difficult, "dysfunctional" families, the conflicts and resentments that, no matter how poetically or historically unfair, have been part of the relations between survivors and their offspring. Other texts portray survivor parents who, far from having been ennobled by suffering, have become callous or embittered, as well as haunted, frightened, and depressed. Art Spiegelman's comic-book memoir, *Maus,* with its parents who have traveled through all the circles of hell and who have emerged severely damaged and severely damaging, can serve as a prototype for this vein of reminiscence. Indeed, it is one of the merits of second-generation writing that it gives such truthful and concrete insight into the personalities of survivors, and that, far from depicting them as noble victims or moral paragons, it dares to show them in their human variety and to evoke the injury to the psyche, or even the brutalization of character, that can follow upon extreme persecution and humiliation. These can be uncomfortable insights, but they are ones we also need to incorporate into our understanding of atrocity's aftermath.

The felt legacy of the Shoah, with its beginnings in enormous loss and mourning, confers on us, aside from its weight and burdens, a profound endowment. An early knowledge of death and loss is terrifying, but it can also be a source of deep instruction. Mourning, after all, is at the very root of much human knowledge—of mortality, vulnerability, the needs for human connection. It is at the root, perhaps, of the reparative urge, the desire to protect our altogether perishable world, to redress some of its harshness and bring to it some healing and consolation.

In my own relations with the most difficult of pasts, it is separation and containment—the two great psychoanalytic goods—that I have found most necessary, and salutary. But if one can dip into the somber past without being swallowed by it, then the past can become a rich vein of meaning. A friend once told me of her eloquent, repeated dreams in which she was carrying a coffin on her back. Gradually, the coffin got lighter; and sometimes, it appeared that it was also a treasure chest. If you can bear the burden of mourning, the knowledge it brings may become a treasury. If you dare visit the shades, you may bring back wisdom. Orpheus's song cannot bring back those claimed by the underworld, but it can become richer for his sojourn there. The urge to rescue, to repair and salve, which we felt so painfully in our early transactions with wounded parents, can transform itself—if it is contained in sufficient frameworks of emotional safety—into the re-creative and reconstructive urge, into the desire for creativity and interpretation. In some of the fictional literature of the second generation—the sharply etched vignettes in *Nightfather* by the Dutch writer Karl Friedman, the delicate stories by the Israeli writer Savyon Liebrecht, or the richly elaborated novels by David Grossman—the mediated but impassioned relationship to the Holocaust past has been a well-spring for imaginative thought.

Others, from being subjects of analysis, have turned analysts themselves, or have followed other therapeutic or reparative professions. After all, psychic pain was the first subject of psychoanalytic investigation, and continues to be the main fount of its insights. This, too, is a way of molding a knowledge of pain so that it can be applied as salve or restoration. In such conversions, our early identifications with vulnerable parents may expand into more considered compassion; the instinctive protest against our elders' humiliation can turn into a broader recognition of everyone's need for dignity and for justice.

.   .   .

The cargo of compressed meanings carried in the first, personal knowledge of the Holocaust has been of the highest density, and it has been susceptible to many kinds of analysis, reflection, interpretation.

But the age of personal transmission, of testimony and documentary discovery, is coming to an end. Sometimes—on rare occasions—there are still revelations. A Polish friend who had always known that her Jewish mother was hidden throughout the war by her non-Jewish, Polish father recently discovered, through a fortuitous chain of contacts, that her father had hidden a number of other people as well; and that some of them were her unknown relatives. For my friend, this has been a life-altering discovery; and it is one of the most hopeful kind—the opposite of the dark information so often lurking behind survivors' secrets. My friend's father was clearly one of the modest great men of this appalling history; and his acts are one clear demonstration that goodness could sometimes be heroic, a true countervailing force to the barbarism unleashed upon the world.

Even after this fantastic delay, this is intensely meaningful disclosure. But such revelations are increasingly rare. The Holocaust is the most documented event in history; the archives groan with information, with transcripts of interviews, videos of survivors, written records. In relation to personal memory of the Holocaust, we may have reached a stage of hypermnesia—as in "Funes the Memorious," a famous story by Borges whose protagonist suffers from perfect and indiscriminate recall of everything he's ever heard and seen, so that he has no way of selecting from or making sense of his memories.

Personal testimony has been profoundly important to our understanding of the Holocaust; but six decades later, it may be reaching the limits of its usefulness. But aside from the power of personal knowledge, aside from our private negotiations with the past, a larger legacy is at stake. In relation to that legacy—to the Holocaust as a historical event—the second generation also stands in a particular position, a vantage point that has its hazards, but also opportunities.

I do not remember exactly when I saw my first documentary images of concentration camps, but I remember very well my reaction to them. Here, in a book of black-and-white photographs, were those grimmest images—images one could hardly bear to look at, never mind really to take in. But aside from a sort of moral helplessness in front of this awful album, I felt another kind of surprise, or internal revision taking place: These images were not the attic. They were not "my" Holocaust. They were the heart of darkness, and I had of course known about them. But our own internal imagery is powerful, and the attic—however it may correspond to the real attic of my parents' hiding—is one of the deepest images I have. It took a forcible impression to modify it. It was not until I saw those stark photographs of bleak barracks and emaciated figures, and the eyes looking out at us with fierce and mute reproach, that the camps became part of my inner storehouse.

For other children of survivors, of course, it was those images that were the given, and my parents' attic that might seem a small, marginal part of the Holocaust topography. The concentration camps are the *locus classicus* of the Holocaust, and some of my second-generation peers have trouble crediting the story of my parents, with their hiding in a Ukrainian village, and their Polish and Ukrainian helpers.

Not "my" Holocaust. The urge to hold on to "our" Holocaust and discount other versions, to claim rights of territory and keep others off—all these are temptations for the heirs of survivors. (A second-generation historian, Norman Finkelstein, for example, seems to include only those who had been in concentration camps—as his mother had been—among the numbers of the Shoah's survivors.)

The danger, in the literal second generation, is not so much a diffusion of memory as its fixity. The images, the stories we were given in childhood, constitute an inner iconography that belongs to our primary geography and location in the world. The transferred fragments we have incorporated are all the harder to modify, revise, correct for being transferred. The childhood prohibition on tampering with the forbidding shards of communication may persist into adulthood in a sort of rigidity of views, or opinion. The call for fidelity in the sphere of interpretation can also be compelling. Something of the taboo that attended our early knowledge of death—a knowledge so much more disturbing, after all, than that of sex—clings to the very subject and idea of the Holocaust. The injunction to remain close to the parental versions of the past can have great force.

There are good reasons for this. Our stakes in this history, after all, are high, and hardly abstract. But paradoxically, if we insist on fidelity to our childhood knowledge, we may run the risk of being unfaithful to what our parents themselves knew. Some time after my parents' deaths, I saw their video testimony, given to the Vancouver Holocaust Centre, about their experiences of the war years. Like their reparations certificates, this document also delivered a jolt of surprise. There is of course always a startling poignancy about such visual records and their capacity, seemingly, to bring back the dead. More than photographs, which capture, above all, the vanishing of arrested moments, film, with its element of motion, seems to recapture (oh so illusorily) the past's concrete immediacy. But the surprise had to do with something else entirely: the impressive coherence of my parents' accounts. Perhaps what I was hearing, in my parents' "official" testimony, was simply the difference between family and public speech. After all, I had not heard them talk about their experiences in a public forum, from that greater, cooler distance. But I confess that, from my own distance, I was almost shocked to realize just how informed and rational they had been in their perceptions of the darkness they had lived through. They had an accurate grasp of the treaties that had decided their region's fate (most saliently, the infamous Molotov-Ribbentrop pact giving eastern territories of Poland to the Soviets, while the Nazis snapped up the western ones); the movements of fronts and armies, the loyalties of the various ethnic populations in their area. My father, especially, understood better than most of his community how much there was to be afraid of; and that in turn allowed him to behave with the kind of will and wiliness that ensured his own and his young wife's survival. When most of his fellow Jews in Załośce refused to believe a seemingly crazed boy who came from another village to tell what the Nazis had accomplished there, my father chose to believe him. When others showed up for the roll calls staged by the Germans ostensibly to recruit people for work, he stayed away. In retrospect, I wish I had asked him how he knew these things, or how he or my mother had decided whom among their non-Jewish neighbors they could ask for shelter and help. For knowing whom to trust, perhaps the very ability to trust someone, was also crucial to survival.

But it took me a long time to start asking such questions, to perceive, outside the vastness of personal pain, the structures of unfolding events, of motive and consequence, cause and effect. As we think about the Holocaust with more developed instruments of understanding, we need, on one level, to restore some of the complexity to our views of the past that many survivors came by naturally.

But as we reach full maturity, I think we need to acknowledge that, in relation to the larger history, as much as to our personal stories, we are now closer to the position of the analyst and interpreter than the perpetually damaged patient. And it may be that the model of the good analyst—in the multiple senses of that word—offers a fruitful paradigm for thinking about terrible histories that are so close to us, but yet are not ours. That is, it behooves us to think about the past with utmost sympathy, or even empathy, for its participants, but without merging with the inner world, or the views, of those participants entirely. It behooves us, with utmost care and compassion, to use our vantage point outside the traumatic history itself in order to bring to it interpretations that may not be available to the victims; and perhaps, even, in our thinking and analysis, to move beyond the point of trauma itself.

We do not come into the "memory" of the Shoah by psychogenetic inheritance, or into its moral rights by historical association. What we do have is an acute, living sense of its human realities. If we want to pick up the wand, if we want to be useful messengers to the future, then I believe we need to transform our living link to the Shoah into a felt, but enlarged, comprehension of history. We need to locate our family stories in the broader context of events, to ponder not only the individual fates of those we know and love, but the larger developments and patterns that propelled those fates.

But further, we sometimes need the courage to depart from a sense of the past conveyed to us through the family, or from the formulations and prejudices to which we have reduced the transferred knowledge, and bring our own perspective to events. We have no choice at this point but to think about the Shoah through retrospective reflection (to use a more accurate term than "memory") and from a perspective different from that of the participants. But such reflection—a detached as well as engaged meditation on the past—can be an enlarging instrument of vision. In a sense, we could not ask for such detached engagement from most survivors, for whom coming to terms with their own experiences and the acute emotions aroused by it is quite enough of a life-long task. But viewing the past through a longer and wider lens can also help us extricate from it an important layer of meanings. In this, our generational vantage point presents certain opportunities. For one thing, an international, cross-cultural, or culturally intermingled perspective comes to us as easily as certain kinds of exclusive ethnic and religious attachments came to our ancestors. Translated backwards, this can lead to a comparative approach to history—something that I believe is much needed in the study of both the Holocaust and the longer Diasporic Jewish past.

None of this means "forgetting" the family stories, or dishonoring Jewish perspectives. The testimonies, the stories and encapsulated sagas we have grown up with, give us access to the realities of the Holocaust, to its moral meanings. They are for us a point of entry into the larger history. At the same time, we cannot understand any single story without grasping the nature of events within which it took place. There is a fructifying dialectic between personal knowledge and historical investigation, between the capacity to grasp one person's suffering and the desire to know what caused or permitted it. Nor does a broader, more comparative perspective imply excessive disengagement, or a recollection of horror in tranquillity. On the contrary, this is the increment of knowledge we can add, the vantage point we can use, to expand our understanding of the past—and, by a further extension of the dialectic, to bring back from the past insights to illuminate the present. If we want to call upon the Shoah to deepen our comprehension of atrocity, then we need to study not only anti-Semitism but the processes of ethnic and religious hatred, the patterns of fanatical belief, the causes of neighborly violence, and the mechanisms through which these can be contained. We need to undertake such investigations, I believe, both within the specific dimensions of the Holocaust and as they occur, and keep occurring elsewhere.

The generation after atrocity is the hinge generation—the point at which the past is transmuted into history or into myth. It is in the second generation, with its intense loyalties to the past, that the danger of turning the realities of historical experience into frozen formulae of collective memory is the greatest; but it is also in that interval that we have the best opportunity of apprehending history in all its affective and moral complexity. It matters that the historical truths of an event as crucial and shattering as the Shoah be preserved from denial and new hatreds, but also from banality, ideological distortion, and vacuous pieties. Paradoxically, I believe that if we are to guard it well, then we need to achieve a certain thoughtful separation from received ideas as, in our personal lives, we needed to separate ourselves, thoughtfully and with sympathy, from our persecuted parents.

The Shoah itself is not a past we can heal or cure, and it would be trivial to imagine that we can perform a therapy on the history. But as the Holocaust recedes from us in temporal distance, it may also be time—to take our retrospective imagination further—to unfreeze our vision of the past from the point of historical trauma and start exploring again the multifarious life before. We need to do this not through denial or dissipation of memory, but, as with the unfreezing of personal pain, through a difficult processing of the past, through full acknowledgment. It may be time to return the Shoah, in our imaginations and collective consciousness, to the *longue durée* of previous and subsequent history.

VI

FROM MEMORY TO THE PAST

With the era of memory, the era of returns. The lifting of the Iron Curtain has made it possible to enter Eastern Europe with new ease, and ever since, people who have not set foot in countries of their origin for decades have been coming back in numbers, to see, to remember, to reconnect parts of life severed by the war, to test their fantasized images of "the Old Country" or confirm their prejudices. Children of survivors and others as well make their "returns" to lands they have never seen and that have remained, in postwar Jewish imagination, a dark, submerged Atlantis. For some of these visitors, the journeys hold surprises, discoveries, conversations. Others, on their brief tours, without a language in which to communicate with the natives, see only what they were prepared to see in the first place.

"The return" is accumulating a literature of its own, one that ranges from essays by such well-known writers as Aharon Appelfeld (who survived, as a child, by roaming the forests of Romania) to such brilliant bouts of fictional invention as Jonathan Foer's *Everything Is Illuminated*. But there are also the standard

EVA HOFFMAN

accounts, written within predictable frameworks of perception and featuring standard tropes: Poland as "one big cemetery"; the mean peasants facing visitors with their closed faces; the gaping sense of absence, of nothingness, where the Jews had once been, the anti-Semitism one can feel in the very air. I am wary of the ready-made metaphors and the prefabricated observations. I am not fond of the Marches of the Living, in which groups of American and Israeli teenagers are taken on whirlwind tours not of Poland, but of concentration camps. It is true that anti-Semitic incidents do occur in Poland and elsewhere. Ugly graffiti disgrace some Polish buildings. Groups of tourists disembarking from their buses to dance the *hora* in the old Jewish quarter of Cracow meet with skeptical looks or sometimes rude jeers from Polish bystanders. But often, it is the power of projection and expectation that attributes generalized anti-Semitism to an undifferentiated mass of humans. How does one intuit anti-Semitism in the atmosphere? How does one sense a vast absence, or presence of the dead, in a place where one has never been?

These are social forms of what, in literary terminology applied to sentimental descriptions of nature, used to be called pathetic fallacy; and in relation to Poland and Eastern Europe, such perceptual conventions still go unquestioned. And it is in relation to Poland, which I have known as a real place, with strata and striations of attitude, human behavior, and political conviction, that I am most aware of the need for knowledge to supplement sentiment, for information to check anecdote and preconception.

But I am not exempt from sentiment, or from a fundamental curiosity about my familial past, the urge to know where my parents and, by extension, my sister and I came from. To see the places in their concreteness, for it somehow still matters, in our globalized world, which spot on the globe we come from. To try to touch on the geography of our family's prewar lives. To think, perhaps, about what might have happened if . . . Who we might have become, for example, if my parents had not decided to leave the Ukraine for Cracow in 1945. To understand, to grasp something—for one's longer historical past begins to matter more as we grow older, as our sense of time lengthens, as we understand that sixty years was not so long ago, and that earlier worlds have formed us, are inscribed somewhere within our bodies and our sensibilities.

And so, after my parents' deaths, I respond to my sister's urging that we visit that mythical village of Załośce—a word that came with my first consciousness, the place where my parents had spent their childhoods and early adulthoods; where they had survived That Time. The urge to go is the next turn in a dialectic that had led me, a few years earlier, to a study of Polish-Jewish relations and a book, *Shtetl*. In my attempt to supplement memory with history, to locate my family's story within the broader events, it was that longer past I needed to know. But this was an undertaking in which the cross-pollination between personal knowledge and historical exploration turned out to be wonderfully fertile. The stories I had heard since childhood, of prewar shtetl life; the anecdotes about daily dealings between Polish, Ukrainian, and Jewish neighbors; the glimpses of intergenerational conflicts between my Orthodox grandparents and modernizing parents: These provided a purchase and a point of entry for reading the intricate canvas of Polish-Jewish history. In the very sensibilities of my parents, their gestures, assumptions, pitch towards the world, I could sense something of the shtetl's atmosphere, attitudes, social textures.

At the same time, as I continued my study of a shtetl not too far from the one in which my parents had grown up, it was instructive in the deepest sense to discover that my parents' lives were formed within an intelligible social context, that the kind of small town, or large village, they grew up in, the schools they attended, the literature they read, and the aspirations they nurtured in their youth, could be seen and located within a marvelously interesting social map of Jewish life in prewar Poland.

Now that it has all of a sudden become possible to do so, I want to see for myself, to pin down concretely the places that have lived such a rich life in my imagination. Oddly enough, although we had grown up so close to Załośce, my sister and I had never been there. Or perhaps not so oddly, since the Ukraine, which had become part of the Soviet Union after the war, was not easy to enter when we were growing up in Poland. Once we emigrated to Canada and the United States, a journey to a Soviet region became even more unlikely. And even when the Iron Curtain was lifted, my parents, for reasons that were not always clear, did not wish us to go. They were obscurely afraid for us. They were committed to the idea of never looking back. My father referred to village feuds. During their lifetimes, this trip would have been a violation of their anxieties and wishes. After their deaths, it became a form of homage and of mourning.

There was also the letter, which suggested that the commitment to never looking back was not complete. I discovered it among the papers my parents had left behind after their deaths. There, on a torn page, written in my father's rather brusque handwriting, was a communication addressed to a man named Hryczko. The name rang a distant bell, and as I read on, I realized that Hryczko was the son of the "professor" whose sobriquet I'd often heard in my childhood—the man whose family had sheltered my parents during the war and thus helped save their lives. The rough draft, written a year before my father's death, was an attempt to make contact after all those years, and perhaps to offer proper thanks. It contained the suggestion that Hryczko's family should be placed in Yad Vashem's roll call of "Righteous Gentiles." It also told Hryczko something he apparently might not have known—how and when my father's brothers died. Both of them were killed when the war was in effect over, in crossfire between the receding German and the incoming Soviet armies. Among the familiar facts, there was a sentence I read with shock: "There was no one to help me," my father wrote. "I had to bury them myself."

"I had to bury them myself." I tried to imagine my father, at the end of the long devastation, borrowing a peasant's cart and taking his brothers' bodies—his loved brothers who had come so close to being wrested from the wreckage—to the Jewish cemetery, where, on his own and without the solace of other mourners, he dug two graves and lowered them in. My father didn't die of this; but I could see how that moment, amidst all the things he had lived through, might have plunged him into speechlessness. It was that speechlessness that I felt as a child, within all his outbursts; a silence he did not fully break until his death. Of this, he did not speak to me. Of this, he could only write on a half-torn piece of paper to a man who was safely on the other side of the world, but who had been there, had seen it all, too. And so my father wrote from the safety of distance, but perhaps with the memory of the intimacy that surely must bind you to a person to whom you once entrusted your life.

It was the letter that consolidated my decision, that made me feel I must go. Hryczko might still be alive, my sister and I might meet him. We did not know whether a revised draft had reached him; there was apparently some doubt in my father's mind that it would.

The trip might have easily turned into a comedy of errors. The town of Załośce did not seem to appear on any maps I could find; and even the Ukrainian historian whom I recruited to the task could not locate it in any of his sources. Mind you, accurate maps were not widely dispensed by the Soviet regime, and the impoverished new Ukrainian government may not have had a chance to catch up yet. Either that or, as the historian suggested, the name of the town might have been changed, as often happened in the Soviet era. Perhaps what we really wanted was "Załoźec," a village in the same general area of the Ukraine. Załośce might have become Załoźec. Or else, I might have made "Załośce" up in the first place, as part of my fairy-tale world. We were, I felt, in a liminal territory, where concrete realities easily dissolve into imaginary entities.

My sister and I were quite ready to go to Załoźec. It was close enough to where this perhaps imaginary Załośce was supposed to be. We might well have gone and found no traces of our parents in reality or in local memories, and we would have gone away saddened, but not surprised. That is how most of these voyages, the returns to small towns, turn out. As it was, the day was saved by a cicerone from heaven masquerading as a former soccer star and coach whom we had hired as our driver for the trip to the putative or real Załośce. In his capacity as coach to soccer teams, which he had guided in his time to all corners of the Ukraine, our driver had been entrusted with detailed local maps—as the historian, subversive academic type that he was, was not. It was our soccer star guide, therefore, who, to our considerable excitement, pointed to the name "Załośce" on one of those maps. He was quite excited himself.

Thus it was that my sister and I arrived in the real Załośce, a pastoral town/village with a primitive economy, a pitiable "main street," and a supply of vodka that began flowing (to our considerable chagrin) at breakfast and did not stop until bedtime. And although we would never have known what we had missed had we not found this unremarkable large village, we now know that we would have missed a lot.

For as soon as we enter Załośce and announce our presence and purpose in the shabby little offices of the "Town Council," the time of a kind of magic begins. We would have missed that uncanny encounter, which takes place a mere fifteen minutes after our arrival, with a pretty peasant woman, blue-eyed and kerchiefed, in whose direction we are pointed by some kindly guide. "The Wydra family," she says, in response to our query about my father's family. Yes, we were neighbors, though I was just a child then. My family went to their inn, and they came to us to have their shoes mended. She stands against a fence and speaks shyly. But who are you, she asks, for to her we must be a very confusing apparition. Sisters, wives, daughters? Ah yes, Boris's daughters. Bucio. Munio, Libko, Bucio, yes? The brothers' names, which she has remembered all this time. I do not always remember them myself.

We would have missed Olga, and her exclamation, on first seeing my sister, "But she's Hava to the life!" Olga claps her hands to her face with the wonder of it as she looks at my sister. Hava was our paternal grandmother, whose face we had never seen, not in life, not in photographs. To know that my sister looks just like her is strangely moving. We had had grandparents once, real grandparents just beyond the time-cut in my imagination; and the information leads into a suddenly fuller, more inhabited past . . .

Olga is a vivid-looking, even beautiful, woman in her eighties; she wears the standard peasant scarf on her head and speaks with a natural eloquence. As she talks, a succession of small, homey details pours out about my parents and their families, about my parents' marriage and the tensions between my maternal grandparents and their new, rebellious son-in-law, and my mother's sweetness and good humor . . . "She was like an apple, she was like a doughnut," Olga says, remembering my mother. Some of her anecdotes tally almost word for word with my mother's memory vignettes: Olga had clearly been a good, even a close family friend. Here, on another side of the world, five decades later, the homey details are confirmed and thereby given new reality by a woman who is a truly faithful repository of memory, who has retained those long-ago friends, once they had left, had disappeared from her horizon, in her mind.

Olga's 101-year-old mother also remembers Hava very well. She is nearly blind, but very alert, and is reading her Bible with the help of a magnifying glass, in Polish, so as to keep up that language. Her husband and our grandmother were friends, she tells us, and sometimes helped each other. They borrowed money from each other, apparently. Olga's mother speaks about human fate, and how we need to accept it. She makes a sign of the cross over my sister and me as we leave, and I feel it as a genuine benediction.

Others, too, use the word "fate" often, as they allude to their harsh lives and the region's horrific history. They seem, however, not resigned, but full of vitality. They walk with us around Załośce, or huddle in groups, speaking with great excitement in a medley of Ukrainian and Polish, our driver translating when necessary, although the two languages are almost mutually penetrable. Everyone tries to tell us something about Załośce and how things had been before the war, whom they had known among their Jewish neighbors, or which of their children had gone where. The Town Council of Załośce, as far as I can tell, seems to cease its functions for the duration of our visit and devote itself to the task of helping us in our memory researches. Maria, one of the council's members, tells us she spent a sleepless night after our arrival because she was so stirred by what we had told her.

It is Maria who, through the local grapevine, tracks down Hryczko, now living in another village, and who takes us, along with another woman councilor apparently freed of her duties, to meet him. And there, finally, he is: a robust, still handsome man in his mid–eighties (the same age as my father would have been), standing in front of his relatively prosperous household (indoor plumbing!) that, however, like all of Ukraine, has fallen on very hard times. We look at each other across a gulf of fifty years with mutual astonishment and then follow him into the house and talk at length, trying to fathom what joins us across the gaping passage of time.

Hryczko fills in the other side of the story, that of my parents' rescuers, the people whose actions had so crucially redounded in our lives, but whose motives I had never known, had never, to my shame, thought to ask about. He tells us that his parents believed in multiethnic coexistence in principle; they wanted to eradicate prejudice among the many groups living side by side in Załośce and the whole region. (It was not for nothing that Hryczko's father, the principal of the local high school and the town's intellectual, was referred to as "the professor.") It was out of such convictions that Hryczko's parents decided to shelter— at the risk of their lives, at the risk of their children's lives—not only my parents but several other Jewish people as well. Among them, Hryczko mentions, there was one Dr. Otto, who was famous for owning the first car in Załośce, and who after the war had also gone to Cracow. Dr. Otto! He was the doctor who took care of me when I was a child, and whose stethoscope and other medical instruments fascinated me greatly as he took them out of his worn leather bag. But I knew nothing of his history or the tie there must have been between him and my parents.

The other side, the one we children of survivors perhaps think about insufficiently, caught up as we are in our parents' stories, in the drama of the overwhelming dangers they faced and eluded. But the rescuers too faced life-threatening hazards— extra risks, which they had knowingly chosen to take on. What must it have been like for Hryczko's family to assume the responsibility of sheltering people whom they had known as neighbors, but who now personified deadly danger? To procure food for them, to walk around one's house knowing that a part of it was in effect booby-trapped? Hryczko tells us that he sometimes slept in front of the door leading to the room where the Jewish group was hidden so as to throw off track an Austrian officer who apparently occasionally visited "the professor." He also mentions in passing that he had to leave Załośce for a while and go into hiding because of suspicions that had fallen upon him.

Taking on such risks on behalf of others is surely one of the highest moral choices one can make, and the rescuers all too often were not properly acknowledged. Sometimes, in fact, they had to conceal their actions both during the war and after for fear of their non-Jewish neighbors. It is unclear why the rescuers were so often condemned by their countrymen, whether it was out of pure anti-Semitism, or political considerations (were they going to stand against other common causes?), or fear that they would reveal others' nefarious acts, or the common man's dislike of excessive magnanimity. Sometimes, rescuers' households were invaded because it was assumed they had acquired Jewish wealth as reward for their acts.

But often the rescuers themselves didn't want to talk about what they had done, and the people whom they had saved did not maintain contact. Why this was so is puzzling. Maybe the silence was part of the general turn away from the awful past. Maybe some of the shame following from the awful events adhered to the bonds between rescuer and the hidden, shame about what was required of them both, the degree of dehumanization that had to be reached in order for the need for such hiding to arise.

Of course, there were also cases in which the bonds survived the war and continued in affectionate and long-lasting friendships. On a more public level, more than a thousand rescuers have been honored at Yad Vashem with the title of Righteous Gentiles. A few books have been written on the subject. But on the whole, this aspect of the Holocaust and of human behavior

EVA HOFFMAN

still remains insufficiently understood. I keep wondering why my parents, who had mentioned the two families that had hidden them so often, did not contact them after the war. (The family of the attic is gone; that piece of internal imagery will have to remain imaginary.) But then maybe they tried to make contact and failed; maybe, given Soviet attitudes, they would have endangered the two families by trying. Perhaps also, during the time of hiding, as they struggled to survive amidst such deadly danger, it was impossible for them to think of those who were hiding them as equally threatened or vulnerable. The rescuers, however admirable their actions, were still, in relation to their Jewish wards, in a position of power, and the Jews, in relation to them, in a position of utter dependence. This, too, unless the period of hiding was negotiated with utmost delicacy, might have left a trail of humiliation. My parents spoke of the people who had hidden them with nothing but affection. But this is one of the aspects, the inward dimensions of my parents' story, that I, their daughter, will never know.

Hryczko has never received the letter. I read it to him now, in the presence of the two women who came with us. Then Hryczko takes my sister and myself to another room. There we talk more privately; and finally, we cry. But then, it is strange and moving to everybody, this unlikely reconnection after more than fifty years, this improbable refinding of an almost lost thread. We are not Odysseuses, my sister and I, and yet, there is something epic about this modest visit—the great sweep of history in between, the most unlikely return, and Olga and Hryczko, waiting for us all this time, weaving and reweaving their memories. "We did not have books that told what happened here," Olga tells us at the end of our visit. "But every-

214

thing is recorded in our memories . . ." The oral tradition, practically Homeric, preserved here because it was so much needed.

The letter, for the duration of our visit, becomes an iconic object in Załośce. The director of the council (a hefty, energetic woman with a Yeltsinian voice, whom we quickly dub "Madame President") makes me read it over and over again, to groups of young people she summons to her office for that purpose. She wants them to know, she says, something of their town's history.

I don't know how that history is really remembered in the stories passed on in the still close-knit families, in the post-Soviet schools, or in the inns where men get drunk. I don't know what is said about the two populations that have disappeared from here—the Jews and the Poles. Before the war, Załośce's inhabitants were equally distributed among the three groups, and Olga remembers ceremonies (this is confirmed by my research into such matters) in which the rabbi, the Catholic priest, and the Orthodox patriarch came out together to greet visiting dignitaries. But it was in villages like Załośce that the knot of interethnic relations got most violently raveled during the war. The hostility between Poles and the Ukrainians (the former being the gentry, the latter peasants in the region's class system) ran just as deep as the local strains of anti-Semitism, and during the war it erupted with murderous viciousness. I remember my mother's stories of Ukrainian husbands who brutally killed their Polish wives, once the hatreds had their day.

How do we think about such ghastly acts, how do we think about them today? Certainly a comparative perspective is informative, for from our unhappily accumulating experience it seems that no group on earth is immune from the possibilities of prejudice or violence. At the same time, cumulative observations should give us some reason for optimism, for peaceful coexistence among different groups is also perfectly possible; it is, in fact—if one looks at the long periods of stability between the punctuations of violence—not the exception but the norm. In villages like Załośce before the war, and Bosnia after, and probably in villages of Rwanda or Kashmir, groups manage to live side by side in normal harmony or benign indifference until some hell breaks loose. We need to take such information into account, to think not only about why groups hate each other but how such hatred is inflamed; and, if we are to be modestly hopeful, how, therefore, it can be contained. We may need to modify our idea of anti-Semitism as a unique prejudice, although it is an exceptionally persistent one, and it may contain elements of exceptionality. But even if only to identify what those extra elements are, we need to set Jewish history alongside studies of other minorities, to ask when interethnic relations succeed and when they fail.

I do not have enough time in Załośce to probe attitudes beneath their surface expression, or what feels to me like genuine good will. I decide not to question memories beyond what people are willing to tell me. Still, the dialectic is working, for although I am merely grazing the surface on this visit, there is much that I can imagine, perhaps even infer, from having studied shtetls such as this. For one of the fascinating aspects of those little microsocieties is how much they resembled each other, and how resiliently the Jewish populations within them organized themselves according to certain models, rules of behavior, calendar markers, and religious beliefs.

But there are also other kinds of signs and sites. Here, our guides tell us, pointing at an innocuous square of ground, was where a massacre of the Jews took place. Yes, right here. The earth heaved for two days afterwards. So this was where my mother's sister died.

Here, right here.

And this used to be the Jewish cemetery. Yes, this grassy knoll on which cows now graze. Nothing remains of it, not a single gravestone. This is where my father must have buried his brothers.

Here, right here.

Here they are again, the people whom I had never known, and whom I cannot imagine. Here they are again, waves of loss, beating against the mind's shore. Loss of what I did not know. The past ambushing me again with its metaphysics of absence. I strain to make the brothers more real, to give loss a content. But there are limits to what the imagination can do. I do not even know what they looked like. I had no uncles. That was my fate. After a while, one has to let this go.

There are other patches of landscape, other moods and associations: the tiny huts, the dirt roads on which the spring mud hasn't entirely dried, the grassy yards over which geese and chickens roam free. Here, says Olga, was your mother's house; and here, your father's. The distance separating them, along a dirt road, is less than a city block. My parents must have known each other from childhood, from always. And here is the river Seret, and the bridge on which the one family picture that had survived was taken: The picture shows my mother's sister with three other young women, in their rather fashionable dresses, striking sexy poses. Yes, there is no doubt, it is the same bridge, and the same river.

And here, says Hryczko's sister, is where your parents hid. The sister, a tiny, gentle-faced old woman, was just a child when the war broke out, but now she lives with her husband in the parental home, in the "professor's" house. She shows us the shed outside the house where my parents and others had hidden during some nights. Then, she and her husband walk with us, they barefoot in the dewy grass, into a thicket of forest not far from the house, and to a spot where they stop and point out a large indentation in the ground, overgrown and covered by branches. This was where the bunker was, the one my father and his brothers had dug out as the Nazi persecutions stepped up. Everyone knew it was here, the sister says. Everyone knew there were Jews hiding in the forest.

Here, right here.

My sister takes photographs. I stare downwards in a state of incredulity. So this was where It started, this cavity in the ground from which my life and the world had emerged. A kind of womb after all, as well as the heart of darkness—though so fresh and sunlit now, and filled with nature's gentle sounds.

One cannot undo the past, redo it, heal it, cure it. And yet, I am consoled by this near-touching of the time before, this near-meeting of parallel lines that, after all these years, seem to be bending towards each other again. I am consoled by so much good will and unforced emotion on the part of everyone we meet, and their intense engagement—even our soccer-star driver's!—with our curiosity, our need, our quest. Of course, it helps that we can communicate easily across our languages, and that such villages are just familiar enough to my sister and me so that we feel comfortable here. I recognize aspects of my parents' personalities in so many of the people we meet. I do not suspect, or find, hostility.

I am also more unexpectedly consoled by the thought that my parents had nearly thirty years of life here, in this pastoral if impoverished village, and among these lively, spontaneous people. There were tensions, of course, among the three populations that lived here, but their prewar lives, from everything my parents had said, from everything I now know, were normal enough. That thought, made vivid by what I have now seen, alters my vision of the horror years: It makes them both more palpably frightening and less infinite in magnitude. The disruption of Jewish lives, of this normalcy, by the sudden viciousness and tides of death must have taxed all powers of comprehension and of endurance. The news, received by my parents in their bunker and the professor's house, of one relative's death after another, one murder after next . . . How could they bear it?

But I now also know that my parents really did have a portion of life before the horror, and uncontaminated by its knowledge. That places the dark interval in a different temporal perspective, permits—nearly—of enclosing it in a sort of bracket.

Beyond that, I begin to sense the leap my parents had to make as they emerged from their hiding and made their trek to the big city. And then, to yet another, entirely unknown, world. In the psyche, it sometimes seems that no time has passed. But as I almost touch the realities of my parents' early lives, I realize how remote this first part of their story is from the present, and with each moment receding into further tinyness as the world becomes larger, faster, more global all the time. Different scale, different forms of human relations, different problems of daily life . . . As in every generation, it has been up to us, the ones who came after, to try to cope with the new problems posed by our world. But the gulf, the ruptures, are in this case very deep indeed, the shadows thrown by the past over the present exceptionally dense and dark. It is no wonder that the present has been sometimes difficult to grasp in its own light.

Still, the visit helps. It helps in measuring the distance between the past and present, and in anchoring that swirling childhood knowledge in solid actualities. And perhaps a kind of task has been fulfilled, for it is not good not to know where your parents came from, and where your ancestors died or were murdered. This was for my sister and me to do: to keep this fragment of the larger story in mind, and perhaps, in some way, pass it on.

.   .   .

The other return is not so much an excursion from the present into the past as an incursion—an eruption—of the past into the present. It takes place on July 10, 2001, in the small Polish town of Jedwabne, some two hundred miles east of Warsaw.

That day marks a commemorative ceremony for events that took place sixty years ago, and that have given the very word "Jedwabne" quite horrific associations. The grim aura is well justified, for sixty years before, on July 10, 1941, Jedwabne was the site of a massacre in the course of which the town's Polish inhabitants turned on the Jewish population, torturing and murdering several hundred of their neighbors. How many participated in the frenzy of collective violence, and how many were murdered, is still unclear. It has also not been definitively established how many Germans were in the town on that day, or at whose behest the massacre took place. But what is known without a doubt is that a few days after the Soviet army re-

treated from the town and the eastern parts of Poland it had occupied, and just as the German army began installing itself in its
stead, a number of Poles, using primitive instruments of killing,
murdered their Jewish neighbors in the most brutal ways, in the
end herding them into a barn and burning them alive.

These are the events we are here to commemorate. I have
come to Jedwabne at the invitation of Ryszard Stemplowski, the
former Polish ambassador to the United Kingdom and now the
director of the Polish Institute of Foreign Affairs. During his
ambassadorial tenure, Mr. Stemplowski was active in encourag-
ing Polish-Jewish dialogue in Britain; and it was his thoughtful
idea to bring a small, informal delegation of Jewish guests to the
ceremonies.

Our group is among several hundred visitors arriving in
Jedwabne on an unseasonably cold and rainy summer morning, among them politicians, journalists, representatives of
Jewish organizations, and a handful of survivors from Jedwabne, as well as their descendants. The contemporary inhabitants of Jedwabne are conspicuously missing, although some
of them—rather woebegone figures in contrast to the visiting
dignitaries—stand on the margins of our enfilade, looking on
with curiosity. We have come here from America, Israel, and
other countries, and I am sure that, as we walk down the bu-
colic, poplar-framed country road towards Jedwabne's grace-
ful, church-dominated central square, many of us are slightly
anxious about what is to follow. As anxious, I suspect, about
how we will feel—how we are supposed to feel—as we are
about our actual heavy feelings. Can we bridge the time gap
with requisite emotion? Can we mourn properly for these
dead who to most of us are strangers, and for the manner in

which they died? It is so, so much later. What does Then mean to us now?

The slight uncertainty that can be sensed among those gathered in the square surely has to do partly with this: the possibility of inappropriate response, of emotional bad faith. Emotion recollected in too much tranquillity, or in not enough, in too much detachment, or in too much rage. But what is the appropriate emotion—the appropriate response? What is the appropriate emotion for me—for those of us who came after? This has everything to do with me, I think; this has so little to do with the actualities of my own life.

And yet we are here to mourn and commemorate the dead.

In medias res, one appropriate emotion, surely, is that of amazement, or bemusement, at the odd mix of fortuitousness and inevitability that has led up to this moment. The ceremonies are a culmination of events that began unfolding a year and a half before and that were precipitated by a documentary film and a slim book. The first, a documentary by the Polish filmmaker Agnieszka Arnold, uncovered what had happened in Jedwabne through interviews with remaining witnesses, survivors, and a few participants in the massacre. The film was a brilliant piece of investigative journalism. But it was the book that followed, a short tome by Jan Gross called *Neighbors,* that caught Poland's and the world's attention. Gross, a sociologist who left Poland in 1968 and has lived and taught in the United States since then, recounts the events of 1941 in unflinching detail, drawing mostly on Jewish testimonies and on court records of trials that took place in the 1950s, and in which some of the massacre's leading perpetrators received sentences of varying lengths. If *Neighbors* affected interested people everywhere, in

Poland it burst upon the scene with all the force of a wide-radius cluster bomb. The book's account of the Jedwabne events unleashed a flood of questions, accusations, rage, remorse, historians' quarrels, conscience searching, and front-page newspaper stories that did not abate for many months and that was, in its reach and pivotal significance, the Polish equivalent of the American debates on, say, Watergate or My-Lai.

Neighbors is indeed shocking, although some of its facts, including the number of those killed, have been legitimately called into question. But even so, the reasons for its explosive impact are not self-evident. The basic truth of the Jedwabne massacre had not been hidden in Poland—but neither had it been noticed. There had been a legal inquest shortly after the war. In the 1960s, there was a book by a reputable historian in which a chapter was devoted to the events. There was Agnieszka Arnold's film, which, while not exactly ignored, did not cause a wider stir. Even Jan Gross's book went initially unnoticed and hardly reviewed before it captured the attention and the conscience of the Polish public. If it were not for some rather mysterious gremlins of history, or of timing, the knowledge of what happened in Jedwabne might well have remained, if not stifled, then at least quiescent.

Perhaps the gremlins felt that the time was ripe, and overripe. During the Communist decades, questions of ethnicity, of Jewishness, of the specifically Jewish Holocaust and of Polish anti-Semitism were among the forbidden, or at least highly censored, subjects. Since 1989, however, the repressed has returned to haunt the Polish polity with a vengeance. On the one hand, there is nostalgia, Judeophilia, the sudden creation of what Ruth Ellen Gruber has called "virtual Jewishness." Only a few days before the Jedwabne commemorations, I attended the Festival of Jewish Culture in Cracow—an annual event that each year culminates in a klezmer concert to outdo klezmer concerts anywhere, an extravaganza of Yiddish music played by bands from all over the world and attended by many thousands of rapt listeners in the charming rectangular square of Kazimierz, the old Jewish district of Cracow. It was extremely hot on the day when I listened to the concert from an upstairs interior of a brand-new Jewish restaurant, and a sense of semihallucination was easy to summon. I remember this square from my childhood as an eerily quiet, whitewashed place, where we came to the synagogue on the High Holidays, where steps echoed and an occasional drunk reeled out of a crumbling building. Aside from the communal gatherings on those holidays, Kazimierz was nearly denuded of Jews already then, as it is almost entirely denuded of them now. So what are these players doing here? Are they impersonations, mockeries, revenants? Their music, with its wonderful, Gypsyish, bluesy rhythms blows over the square as if trying to bring back the past, re-create it, reenact it; and enacting, at the same time, the postnature of this historical moment, its own secondariness.

On the other side of virtual Jewishness, there is virtual anti-Semitism, or anti-Semitism practically without Jews. Practically, since the official statistics have revised the numbers of Jewish inhabitants in Poland upwards to around 30,000, and, miraculously enough, there is quite a sturdy revival of Jewish life going on mostly in Warsaw, with its own schools, summer camps, publications, and even—that is how one knows Jewish life is thriving!—quarreling rabbis. Still, none of this accounts for the upsurge in anti-Semitic rhetoric since 1989, for the conspiratorial theories or the finger pointing at putative Jews, who have included—in the anti-Semites' overheated imagination—a Catholic bishop and an observant Catholic president. This, too, is the return of the repressed, in strangely contorted, even hysterical forms.

But amidst the vicissitudes of virtual Jewishness and virtual anti-Semitism, the end of censorship has also yielded the kinds of positive results that should theoretically follow from the lifting of repression—foremost among them a serious examination of the Polish-Jewish past. Since 1989, there has been an ongoing discussion, in the press and other public forums, of Polish-Jewish relations throughout history, touching on a spectrum of sensitive matters and extending itself to such sacred icons of Polish memory as the Home Army, that heroized and often really heroic movement of resistance against the Nazis. The Home Army included a range of political sections, some of which actively helped Jews during the Holocaust and delivered arms to the Warsaw Ghetto during its uprising; but it also included right-wing units that—it is now revealed—were active in persecuting and sometimes killing Jews.

Still, nothing had shaken Polish public opinion like Jan Tomasz Gross's book. I confess I was shaken by it myself. With all my studies of Polish-Jewish relations during the Holocaust, and the unhappy and ugly aspects of Polish behavior, I was not aware of anything like the Jedwabne massacre and did not know how to absorb it into my picture of Poland under the Nazi occupation. What has been known about and often described were acts of individual informing and small-time banditry, attacks on Jews under the cover of night, or vendettas by rightist partisan groups on Jews suspected of Communist sympathies. But not this open unleashing of brutality, in the light of day, di-

rected against the entire Jewish population of a town and perpetrated by the town's ordinary citizenry.

And so the revelations bring up once again the essential questions: not only what happened but why; what are the dynamics
of such events, and from what sociopsychological soil do they
spring? Was the Jedwabne massacre caused—or enabled—by
long-standing, home-grown anti-Semitism that had always harbored virulent or even annihilationist undertones? Or was this
"action" prompted by the specific circumstances of the wartime
years? Was it seen by its perpetrators as a species of revenge
against the Jews for their supposed support of the Red Army
when it invaded from the east and their brief hold on local positions of power under the Soviet occupation? Did the massacre
happen in a spontaneous outburst of rage, or was it engineered,
prompted, dictated by the anti-Semitic Jedwabne powers in collusion with, or with permission of, Nazi bosses? Did the impulses of murderous aggression have to be aroused, and a sense
of conscience numbed, by considerable quantities of vodka?
How does sour, petty, unpleasant prejudice get whipped up into
an orgiastic frenzy of violence?

These are unsettling questions, but they have to be asked if
we want to understand not only the Jedwabne massacre but so
many others that have occurred before and since; episodes of extreme brutality that keep surging up like wildfire in disparate
countries and cultures, claiming lives, leaving scarred survivors
and waves of wider disgust and disillusionment. How is it possible that, after all of our historical experience, after international laws, unexceptionable political ideas, endless debates and
diagnoses, we keep doing this to each other?

The discussion that followed the publication of *Neighbors* in

Poland was, for the most part, serious, searching, and candid. It was also at times fiercely angry, or fiercely anguished, with an intensity that suggests that this part of the past is not at all past, that this history lives and rankles as if it had just happened. Why is that, why does the past refuse to recede into the background, into the space of memories recalled with calm and events analyzed with some detachment? One reason, surely, is that this past has, for so long, been suppressed and repressed. And it seems that, in collective, no less than in individual, memory, repression never works completely. As long as there are people still alive who witnessed or lived through the events, as long as there are descendants for whom this past is still palpable, the repressed, or the suppressed, will surface, sometimes with the momentum of long pent-up passion.

The long silence, the shocking revelations, the fierce debate: All of this informs the moment as we wait in the small Jedwabne square, under our mundane umbrellas, and in somber, sober quietude, for the commemorative ceremonies to begin.

The ceremonies themselves unfold through the long day like a ritual drama in several acts leading up to moments of great emotion and even catharsis. After the mayor of Jedwabne and the Israeli ambassador to Poland make their speeches, it is the moment for Aleksander Kwaśniewski, the president of Poland, to ascend the tiny, improvised podium. His address has been much awaited and its potential content much disputed. But the speech lives up to the occasion both in content and in style. The periods are rounded, the sentences marked by balanced parallelisms and escalating repetitions. This is political rhetoric that comes close to a kind of poetry. Or perhaps this is the kind of event, the kind of moment, in which we rediscover the origins of poetry in public rhetoric. The president seems to be fully aware of this. He speaks with a steady, almost classical gravitas. His tonalities are communicative, immediate, and perfectly controlled. He addresses all the issues, the sensitive points, and the horror of what happened firmly, but with some subtlety. What took place in Jedwabne, he tells us, was a crime not only against Jews but against Polish citizens and the Republic of Poland. Still, we must not apply to the inhabitants of Jedwabne today the principle of collective responsibility. And yet, can we say this was a long time ago? Can we say, "Those were the others"? No, we must try to understand this as part of our own history. We are not doing this because the world expects it of us but because of what is in our hearts.

Mere rhetoric, perhaps. That is exactly what some would—and do—say. Undoubtedly, the president practiced his speech for maximum effect and drafted it with somebody's help. And yet, there seems to be just enough integrity in his voice to give credibility to his sentiments—or at least, to give credence to his wish to express those sentiments. Which is perhaps why, when he comes to its culmination and utters, in a clear and unhesitant voice, the sentences that begin with the phrase "We apologize . . . We apologize . . . We apologize . . ." I feel as if some internal burden has been both located and shifted.

I have been skeptical about the ritual of apologies, and I think there are good reasons to be. It has become too easy for politicians to express remorse for something their countries have done long before their tenure in power. Official apologies, having become fashionable, exact nearly nothing in moral cost, and they earn quite a bit in moral credit. Saying you're sorry has become one of the rites of entry into the Western, liberal, democratic world.

Why, then, should Kwaśniewski's phrase, repeated in a crescendo of controlled intensity, be so penetrating? Why should a sense of salutary relief wash over my mind, overcoming and disarming my critical controls? It is not that the horror of Jedwabne dissolves in the president's words. Nothing can accomplish that time-reversing feat. The relief comes from something else: from the public recognition—before the world—of the dark things that took place here; but even more, perhaps, from the symbolic gesture of power bowing (even as the president's voice ascends) before suffering.

In a way, what we are witnessing in the Jedwabne square is an event typical of our time; but the meanings that have accreted around these ceremonies lend to them a density and an intensity often missing from occasions of this kind, the routine rituals of remembrance that have become a hallmark of the era of memory. This is the first time that the Holocaust is being commemorated in Poland as part of Polish rather than Jewish or German history, and there has been nothing routine or easy about the struggles that have led up to this day.

One of the issues most fervently debated in Poland in the months leading up to the commemoration was precisely the question of apologies. There were many who said that Poland had nothing to apologize for, that the Holocaust was not a Polish issue and there was no Polish policy towards the Jews as it was taking place because the country had ceased to exist as a sovereign entity. There were others in the debate who wondered to whom the apology should be delivered: the descendants of those murdered? Polish Jews? all Jews? There were some—those on the extremist fringe—who suggested that it was Jews who should apologize to the Poles for welcoming the Red Army when the Soviets marched into Eastern Poland, and many previous sins as well.

All of this informs the president's rhetorical gestures and adds to the impact of his reverberating phrase. In contrast to many other rites of apology, this one has carried risks and costs. Uttering those words required a difficult political decision on Kwaśniewski's part, and perhaps some personal courage.

An apology, if it is authentic, almost never comes easily—not to adults, not to those in power. It is nearly always achieved against internal resistance, against our wish to preserve the conviction and appearance of rightness, and our pride. And, if it is authentic, an expression of remorse therefore betokens a sort of bending towards the other—an acknowledgment of the other's point of view and subjectivity. It carries within it a recognition both of having committed a harmful act, and of the other's capacity for being hurt. It is that quintessential moral drama that is being symbolically enacted in the president's words and his voice. The others—those ordinary, insignificant people who weren't quite "us"—were here and they were fully real. The harm done to them was a crime; their hurt was great, and it counts.

After the president's speech, we walk in a silent procession through Jedwabne's unpaved streets, lined with low, tiny houses, to where the town gives out onto open fields and meadows and, farther behind them, a line of a denser, darker forest. Here, where an improvised stage and a few rows of chairs have been set up, was where the fated barn once stood, in a farmer's field. And it is here that the next part of the ceremonies—a Jewish service of mourning—takes place. A rabbi, ancient and frail, his shaking hand supported by a cane, delivers a speech that is also a kind of sermon, and a Talmudic disquisition. He is Rabbi

Baker, and he is himself from Jedwabne, although he left in
1937, before the catastrophe. He does not glide over the horror
of what happened on the site where we now stand. He had
heard first-hand accounts of it from the few surviving Jewish
witnesses, and his beloved rabbinical mentor was among those
killed. But his message, couched in Midrashic parables and ex-
empla, is about the greatness of humility and the possibility of
actual forgiveness. "The one who lowers himself before a mar-
tyr becomes great," he says. "That is why our dear president
today performed a great act." The intimacy of "our dear president" is touching, but it also suggests a kind of spiritual self-
confidence. In this terrain, the rabbi feels himself to be the equal
of the president. But, as in various ways he reminds us, the
physical terrain on which we stand—these fields and forests—
used to belong to him as well. His presence here is like a magical return, for one brief moment, of something there once was:
a rabbi delivering a Talmudic lecture amidst this Polish landscape, which he clearly loves. In the time Before, he would have
spoken in a synagogue, of course; but many a Talmudic parable
was probably shared and analyzed by Jews walking through
these fields in their black garb, conversing in Yiddish. Indeed,
the rabbi tells us, Jedwabne was famed for its scholars, some of
whom became renowned throughout the world. He's speaking
of scholars who wrote in Hebrew, of course, and who were apparently famed in their Orthodox Jewish cosmos. Very few Jews
are aware of such figures anymore, and the Polish inhabitants of
Jedwabne would not have known what to make of them at any
time. And yet, here they were, studying in the Jedwabne yeshiva,
which was apparently an institution of some stature, and undoubtedly often discussing the all-important questions of tex-

tual interpretation in this rural, lyrical landscape. Intimate and separate worlds: There is a whole Jewish map of Poland with its own points of reference, layers of association, and sometimes different names for rivers and towns. A separate Jewish map that is yet inextricably of Poland, and interwoven with Polish fate.

A cantor sings a beautiful lamentation, a song that is close to a primal wail of mourning, but shaped into a long, ancient line that rises and falls and extends itself beyond ordinary sorrow and travels over the fields and into the bordering forests. Afterwards, Polish soldiers do a four-cornered salute of honor. And then, the kaddish is said.

Sixty years after the event itself, this commemorative ritual revives the contradictions of interwoven destinies, which ended in the tragedy of violence, in this modern incarnation of Cain's murder of Abel. But the ritual also attempts to enact the gestures of recognition, remorse, and forgiveness.

For me, the day condenses all the contradictions that haunt all of us who came after. The survivors and witnesses here are few in number, although the woman who saved seven Jewish people from the mob's fury and certain death has lived to see this day, and is later honored by the president in his own palace. But mostly it is the direct and indirect descendants of survivors and saviors, of witnesses and, yes, the perpetrators, who are here, and who are responsible for this moment. But what is our role? Is it in our power to forgive—or not to forgive?

Some of the descendants here are unyielding in their anger. Others point out that representatives of the Catholic Church were absent from the ceremonies. A survivor's granddaughter suggests that to think a ceremony could redress the horror or lighten Polish conscience is to add insult to injury. "Do you think we have done enough?" a journalist asks her. "Enough?" she responds in a voice cold with fury. "Do you think an apology is enough?" It is true that no gesture is commensurate with the crime that took place here, or offers sufficient redress. And yet I must admit I wonder how she—from her vantage point, in her generation—has come to feel she has earned the right to this moral high ground. And I wonder what would be enough.

As for me, throughout the day, I think—feel—how much my own life has been shadowed by this past, despite all my attempts to escape it. And how long it has taken me to unravel and then braid together its raveled, knotted, cut, and fragmented threads until I could distinguish shadows from realities and fable from history.

It has been one of my life's major tasks, and it has exacted a considerable price. And yet what more can I ask of others than this? What is the appropriate response on their part? If there is none, then we cannot ask for it; we must simply separate ourselves from our interlocutors. But if we do ask for something— examination of prejudice, acknowledgment, apologies—then we must respond to the gestures of good faith when they are made; we must recognize the recognition. We cannot ask of others what we might not be able to do ourselves—or what is impossible to accomplish. Sixty years later, what was so horrifically and still puzzlingly done here cannot be undone. Sixty years later, I feel, this is the only thing that can be done: to acknowledge, turn, bend towards the victims rather than away from them. There can be no other recompense, no other closure. Sixty years later, I think, and after all that can be done has been done, it may also be time to turn away, gently, to let this go.

VII

FROM THE PAST TO THE PRESENT

It was almost exactly three months after my Jedwabne visit, on September 11, 2001, that the beginning of a new era was announced, as surely as if a giant, glass-shattering gong had been sounded.

For me, as I turned on the television that afternoon in my London flat and stared at the inexplicable images of airplanes crashing into the World Trade Center and the Pentagon, nothing except the date of my confusion was clear: September 1, 1939. That was my point of reference for global terror, for the overturning of the world. For the War. Here, I thought, it was. A childhood expectation confirmed. In some shadowy way, I felt well prepared. In other ways, it turned out, I was not at all.

As it transpired, September 11, 2001, did not turn out to be September 1, 1939. But whatever the twenty-first-century date will come to stand for, however it will be understood, the apocalyptic, silent images of that day—images of events that this time we could never say we did not know about—delivered their own, instant mega-information. The information concerned many things; but one of them had to do with the witnessing of catastrophe *in medias res*. I had grown up with the subliminal expectation of catastrophe, and the received "memory" of mass death in my very bones. And yet expectation is not the same as reality, received knowledge not the same as the direct kind. As my mind reeled in front of the television set, and as a sudden, sodden despondency settled over my body, I understood palpably what I had until then known only imaginatively: what it is like to have your entire world shaken at its very foundations; what it is like to wait, in concentrated calm and submerged fear, for the unpredictable unfolding of events; what it is like to feel, in a flash, that the defining parameters of your world have just been rendered irrelevant, and that there is no way to predict what awaits you.

The information continued to be delivered in mind-jolting doses in the course of the following days. I was learning quickly about the psychic impact of large-scale violence, when it touches on your identity, however impersonally or symbolically. I understood the dulled disorientation that follows the helpless, hopeless witnessing of collective death. Especially if the witnessing takes place in simultaneous time so that you know you are watching another human creature—multiplied by so many—in the throes of death, and that you can do nothing about it. I was beginning to be familiar with the impotent anger that comes from being the object of gratuitous hatred, even (or perhaps especially) if one is hated in the abstract, as a member of a group. I was beginning to experience, in other words, the power of collective shock, with all its malodorous sensations: agitation alternating with numbness, inchoate rage oscillating towards grief, vengefulness turning to powerless resignation, the spectacle of murder breeding inner deadliness. All of this I had known in a mediated, imaginary way; but now, I was confronting it in its penetrating, flame-illumined immediacy.

For those of us who were not directly involved, who were fortunate enough not to lose relatives or friends in the conflagration, September 11 delivered a large shock rather than trauma. The events of that day were a discrete occurrence, and their effects, while profound, were not cumulative enough to embed themselves in the collective consciousness in the form of sustained suffering. But the days, weeks, and months following the event were an education in unknowing. How was one to understand what was happening, how could one analyze causes or gauge possible consequences? If September 11 was not September 1, 1939, was it perhaps November 9, 1938—a Kristallnacht of a globalized world, with the shattering of glass effected across borders rather than within the country of terror's origin? Or was it, even more worryingly, something like 1933, an early warning signal whose real meanings would not emerge for several years? It was impossible, in those first weeks and months, to know, and it is undoubtedly risky even in the longer range to draw parallels. "Learning from the past," when it involves specific prophecies, is a notoriously tricky exercise. Each event is so multiply determined, each historical development grows out of such intricately interwoven factors, each moment of the historical present can unfold in so many ways into the future, that analogies between the past and present need to be made with great discrimination.

And yet for a person like myself, perhaps for anyone who grew up in the shadow of the Second World War and for whom that devastation was the Event, it was hard not to read the

tremors of the present through the prism of the earlier earthquake, not to discern parallels, or worry about their implications. Certainly, the psychic links seemed inescapable. A
daughter of Holocaust survivors told me that September 11
pierced through a carefully erected shield of defenses to
reawaken disabling anxieties she thought she had long put to
rest. A German woman who was a child during the war reported that after the attacks, all those decades later, she began
dreaming for the first time about the savage bombardments of
German cities she witnessed at the end of the war. It would be
self-indulgent in the extreme to think that children of the war
were especially affected by September 11; but we undoubtedly
have our associations. It seems that what I feared most, or felt
most closely in the violence and passionate agitations of that
moment, was the crumbling of a protective, shared rationality—of that "veneer of civilization" which my parents and others like them had found to be so thin—and the uncovering of
that irrational universe which had roiled so darkly in my childish mind.

One cannot—should not—draw conclusions from nightmares. For one thing, it would be wrongheaded to bring the
same historical analysis to the dreams of a German and a Jewish
childhood. The dreams may be equally disturbing; but their
larger causes are very different, and taking note of that difference is as crucial for a rightful understanding of events as compassion for individual suffering.

Insofar as history is a nightmare, it is one from which we
need, soberly and consciously, to keep awakening. But the
shock of September 11 and the uncertainties of its aftermath
gave me an instant new measure through which to contemplate

the cataclysm of my parents' generation. The attacks on New York and Washington were the first events in my own lifetime that seemed to me as primary in their significance as the Event that overshadowed my consciousness ever since I can remember. It is not that the two atrocities are comparable in scale or kind. The terrors of terrorism are not like the horrors of the Holocaust. Nevertheless, September 11 was an event of first-order magnitude in that it seemed to signal a fundamental transformation in the arrangements of the world, the manifestation of a fault line whose opening released demons, and whose further opening could tear everything apart. Perhaps it was that dizzying upending of basic assumptions, as much as the sights of destruction and death, that produced the impact of those surreal acts, the blow to the mind and the psychic girders. The world was all of a sudden changed, changed utterly—its present, future, even its past. For, like some newly introduced bit of code that travels backwards through an entire text, the opening salvo of the twenty-first century seemed also to insert itself into the past and add its own information to my reading of my generation's story, and history.

.　　.　　.

Our history has been, mostly, a psychohistory. Insofar as we identify ourselves as children of survivors, our narratives have been structured mostly by our relationship to the past. The milestones in our pilgrim's progress have marked stages of an internal journey. But with the quake of September 11, our reentry into immediate history—if history is defined as conflict and violent change—has begun. In that sense, too, the wand is being passed on to us, the second generation and the postgeneration as a whole.

The era of memory is ending, thus throwing a whole landscape of intervening time into an altered perspective. In my mind's eye, the postwar era will now be always bracketed by two images: the exposed scaffoldings of Warsaw, and the other-planetary scaffolding of the World Trade Center. In between, for my generation in the West, there was a long period of exceptional if uneasy peace, of ever-increasing prosperity, and of safety and a level of public security that we may never again be able to take for granted. In subjective terms, a period that—because it was relatively peaceful—allowed for a certain kind of retrospective reflection on the enormous events from which our world had emerged.

It is interesting, and it may be no accident, that the veritable obsession with "memory," and particularly memory of the Holocaust, reached its apogee in the 1990s as the Cold War era abruptly came to its end and "the end of history" was confidently and ludicrously declared. Memory stepped in at the very moment when the old geopolitical arrangements defining our world gave way, and no new "meta-narrative," no new frameworks for perceiving the world, had yet emerged. For a while, there seemed to be, in our increasingly prosperous and protected West, no urgent pressures or conflicts against which to pit our ideas, no structures of necessity, or indeed, of shared meaning, to support errant theories. The past, for a period, seemed to have greater, more compelling, more serious reality than the present; and the very sense of reality seemed to be transferred to the past. Among its many other aspects, "memory," as a category of collective experience, suggests a relationship to the past that is conducted via looking backwards, and a preoccupation with the processes of imaginative construction and deconstruction. At the same time, the very term "memory" suggests a longing, a nostalgia for history, for the object of our remembrance. In other words, the emphasis on "memory" may have expressed the postgeneration's mediated and questing relationship to history, its proximate distance from the awful and awe-inspiring events of our time.

If the privileging of memory led, at times, to excesses of sentiment, intellectual hypertrophy, or ethical etiolation, it also gave us the space to reckon with the formative events of the twentieth century, and above all, with the enormity of the Holocaust. But the uses of "memory" cannot last forever; the lines of meaning drawn out of the past cannot retain their strength as a scaffolding for present significance.

In that sense, perhaps it is not too fanciful to suppose that the sequence that led straight from the Jedwabne commemorations to September 11 may not have been entirely adventitious, that the gremlins of timing in this, too, were following their own logic. Sixty years after the Holocaust, the Jedwabne commemoration was surely one of the last events of this kind to carry its powerful emotional charge. There will not be many more like it, nor many to attend them who have living memories of the events to which they refer. There are surely not many episodes within the Holocaust, or World War II, that we do not know about, that have not been recorded, decoded, or commemorated.

The statute of limitations on the great cataclysms of the twentieth century is running out. The soldiers and victims of the Armageddon are reaching the end of their life spans. The memories of the heroic battles and the unbearable atrocities are waning in their power. The underlying mythos that emerged in the cataclysm's wake and that ordered the world for a while—the symbolism of the West's struggle against Fascism and Nazism, and of America as the defender of democracy and freedom—is losing its force. The gong that struck on September 11 announced, among other things, that the structures and centers established at the end of the Second World War were no longer holding. What had been unthinkable within that order—a direct attack on America—happened, and it happened in part because it was now possible to persuade large masses of people in various parts of the world that America, far from being the harbinger of hope, a refuge for the dispossessed and repository of all the good things in life, was instead a sort of Darth Vader of our universe, a nation as all-powerful as it was corrupt, greedy, and rapaciously hegemonic. Whatever the grains of truth in such a vision of America, this is mostly the stuff of psychopolitical fantasy; but it is the nature of the fantasy—or the ideology—that suggests, as much as anything else, that the worm has turned, and a new epoch has begun.

Was the interval in between well spent? Has the era of memory yielded any lessons that might be applicable to present conditions? And does the second generation's experience, or the messages of its internalized past, have any bearing on the issues and problems of the contemporary world?

How such a transposition—from history to contemporaneity, or from the personal to the political—ought to be made, even in principle, is far from obvious. Unfolding events are always contingent and made up of specific circumstances. If one superimposes patterns of past events on the unfolding momentum of the present too mechanically or rigidly, one can fail to perceive what is happening in front of one's eyes. Consciousness is always in danger of lagging behind reality, as Karl Marx well knew, and this is at no time truer than in periods of exceedingly fast and explosive change.

As for the more horizontal transposition—from psychohistory to external events, from personal experience to politics—this is also an uncertain and hardly straightforward process. "The personal is the political" has always been much too glib a motto. The personal becomes the political only sometimes, and even then, the relationship between the two categories of experience is rarely direct or unvarying. Different people can draw very different conclusions from similar experiences; and often enough, personal motive and morality stand in marked contradiction to political posture. At the same time, the structures of collective bodies are not homologous with the structures of a single subjectivity; the needs of societies do not correspond exactly to the needs of individuals. The translation from the personal to the political, from one level of analysis to the other, needs to be made with considerable caution.

In addition, in the specific case of the second generation, there is a large factor that makes the transposition from the past to the present, from history to politics, particularly problematic: We are not in situ in relation to the relevant events. In this way, the post-Holocaust second generation is different from many other heirs to ethnic or religious conflicts. For second generations coming into adulthood in Cambodia, Bosnia, or Rwanda, one of the most daunting dilemmas, surely, is how to continue living in the same society as the perpetrators without falling into hard bitterness, or reigniting rankling memories into impulses of revenge. But while the challenge is undoubtedly demanding, the nature of the task, for such groups, or at least the arena in which their experience has immediate applications, is in a sense clear: The need, as we have learned from so many difficult pasts and the "transitions" out of them, is to establish, within societies riven and infected by great injustice, sufficient instruments of justice so that the victim's justified grievance does not erupt in wild retribution. It is to attain, within the "hinge" generation, enough rectification for wrongs, or benign forgetfulness, or social rapprochement, so that the pressure of collective memories does not build up to the next outburst of futile violence.

But as descendants of Holocaust survivors, we are dispersed throughout the world; therefore, it is not clear in what arena our "collective" as opposed to individual identity might express itself, where we might act as a community or political body. In one way, of course, the task for us is the same as for other children of atrocity: We, too, have had to come to terms with the complex of received memories, our emotions about the perpetrators, our feelings of hatred and fear. But in a sense, such feelings can only hurt ourselves. We have not been tested, as a group, by having to live in the same society as the perpetrators (except for the few who have done so by choice); nor has the possibility of direct revenge for the wrongs done to our predecessors been open to us. At the same time, our energies could not be directed towards rebuilding a better society on the ruins of the old. The separation from the geographical and political locus of our history has been accomplished perforce.

"Politics" in its most obvious guise as "current events," and the reactions to them, can be the most depthless layer of action and thought, the most reactive to sensational events, and most susceptible to passing winds of opinion. And yet, there are moments when politics becomes the crucial realm of ideas, and when intense passions accrue to impersonal events, because so much is at stake. There are moments when we are forced to see ourselves, however reluctantly, in terms of "collective" as well as individual identity; and when it is impossible not to take positions on certain issues because they are tied up with longer currents of history and deeper strata of affiliation, and because they touch on what matters to everyone—the emerging shape of the world—and also, on our very lives and selves.

One such issue, for any Jewish person minimally conscious of the world (and, it turns out, for just about everyone else), is Israel. Of course, Israel is also, more than any country, seen as the "inheritor state" of the Holocaust, and thus it is at least notionally tied with the second generation's trajectory. Indeed, it has been regularly suggested that Israel *is* the arena on which post-Holocaust history has played itself out, that the cycles of feud and revenge, of persecution turning into defensiveness and vulnerability into aggression, have been transported precisely to that nation. In that interpretation, much of Israel's political behavior, whether desperate, defensive, assertive, or aggressive, is seen as a sort of compensatory symptom—a giant abreaction to the victimization suffered by the Jewish people in the Holocaust.

Is there a special, an intrinsic link between the second generation and Israel? Or between the legacy of the Holocaust and that state's political behavior? On one level, there is probably no

one among children of survivors who does not have strong
views or feelings about Israel, even if this is only a desire for dis-
affiliation. But I do not believe there are "representative" opinions on such matters in the second generation, any more than
among the larger Jewish (or non-Jewish) world; nor do I think
that "our" opinions have any special status or legitimacy in this
area, unless we live in Israel—as only a portion of us do.

Nevertheless, it cannot be said that Israel is not, in some
manner, linked with the larger postwar Jewish history, or questions of Jewish identity today. Certainly, it is not a neutral site
in my imagination. Why and how? What is Israel to me, or I to
Israel? I have been there, of course, but not often. It is not a
place I know well, or for which I feel a cultural affinity. But it
cannot be denied that I feel an extra measure of identification
when Israel's existence is threatened, and an extra dose of shame
when it engages in what I consider unjust aggression. I experience the images of carnage left by the suicide bombings executed by Palestinian terrorists almost as a body blow—as does
not happen when I see similar images from Kashmir. When I
look at the images of Palestinians killed by Israelis, I feel an extra twist of sadness and remorse—as I do not when I watch
footage from Kashmir. This may not speak well for the capa-
ciousness of my compassion, but I note that it is so. Possibly,
none of us have a capacity for universalized emotion, though we
should have the ability for universalist thought. Possibly compassion, if it is to be real, has to attach itself to concrete entities.
Our capacities for response, as our memories, are "thick" or
"thin." Of course, when faced with images of murders and massacres in Kashmir, I wish they did not take place—and I hope
that somebody is taking care that they might not. But I grasp

those horrors abstractly; I feel the tragic knot of what is happening in the Middle East palpably.

This is not purely personal, nor yet ideological. Perhaps, on the analogy of Freud's preconscious, as opposed to the unconscious, my feelings about Israel could be described as pre- rather than nonpolitical. Israel was the place where my family had almost decided to go when we were allowed to emigrate from Poland. It was a place where a lot of our family friends did go. I remember the first letters arriving from the closest of those friends and being read around our Cracow kitchen table—letters that breathed an unaccustomed energy and hope, and that conveyed an unabashed excitement not so much of nationalism as of participation in the project of building a new state—a state that would also be a home. Israel was the place where several of my childhood friends were killed or badly wounded in the country's defensive wars. It was a place to which my parents made a pilgrimage, as if it were a sort of spiritual duty, and from which they returned with certificates of a duty fulfilled. I do not know whether they felt something like guilt for not having chosen to live there, for having taken a supposedly easier option. Occasionally, I feel a twinge of self-doubt too, for as an adult, I also have made choices that have sprung out of personal preference rather than patriotic solidarity.

An alternate fate, then, an imaginable shadow history. Perhaps it could be said that Israel is a symbolic location around which some of my feelings about Jewishness—some of my choices about that aspect of my identity—gather. At the same time, it is incongruities and lines of fracture between European and Israeli Jewish identity I most vividly feel when I visit Israel and observe its human and cultural landscape. A sort of bemused amazement at the unsuitability of Orthodox garb—initially borrowed from Polish nobility!—to the swelteringly hot climate of a Middle Eastern country. A bemused sadness at the beautiful, recently erected monument at Yad Vashem, where the names of the lost Jewish communities of Europe are inscribed into sunlit, white Mediterranean stone. The intention of Yad Vashem is to commemorate the Holocaust within an Israeli context, to transport its legacy, so to speak, to the Jewish state. But the setting of this monument, the glaring sun and white stones, renders the transposition poignantly implausible. Israel, it seems to me as I contemplate the familiar village names, is the inheritor state of the Shoah by default, not deep association. All my deeper association, my linkages and bonds to the Holocaust, take me in other directions: to Poland, Germany, even America.

This seems to me to represent at least an important part of the truth about the relationship between Israel and the Holocaust—a relationship that itself is made up of fractures and incongruities. For while the awful fact of extermination undoubtedly played a role in the world's decision to establish a "Jewish state," the Shoah was hardly the new state's raison d'être, or its main foundational myth. The sensibilities of Holocaust survivors, among other immigrant groups, have naturally influenced Israeli society. But survivors have never represented a political majority in Israel, and the story of their reception in that country was hardly happier than elsewhere. Indeed, they were initially a denigrated minority as Israel tried to revise Jewish stereotypes and self-image and create an Israeli version of the "New Man"—more hardy, physically active, and fearless than the Talmudic Eastern European archetype. In the first years and even decades of Israel's existence, Holocaust survivors were seen as an embarrassment to the country's new image, and belittled in sometimes callow ways.

It is likely, nevertheless, that in the early stages of Israel's establishment, the consciousness of recent catastrophe added an extra element of desperate determination as Israel fought its difficult wars. But those wars, after all, were started by neighbors intent on wiping out the state's very existence. "Never again," when it applies to the possibility of renewed elimination, seems like an entirely reasonable proposition. In later decades, the Holocaust was more deliberately summoned up to marshal patriotic feeling and allegiance to Israel among Jews everywhere. Undoubtedly, Israeli politicians were not above using potent allusions to that tragedy as a chip in a loaded game, a card meant to recharge the world's sense of obligation and guilt. But the card has been less useful and less frequently played of late. In any case, the actual situation in the Middle East has its own horrible momentum, far removed by now from mid-twentieth-century events in Europe. It is surely the realities of that situation that are driving the policies of both parties to the conflict, rather than the symbolic politics of Holocaust memory. The memory—or rather memories—that have immediate bearing on the situation, because they belong to the conflict's historical continuum, are the fiercely contested memories of post–1948 Middle East.

For all those reasons, I feel the rise of objection when the Holocaust is blamed for current Israeli policies, or the failure of that country to become a saintly state. That, too, seems to me a tendentious use, or misuse, of Holocaust "memory." Nor do I think there is any causal link between my membership in "the second generation" and my opinions on contemporary Israeli politics. I have my views about the Middle East conflict (which include a fervent wish for Israel's withdrawal from the occupied territories and a strong conviction that the Palestinians are in large part responsible for their fate). But these are certainly not representative of the "second generation," which is as divided on these issues as the rest of the world, nor are they in any intrinsic way connected with my relationship to the Holocaust legacy.

If there is no predetermined, generalizable connection between the dispersed children of survivors and Israel, what of the second generation within Israel itself? Some of what I know of this comes from my friend Gila, whose biography encapsulates one kind of second-generation trajectory within Israel, and the ways in which the Holocaust legacy was absorbed into Israeli life. Gila is a daughter of German and Polish Holocaust survivors, and her memories of familial childhood echo those of many other second-generation progeny. At home, there was silence, indirect revelations, felt scars, the passage of pain. In school and among her peers, there was unease, awful jokes, awkward embarrassment. Certainly nothing like information or discussion. This changed much later, as it did everywhere else, and Gila became involved in second-generation groups and intensive and rigorous psychotherapeutic dialogues with second-generation Germans. In the meantime, she served in the army and became, for all intents and purposes, a sabra. I am impressed with her stories of running across the enemy lines in 1967 to retrieve her pair of reading glasses. She is also a patriot, someone whose feelings about the country and all the terrible violence it has undergone and caused are immediate and ardent. Gila does not wish her children to avoid military service. At the same time, she is one of the women who, quietly and without publicity, have taken upon themselves the difficult and ungrateful task of monitoring the behavior of Israeli soldiers at the Palestinian checkpoints. The women try to hold the soldiers to standards of civilized comportment, of politeness and respect. If they think the soldiers are treating the Palestinians harshly or humiliatingly, the women try to restrain them. For Gila, this is a heartbreaking task, for she knows that the soldiers' duties are onerous enough; nevertheless, she feels this is her contribution to maintaining some standards of rectitude and fairness in a situation of virtual war. But she feels wrenched by the very idea of Israel as an occupying power, and by what she sees as the decline of compassion and sensitivity in Israeli society. This seems to her somehow "un-Jewish." But then, perhaps her idea of Jewishness is partly imported from Diasporic life, and from circumstances in which the exercise of power was not an option.

Possibly, if one examined the question statistically, one would find that the second generation tends to be more humane than the average in its political views, that a personal legacy of the Holocaust inspires a feeling for justice. It is certainly my impression that this is so. But there is undoubtedly, among the Israeli subset of the second generation, as among others, a variety of views and political analyses. In any case, as a child of survivors, Gila belongs to a small minority within Israel. Of course, her sensibility—partly formed by the Shoah, partly by the longer Diasporic history—informs the tones and textures of Israeli society. But that sensibility is also becoming an endangered species, and, in any case, has been transmogrified into something new and unique by the conditions of Israeli life.

.   .   .

Just as the Holocaust was not a national event, so the second generation's collective "identity" is not of a classically political, national kind. But in one sense, the fact of Israel's existence has been tied up with my sense of myself as a Jewish person, and perhaps with the identity of the larger postgeneration as well. That link has been quite paradoxical; for, having grown up after Israel was established, I could, however subliminally, take its existence, and the basic reassurance it offered, for granted. This, I have learned from many conversations and observations, is in marked contrast to the feelings and assumptions shared by much of the older generation. For many Jews who grew up before the war and witnessed the breakdown of all civilized norms and protective laws in relation to the Jewish minorities in Europe, the creation of Israel meant the establishment of an existential guarantee. As long as Israel exists, this line of feeling and reasoning goes, as long as there is a place of assured asylum and refuge, Jews elsewhere need not feel fundamentally insecure or threatened. It therefore follows that a threat to Israel's existential safety is perceived by some—and not wholly irrationally—as an indirect threat to the well-being of Jews everywhere.

It might be reasonably inferred that for children of survivors, the sense of collective vulnerability and the need to think of Israel as a bulwark against Diasporic dangers would run deeper than among most Jews. But in fact, just the opposite may be true. The convergence of Israel's birth with our own entry into the world has meant that, among all the insecurities we may have absorbed with our postwar condition, the insecurity of political survival has not been one. We have not known a world in which Jews were notionally stateless, and in which the safety net of a national homeland and assured citizenship did not exist.

We have not really known what it is like to live with the age-old Jewish awareness, no matter how subliminal, diluted, or irrelevant to current circumstance, that the political existence of one's group is dependent on the good graces of others, that it remains, when all is said and done, provisional and precarious.

The irony may be taken even further, for, coming into the world after the Holocaust, we of the postgeneration may have grown up with less fear of anti-Semitism than almost any Jewish generation since, perhaps, the Spanish exile. For all the seeming incongruity of such a statement, this was an indirect outcome of the Holocaust: For a while, the horror of the Shoah made the prejudice that gave rise to it unacceptable, and the public prohibition on this sentiment (at least in the Western, democratic countries) so total as to render anxieties about this ancient prejudice seemingly obsolete.

The reprieve from such anxieties made it possible, for those who wished to do so, to spring the trap of automatic tribal belonging and the narrowness of parochial concerns without incurring undue opprobrium, or accusations of betrayal. It was possible to get away from "the elephant and the Jewish problem" and to think about Jewishness without the elephant, or even, the elephant-in-itself. In his provocative and astute analysis of post–1960s Jewish identity, *The Imaginary Jew,* the French philosopher Alain Finkielkraut notes that the relationship of his French Jewish contemporaries to their Jewishness is the exact inverse of that which obtained among their predecessors. In the nineteenth century, French Jews tried to appear French in public, even if they remained Jewish at home. For his peers, it became desirable to appear Jewish in public, even if they were perfectly French at home. But if some European and American

Jews decided to emphasize their Jewishness for their own reasons and in their own eclectic ways, it was also possible not to make that aspect of "identity" central to one's self-definition at all. And it was possible to choose all such tactics of selfhood with a confidence and ease that, I believe, really are a sign of inner liberty and of full, self-respectful dignity.

.   .   .

Such freedom from obligatory concerns about Jewish identity, or anxious concern about anti-Semitism, has become much less possible since September 11. For one of the phenomena made dismayingly evident by the time-dividing date has been the reemergence of that prejudice on a global scale and sometimes in unabashedly open forms. In the Arab and fundamentalist Islamic world, anti-Semitism is actively encouraged, sometimes in violent and virulent ways, ranging from injunctions by fundamentalist imams to kill all Jews everywhere to government-endorsed promotions of *The Protocols of the Elders of Zion* (the old anti-Semitic canard, concocted in tsarist Russia and masquerading as a real record of a "Jewish conspiracy") and articles in the mainstream Saudi Arabian press expounding the medieval superstition of blood libel. But closer to home as well, incidents ranging from physical attacks on rabbis and school kids in France to blatantly anti-Semitic statements by senior European politicians and assaults on Jewish students on American campuses to yet other nasty, if minor, episodes, make the conclusion unavoidable that anti-Semitism is on the rise.

It does not help that some exponents or defenders, of anti-Semitic actions or views claim that such manifestations are really a protest against Israel's policies towards the Palestinians. Those policies have often been oppressive and sometimes onerous, and they should be susceptible to criticism by Jews and non-Jews alike. But, after all, people associated with other nations whose political behavior we deem objectionable are not routinely attacked abroad because they belong to the same national group as those countries' governments. Indeed, the very conflation of Israel with Jews everywhere already smacks of anti-Semitism. Moreover, while criticism of Israeli policies is certainly legitimate, it would in some cases take quite a few angels dancing on a pin to distinguish the exceptional, bilious antagonism directed at that country from anti-Semitism pure and simple.

The reasons for the return of this antique prejudice are undoubtedly multiple; but at least one, highly ironic strand of causality seems linked with September 11, and with some of the ideas swirling in the agitated reactions to that event. Those reactions, in the countries of target, of course ran the gamut: from the expected "hawkish" calls for immediate retaliation to sympathy for the victims and the newly exposed American vulnerability; and to the understandable human response of sheer fear at the sudden, yawning opening of hitherto dormant fault lines, and a hope for some form of protection from the forces revealed thereby.

But among those who pride themselves on politics of conscience rather than raw emotion or national self-interest, the instant diagnosis in the wake of Al Qaida's attacks could be summarized by (and was often literally expressed in) the following set of propositions: They are right, and we are wrong. We brought it on ourselves. If they hate us so much, that means we

EVA HOFFMAN

must be hateful. Therefore we must learn our lessons. In the most extreme formulations, a more acrid addendum was made: America (or we) had it coming. It (or we) deserves just what it got.

I am hardly an American nationalist, but I must admit that I was puzzled and even dumbfounded by this genre of critique, disturbed by the dizzying upending of causality, which seemed to me evident in the vehement assertions of American aggression and omnipotence at the very moment when that country became the target of aggression, and its vulnerability was so extravagantly demonstrated. I was frightened, even, by the seeming legitimation of irrationality in the heat of the moment, the puncturing of *that* veneer, at the very time when rationality was so much needed. This is not to discount the realities of American power, or to suggest that its uses are always altruistic, or to ignore the demoralizing disparities of wealth between the developed and the underdeveloped world, or the lessons that the world's mightiest nation does need to learn. I have hardly been a standard American patriot, nor am I unaware of that country's tendencies to a kind of moral arrogance.

But as a blank and blanket assumption, as an instant diagnosis of a new and murkily complex situation, the idea that America was responsible for the attacks on itself seemed to me perplexing in the extreme—especially since this diagnosis had so little in the way of empirical fact or actual analysis to offer. Certainly, if you looked for insights into the rise of Islamic fundamentalism, or the sources of bin Laden's rage, or the contributions of American policies to the state of the Arab world, or the state of that world in itself, the new *bien-pensant* orthodoxy was not going to be of much help.

Was it schadenfreude that could be perceived in this critique, especially as it came from the European left—the satisfaction of seeing the giant, however temporarily, brought down? Or could one speculate about an unconscious "identification with the aggressor"—a perennial if hardly noble impulse in human nature? But, of course, within the gestalt driving this diagnosis, its exponents were identifying not with the aggressor but with the real and quintessential victim. For within the terms of this critique, "America" is always and necessarily the all-powerful oppressor and aggressor, no matter what the concrete facts of the case. The Other, even if they are perpetrating ruthless and unprovoked attacks, are necessarily and essentially "our" victims. Indeed, it seemed to me that perhaps the strongest sentiment discernible within this mode of analysis was not so much approval for the aggressor as a kind of disillusionment, or even disgust with "ourselves," a sense that "we" or "America" are à priori guilty, that badness resides in us, and that goodness, or rightness, is elsewhere. This seemed to me to involve a kind of inverse projection—the attribution of all good qualities to the Other, especially if the Other is seen as victimized. If the diagnosis could be offered so instantly, that was because it crystallized a climate of opinion that had been long brewing—a kind of gradual but decisive shift in the postwar decades from the older politics of triumphalism to the politics of trauma, from the belief that victory vindicates to the conviction that victimhood confers virtue.

This is a change in which the cult of "memory," and of Holocaust memory in particular, has been not unimplicated. And clearly, given the West's histories of colonization and collective violence; given its uses and abuses of power—given the

Holocaust—a change of heart and mind was much needed. The notion that might is right could not, in the face of the twentieth century, be decently sustained. Sympathy for the victim surely represents a moral improvement over automatic respect for the strong.

But if "identification with the victim" seemed to reach its apogee in the Holocaust cult, in the wake of September 11, it was the other side of the coin—self-blame and righteous guilt (we are contaminated; we had it coming)—that was brought into the foreground and taken to new lengths; to that extreme, in fact, where opposites meet and putative empathy for the victim is transmogrified into an alignment with the actual aggressor; and where putatively progressive views begin to be used in the service of rationalizing the world's most retrograde and regressive ideologies.

But, as we have learned from a close study of responses to the Holocaust and the oscillations of attitude towards its survivors, the ostensible idealization of, or identification with, the symbolic "victim" can disguise much less worthy sentiments. After all, no responses such as followed in the wake of September 11 would have been possible, or even thinkable, if the attacks had been perpetrated by any nation, faction, or party we recognized as belonging to "our" world and moral community. Had that been the case, we would surely have condemned the actors in the assaults unequivocally and without hesitation or elaborate excuses. But that is because we would have recognized them as agents capable of deploying power and responsible for the character of that deployment. The impulse to absolve and justify the perpetrators in this case—to construe them, indeed, as the real victims—could only have proceeded from an underlying vision of them not as agents, but as vehicles, literally, of blind reaction; not as persons expressing in their actions a set of intentions, beliefs, and agendas, but as a sort of elemental force erupting out of a miasma of historical inevitability and expressing the victim's impotent and necessarily justified rage. In this view, all agency and intentionality is in the hands of "America"; all passivity and impotence on the side of the other. Such a view suggests a very long distance from the objects of our supposed sympathy, and an unwitting condescension. It also suggests a fundamental disavowal of the reality, or realities, of other collectivities and groups, once they are construed as Other—a discounting of their home-grown inequities, internecine oppressions, conflicts of ideology, and of power. This is not so much sympathy for the other as an odd dehumanization, a reproduction of that "production of distance" that throughout history has wreaked such untold harm by other means.

But there were further ironies still. The sentiments driving the progressive response may have been an extension of the earlier "politics of trauma" in which the Holocaust was a central sanctity; but in the wake of September 11, the positions and alignments driving victimological identity politics contributed—through a series of almost diagrammatic ideological turns—to the rise of brand-new anti-Semitism. For, within the symbolic configurations following September 11, it is the Muslim and Arab world that has come to stand for the oppressed and the archetypal victims; and since so many members of that world consider Jews to be the archenemy, it follows all too easily from this that Jews must be the oppressors and the villains of the story. The shifts of alignments within identity ideologies are often highly abstract, and in the newest twist, Jews have become

(mutatis mutandis) the oppressors of "our" victims—and therefore as delegitimized, as suspect, as we are. In the new rhetoric,
Jews are configured not as outsiders, but as hyper-insiders and
figures of power—the allies of America, the profiteers of its
wealth, and the hidden agents of its influence. In the Middle
East, of course, Jews are seen as the local imperialists and, no
matter what the actual events, the unilateral aggressors.

Indeed, if many Jews find it difficult to address such sentiments energetically, that is because certain forms of anti-Semitism have become so difficult to distinguish from the broader
assumptions of supposedly right-minded politics. The politically correct complicity with expressions of anti-Semitism in the
West—the widespread disavowal of what is obvious and insidi-
ous—comes in part, I believe, from a sort of cognitive confusion as to what Jews have come symbolically to represent. To
some extent, they are still Other, and in some cases associations
of the Holocaust still attach to them. But insofar as they belong
to "our" world in which they hold some power; and insofar as
today's new hyper-victims consider them the hyper-enemy, Jews
have turned from being symbolically untouchable to becoming
fair game for symbolic attack.

How broad is the new bout of this familiar bigotry, and how
dangerous? For my part, I find myself not so much threatened
by it as outraged, astonished, and deeply saddened. I am an-
gered by the religious fanaticism and polite prejudice that make
expressions of anti-Jewishness once again possible, and by the
collusions of those who would excuse, explain, and turn a blind
eye to these unpalatable phenomena in the name of supposedly
noble sympathies. I resent the fact that there are now whole
swathes of the world where it is dangerous for me to travel be-

AFTER SUCH KNOWLEDGE

cause I am Jewish. But it also makes me profoundly sad to think that my generation has not attained full freedom from the constrictions of Jewish history after all. I deplore the fact that, once again, I have to place questions of Jewishness at the center of my moral consciousness. This, when it is caused by anti-Semitism, is a restriction on my inner, as well as external, freedom.

But speaking more generally (and I believe we all need to think not only from our own "identity positions" but on behalf of each other, on behalf of us all), if the recent swings of the ideological pendulum illustrate anything, it is that the politics of trauma is not an adequate antidote to the politics of power; nor is prejudice in reverse much of an improvement on prejudice plain and simple. The idealization of the Other and the putative victim is not much of an advance on reflexive demonization. Again, this is not to deny the dangers of a unipolar world, in which one nation exercises disproportionate power and wields disproportionate weight. Certainly, the critique of that power should not be abandoned, and our own proclivities for violence should be closely watched. But this cannot lead to a denial of others' aggression, or a proper evaluation of their intentions. The limits of toleration are also imposed by a kind of recognition—recognition of declared enmity, irrational hatred, desire for power, independent motive, and autonomous intention on the part of the Other—even if the motive is sometimes utterly deplorable and the intention unacceptable.

Finally, in our collective transactions with each other, the only criterion sufficient to the occasion, and to the complexities of our internecine and international transactions with each other, is surely the criterion of justice. Justice, after all, is the principle of mediation between people who are not necessarily

263

conjoined by bonds of mutual affinity or shared histories, but who yet need to coexist together in the same society, or to negotiate their interests across national borders. The French-Jewish philosopher, Emmanuel Levinas, who based his entire body of ideas on a vision of intersubjective recognition of others and the deep obligations that follow from this, thought that justice was a necessary counterpoint, or corrective, to individual compassion. When we are faced with the suffering or vulnerability of another human being, our obligation of empathy—sometimes our instinct of empathy—is absolute. But such empathy could blind us to the needs and rights of others. Exclusive compassion for one person—or tribe—can lead to injustice towards those outside the sphere of our immediate attachments.

Personal justice—the recognition of another's experience and feelings—can only be accomplished through sympathy and love, through privileging each person's subjectivity as if it were the world. But the arenas of collective life are a terrain that is not so much intersubjective as interobjective; that is, a space in which we negotiate interests across our differences, and in which we cannot claim special privileges because of special traits. In that arena, justice has to follow not the laws of love, but the sterner deity of the categorical imperative: the demand that we judge all in the light of the same standards, and as accountable to the same standards of basic dignity and responsibility.

These are very old, time-honored ideas, but they bear reiteration in our time of identity politics and tribal sentimentalisms. From the perspective of the second generation—that is, the vantage point of those who grew up in proximity to the victims of most profound injustice—the lesson is only reaffirmed; for if we study our parents' history, we will know that the unleashing of hatred is enabled by the tipping of rationality towards projection and that the mechanisms of justice afford the only means of protection sufficient for all, including groups that labor under social disadvantage, or that are potential targets of abuse.

One hopes that the historical experience of trauma, humiliation, finding oneself on the receiving end of wrong, may instill in its victims and their descendants a powerful longing for justice. The desire not to repeat wrongs is also one of the uses of the Holocaust.

But our criteria of judgment ought not to change when it is we who are the targets of injustice or violence—even if "we" stand in a position of relative privilege. If, in our abstract privileging of others—especially those we consider victims—we declare ourselves *à priori* and essentially illegitimate, that leaves us with no standards from which to defend ourselves; indeed, with no standards at all. That is politics of trauma eliding into politics of self-abnegation, or inverted injustice. If the categorical imperative requires us to treat others as we would treat ourselves, then it also demands that we treat ourselves as we would treat others. That is the only position from which we can extend respect to others without falling into the sins of thoughtless superiority or mindless guilt. If we refuse to acknowledge others, then clearly all possibility of such relations collapses; but if we yield our own stance or principles too readily, then we have no standpoint from which to enter into interaction either. And if, further, in our efforts to privilege "the Other," we fail to recognize ourselves, so to speak; if we accept at face value the diagnosis of our wrongness when it is made in hostility and hate, then we are engaging not in a moral act, but in self-betrayal. This is equally true when it applies to Polishness, or Americanness, or, for that matter, Jewishness.

.   .   .

The statute of limitations on the Holocaust is running out, as it must. Living memory fades, the fierceness of feeling subsides. Even with events of the Shoah's magnitude, this is inevitable. We must reflect on the past, but we cannot dwell in it forever. But how we turn away from the Holocaust matters. For those who lived in its proximity through personal history, it matters for our own sake. But it matters also for the sake of historical fidelity. Once again, the dangers of distortion—of sheer forgetfulness or mythologizing, of partial denial and willful misinterpretation—are considerable. It matters enormously that we do not use the Holocaust for our own self-serving purposes, or pervert its facts for newly hateful ends.

On one level, extreme events teach us simple lessons: Virulent prejudice breeds virulent results. Deadly ideologies permit deadly deeds. The dehumanization of the other leads to mass murder. On the other hand, the claims made for the uses of historical memory have to be modest. The Irish poet Seamus Heaney, in a clearly pessimistic moment, observed that it sometimes seems we can learn as much from history as from a visit to an abattoir. And, in relation to our collective histories, pessimism sometimes seems the only form of realism. Certainly, as we have watched the genocides in Cambodia and Rwanda, and as new methods of atrocity and terror have started presenting themselves at the beginning of the twenty-first century, it is all too clear that to learn from history is not the same as to cure or prevent it.

Nevertheless, we must keep trying to learn; we must keep trying.

Moreover, sometimes, by small increments and not always in dramatically visible ways, we do seem to learn something. It seems to me that in some areas, the concentrated thinking about atrocity we have been forced to do, perhaps especially about the Holocaust and its aftermath, has led to greater collective awareness. One of those areas in which we have tried, at least, to deal with large-scale problems with greater sensitivity has been, precisely, the aftermath of enormity and collective violence.

For one thing, we have come to understand that great crimes and wrongs cannot be left unaddressed; that unless some acknowledgment and recognition of what happened takes place, the suppressed past will rankle and return. Among the ravages of atrocity are the ravages of the moral sense—the moral world—of those so gratuitously injured; and the first need of the victim after such violence is for a restoration of that moral world and moral order through an acknowledgment that wrongs have been committed, and the punishment of those responsible. The need for societies as a whole is also to invert the perverse order of atrocity—its principled injustice, one might say—by establishing the very principles and norms of justice. Whatever the specific criteria of judgment or punishment, the first task after great wrongs have been committed is to name those wrongs *as* wrongs.

At the same time, it has been increasingly recognized—from so many instances of dealing with the aftermath of great wrongs—that large-scale justice in such situations is difficult, in fact impossible, to attain. In recent years, there have been interesting experiments, the most notable among them South Africa's Truth and Reconciliation Commission, in administering symbolic justice instead. The commission, for all its shortcomings and compromises, was a stirring attempt to achieve justice through the symbolic processes of recognition—through bringing the executioners of apartheid face to face with the people they had injured and giving them the opportunity to gain amnesty by telling the full truth of their deeds. Although this was hardly a perfect instrument of redress, it was nevertheless as effective as could perhaps be hoped for in the wake of the great and longstanding evils of apartheid. For some of the victims, at least, the opportunity to face their tormentors and executioners and force them to recognize the victims' pain—in some cases, the expression from the perpetrators of awareness and even remorse for what they have done, seemed to be reparative and cathartic. The balm of recognition seemed to do its work: The South African experiment has become a model for other efforts to cope with the aftereffects of enormous crimes.

Possibly, in some instances, second-generation meetings can also have a salutary and even, in the longer historical range, preventative effect. One can imagine the potential for this in Rwanda or former Yugoslavia. One can imagine the necessity of it, if that bitterest of conflicts ever gets resolved, in the Middle East. It may be that the German-Jewish dialogue in the decades after the Holocaust could become a model for such encounters. Of course, "Memory and Reconciliation" is a less urgent and a less bold proposition than Truth and Reconciliation. But in some contexts, even delayed dialogue may shortcut new cycles of vengeful violence.

Aside from becoming more subtle about the needs of societies in the wake of violence, we have become much more aware of the effects such events have on individual victims. We have come to understand, at least in principle, that those who have been through situations of atrocity are deeply affected, and that this is not a sign of pusillanimity or weakness. Soldiers who had been undermined or even maddened by the war in Vietnam were, at least notionally, objects of concern rather than scorn. Notionally, because of course the level of actual tolerance for their behavior varied. But in normative terms, their condition was understood to be the result of trauma rather than bad character.

At the same time, after a period when "trauma" was the unquestioned term of explanation for all forms of postviolent conditions and all cultural contexts, in recent years, in the next swing of the pendulum or conceptual correction, a fledgling critique of the "trauma discourse" has begun to be advanced. The critique comes mostly from a very interesting source: the cadres of humanitarian aid personnel and assorted counselors who have been exported by Western countries to sites of war and violence all over our perennially violent globe. On the basis of their first-hand observations, these fieldworkers in landscapes after battle have begun to note, and to tell us, that reactions to atrocity do not always follow a course that can be easily classified under the rubric of "trauma"; and that, even if they are administered with the best intentions, the Western, psychological models for addressing loss and mourning are sometimes entirely inappropriate to the local cultures. To the villagers of Bosnia or the Congo, "the discourse of trauma," with its vision of the resolutely separate self, and its techniques of depth-psychological probing, may seem a very strange—indeed, an alien—invention. Various societies may have their own ways of dealing with grief, which may include, for example, communal mourning, or the reclamation of family hierarchies and social status, or religious rituals. In the light of such close cross-cultural observation, the human rights workers have begun to note the extent to which the theories of trauma and PTSD are themselves permeated by certain cultural assumptions—most saliently, a highly individualistic conception of selfhood—and the degree to which they miss or ignore the importance of other elements, such as social roles or communal relationships, in coping with the aftermath of catastrophe. Not everyone expects talk to save them, or individual freedom to be the final balm. In the eyes of some of the human rights workers who have become, willy-nilly, informal anthropologists in far-flung corners of the earth, the globalization of psychological, no less than material goods, holds the danger of another kind of "imperialism"—an unintended but nevertheless presumptuous superimposition of our own, rarely questioned values on other systems of selfhood and sets of beliefs.

.   .   .

The large and simple lessons of atrocity are the first ones and they need, again and again, to be instilled in our minds. But beyond that, as the period of primary documentation and direct testimony comes to an end, there are, specifically in relation to the Holocaust, more complex and more fundamental questions that arise from that time—questions that demand both a more stereoscopic and a subtler vision. History is a race between education and catastrophe, it has been said; and this is at no time more true than in the interval of the second generation. In that prolonged aftermath, the human meanings of events still course in our veins, and history still speaks to us in eloquent ways. To us, the horror of the Holocaust is more than an impersonal abstraction; but at the same time, we have sufficient distance so that we can view its forbidding terrain not only from within personal narratives but also with a wider lens.

The first need was to put together a factual picture of events and to acknowledge as fully as possible the fate of the victims; but several broad areas can still bear a deeper exploration: The question of German and Nazi behavior has started to come under close scrutiny, both in studies of high-ranking Nazis and of ordinary Germans. We still need, however, to understand much more about the perpetrator mentality: how people are led towards systematic sadism, how the mind converts ordinary ambivalence into extreme cruelty, and in what cultural circumstances such forms of feeling coalesce into collective movements. Conversely, we also need to ask how ardent ideologies of hatred are fanned by leaders and communal institutions; and what political and emotional needs fanaticism serves that more moderate systems of value do not.

In our disbelieving age, we may be particularly ill-equipped to understand such phenomena, or even to credit them. The temptation is to transpose the very idea of belief into other categories of explanation—reaction to oppression, political strategy, etc. There may be elements of all such things, of course, in militant faiths, whether ideological or religious. But the fueling quality of belief itself—as we are seeing once again in the rise of Islamic fundamentalism—cannot be underestimated. On a collective level, it is belief rather than errant passion that most decisively underwrites extreme deeds. We may have thought, as perhaps every generation since the age of Enlightenment has thought, that in our times the force of absolutist, or "blind," faith had subsided; but by a strange turn of a historical wheel, the problem of such faith is once again gaining relevance and urgency, and we may need, however reluctantly, to grapple with its inner workings and its meanings.

At the other end of the moral, or the human, spectrum, we need to learn more about patterns and motives of rescue: Who rescued and why? What part did positive ethical—or religious—belief play in the rescuers' acts, what part individual bravery and kindness, or deeply instilled cultural values? To what extent does the motive of rescue spring from a personal relationship with those in need of help—or, for that matter, the tenor of human relationships among different groups altogether?

In all these areas, I believe we need to broaden—and deepen—the questions through a comparative approach. We need to study genocidal violence in Cambodia and Rwanda as well as in the Holocaust; to look at the explosions of murderous interethnic violence in the villages of Kashmir as well as of Poland. In what circumstances does such violence flare up between neighbors—and what are the mechanisms for containing it? Conversely, what are the patterns of moral resistance in such situations, and in different kinds of war?

There are even more ethically intricate quandaries that still haunt us, still require reflection. The ravages visited upon Germany at the end of the Second World War—the wholesale bombardments of German cities by the Allies, the wholesale rapes of German women by the Red Army soldiers, the expulsions of ethnic Germans from Czech and Polish territories—these unsettling sequelae of the war are becoming a subject of address not only within Germany but from the vantage point of the victors. This is one of those areas where instinctive response and considered thought pull in opposite directions. We can sympathize with the instinct of retribution, for wrongs as immeasurable as those that were inflicted on the world by Germany. In moral terms, retaliation does not have a meaning equivalent to the initial aggression. And yet, wild revenge cannot be sustained as a value and, as we have seen again and again, leads to further wrongs. It further slackens the restraints of civilization already loosened by war, especially when it is visited upon an enemy who is already defeated.

Finally, I believe we need to enter more boldly into that most taboo of areas—the range of Jewish behavior during the Holocaust. Were there possibilities of more resistance in the early stages of the Final Solution—and why were these not pursued? Some interesting suggestions have been made about structural reasons for the absence of active Jewish leadership in the shtetls of Eastern Europe as the Holocaust loomed. (I remember my father's voice: "Where was the leadership? Why did nobody gather us together and organize us? We would have fought—we would have fought with anything that came to hand.") Traditional Jewish nonviolence may have played a part. But also, the war came at a time when the shtetl communities were making the transition from orthodoxy to modernity, and from the older modes of religious authority to still untested forms of modern, party-based politics—resulting in a temporary vacuum of power and of trusted structures. Within the larger, ghastly situation, what were the patterns of survival, aside from the all-important element of luck? Again, close statistical studies are just beginning to be undertaken in these areas; but from informal readings of a large body of testimony, it seems that there are extremely delicate issues of education and acculturation to be looked at here. It helped, in the inferno of wartime Poland for example, to be able to speak Polish and move around without the fear of being immediately identified as Jewish; it helped, in some proportion of cases, to have non-Jewish friends. On a larger scale, how much did the historical insularity of Jewish communities in the shtetls of Eastern Europe redound on the behavior of others towards their Jewish neighbors? Such questions touch on the most sensitive problems and feelings; and they should not be construed as shifting any sense of responsibility to the victim. The responsibility for the Final Solution lies in one place only: Once the war started, the course and success of the extermination followed inevitably from the Nazi intention to carry it out.

But the more nuanced questions also need to be raised if we are truly to learn from calamity. The Jews of Europe were in many ways in a unique situation, in being a Diaspora without a state, a minority in habitually homogeneous countries, and a group with a long history of persecution. And yet, patterns of Jewish interaction with majority populations can be usefully compared with other interethnic relationships. As we see the tensions inherent in such relations flaring up with such frequency into deadly conflicts, we need to think as realistically as possible about the formation of majority attitudes towards the internal Other and the obligations of majority populations to the minorities in their midst. At the same time, we need to look squarely at the more delicate and less-examined side of the coin—the patterns of political attitudes (and for that matter, prejudices) among minority groups, as well as the obligations of such groups towards the host countries and the needs of societies as a whole. We need, most of all, to be able to talk to each other with honesty and some boldness across our differences; and to think as strenuously as possible about social forums and frameworks of commonality that can contain such differences. Given our historical experience, our aspirations for preventing conflict have to be modest. It would probably be foolish to think we can eliminate the instinct of aggression through a collective project of human improvement. But we can, I believe, fruitfully think about structures to restrain such instincts, and contain our separate interests through a conception of common interests.

But beyond historical questions, the heuristic power of the second-generation perspective inheres in what has been most difficult: our proximity to the aftermath of suffering, and to victims of extreme brutality and injustice. It is from within that intimacy that we need to begin our reflections, to think about the oldest of questions—how we might treat each other as suffering, vulnerable human beings. A culture that does not give a place to suffering loses a part of wisdom about human experience. But our attitudes towards vulnerability and pain are often inconsistent and confused. Much in our time and in our world militates against the acceptance of suffering, or of incorporating it into our vision of the human lot. Our ideals of control, self-improvement, freedom from dependence, and the very speed of middle-class life do not leave much room for frailty, or for solidarity with those who may need our help. Our lives are so structured that we depend increasingly on mediating institutions for the care of the vulnerable. At the same time, our rhetoric is ever more pervaded by the professional and sociological vocabulary of victimhood—and in that vocabulary, suffering becomes reified into pathology or aggrandized into martyrdom. Suffering becomes Trauma; a person who has experienced adversity or been treated harshly becomes the Victim.

Indeed, it sometimes seems to me that the excesses of identity politics and the politics of trauma are themselves a kind of displacement, wherein the actualities of suffering are placed at a safe distance and relegated to the sphere of abstract compassion and morality. But victimhood is not—for all that we would wish otherwise—a conveniently moral condition. If we lose our sympathy for suffering we lose part of our moral being. The bearers of atrocity's scars deserve our help, understanding, the alleviation of pain. On a personal level, if we are to be of help to those who have been *in extremis*, then we need to remember, or perhaps relearn, the very old arts of simple sympathy and empathy: the ability to take in a story without excessive comment, to imagine what the other feels without diminishment or exaggerated sentiment; most of all, perhaps, to imagine the reality of the other person's situation accurately; and sometimes, to help the sufferer see more accurately as well.

But if we are not to engage in yet another displacement or a renewed "production of distance," then we need also to remember that to deserve our sympathy or help, the victims of atrocity do not have to be especially virtuous, nor saintly—nor should such virtue be expected of them. Persecution is not a character-improving process, and collective suffering cannot assure collective merit. This is why the leap from the personal to the political is so difficult, and why an ethos of martyrdom cannot serve as a basis for a decent society. After the collective memories have been excavated, and the individual narratives recounted, we need the restoration of principles that will assure mutual respect, even if we do not share enough past to warrant mutual love. Otherwise, the memories of pain will soon turn into someone's rage, and the conflicting narratives will come into possibly deadly conflict. Sympathy for those who suffered is our moral duty; but we cannot cease to treat the victim as a moral being. The recipients of great wrongs need, for the restoration of their moral world—and a shared moral world—a recognition of those wrongs; but they cannot be placed outside the community of justice and reason.

Perhaps, after all the causes and mechanisms of the Holocaust—and other atrocities, for that matter—have been examined, the urgent question we are left with is how to establish normative principles and structures that can form a mainstay against eruptions of hatred. For this, neither victimology nor demonology will suffice; neither the idealization nor the denigration of the Other will in the long range assure harmony. Moreover, on such issues, we need to think not only on behalf of our own tribe, or from particular sites of identification, but from the imagination of norms that apply to all. We need justice for others—and for ourselves. We need the kind of tolerance that does not dissolve either others' or our own integrity or legitimacy.

But beyond keeping compact with the past and contemplating its stern lessons, there is one thing that we, as members of the second generation, need to do for ourselves—and that is to disentangle the spectral memories that have inhabited us from the realities we inhabit. It was in the United States Holocaust Memorial Museum that I had my strange epiphany. As I walked through this most daunting of museum exhibitions, and as I entered into its hellish world as into a familiar element, I suddenly thought: But there must also be something outside of this. There must be a reality that is not horror, but that is equally foundational. The Holocaust cannot be the norm that defines the world. It is, of course, symptomatic of my second-generation condition that it would have taken so long—half a lifetime—for such an idea to occur. For me, in the beginning was the war, and the Holocaust was the ontological basis of my universe. And indeed, the Holocaust continues to stand as a kind of limiting condition of experience, and therefore, a necessary part of our knowledge about human nature. It is because the Holocaust exposes the negative extremes of human possibility that it has been taken as philosophically central not only by childhood minds but by so many thinkers of our time. Hell, especially if it is of human making, is surely one clue about the human condition—and the Holocaust extends our knowledge of the human hell.

And yet, unless we want to fall into permanent melancholia or nihilistic despair, we cannot take the Holocaust as the norm that governs human lives. We cannot start from it as a basis, or move towards it as a form of transcendence, even of the darkest kind. That is why it is necessary to separate the past from the present and to judge the present in its own light. For me, as for many direct inheritors of that wounding trauma, this has been the difficult and necessary task. After the dark logic of the Shoah, acceptance of a benign world does not come easily. The "normal" may seem suspect, or it may seem thin. How to find richness, authenticity, depth in the temperate zones of ordinary life? How to find sources of significance that do not derive from extremity and to endow with value not only great losses but modest gains? In a sense—as with all aspects of second-generation experience—this is a question that arises in every transition to maturity but that, for children of survivors, is sharpened to a fine acuity. For the inheritors of traumatic historical experience, the ability to separate the past from the present—to see the past *as* the past is a difficult but necessary achievement.

The moment of that separation, of letting go, is a poignant one, for it is akin to the giving up of mourning. There is pain in the very diminution of pain, the danger that time will dilute morality as it dilutes passion. We do not, generally, forget the facts; anyway, these are always available as information, in books or on the Internet. What we do forget, imperceptibly but inevitably, are the sensations accompanying the facts: the rightful rage, gratitude where it is due, the anguish of loss for the loved ones' death. This has to be accepted as part of time's work and its passage. But if we do not want to betray the past—if we want to remain ethical beings and honor our covenant with those who suffered—then moral passion needs to be supplanted by moral thought, by an incorporation of memory into our consciousness of the world. There is a Jewish tradition that says we must grieve for the dead fully and deeply; but that mourning must also come to its end. Perhaps that moment has come, even as we must continue to ponder and confront the knowledge that the Shoah has brought us in perpetuity.

SELECTED BIBLIOGRAPHY

Antelme, R. *The Human Race.* Evanston, Ill.: Marlboro Press, 1992.

Appelfeld, A. *Beyond Despair: Three Lectures and a Conversation with Philip Roth.* New York: Fromm International, 1994.

Applebaum, A. *Gulag.* London: Allen Lane, 2003.

Appignanesi, L. *Losing the Dead.* London: Chatto & Windus, 1999.

Barker, P. *The Regeneration Trilogy.* London: Viking, 1997.

Bar-On, D. *Legacy of Silence: Encounters with Children of the Third Reich.* Cambridge, Mass.: Harvard University Press, 1989.

————. *Fear and Hope: Three Generations of the Holocaust.* Cambridge, Mass.: Harvard University Press, 1995.

Bauman, Z. *Modernity and the Holocaust.* Cambridge: Polity Press in Association with Basil Blackwell, 1989.

Ben-Cion, P. *Shtetl Jews Under Soviet Rule: Eastern Poland on the Eve of the Holocaust.* London: Basil Blackwell, 1990.

Berger, A. L., and N. Berger, eds. *Second Generation Voices: Reflections by Children of Holocaust Survivors and Perpetrators.* New York: Syracuse University Press, 2001.

Bergman, M. S., and M. E. Jucovy. *Generations of the Holocaust.* New York: Columbia University Press, 1982.

Blumenthal, M. *All My Mothers and Fathers: A Memoir.* New York: HarperCollins, 2002.

Borges, J. L. "Funes, the Memorious." In *Ficciones,* edited by J. Sturrock, pp. 83–91. London: Everyman, 1941.

Borowski, T. *This Way to the Gas, Ladies and Gentlemen.* Harmondsworth: Penguin, 1980.

Bracken, P. J., and C. Petty, eds. *Rethinking the Trauma of War.* London: Free Association Books, 1998.

Brison, S. J. *Aftermath: Violence and the Remaking of a Self.* Princeton: Princeton University Press, 2002.

Brittain, V. *Testament of Youth: An Autobiographical Study of the Years 1900–1925.* London: Virago, 1992.

Brodsky, J. *Less Than One: Selected Essays.* New York: Farrar, Straus and Giroux, 1986.

Bukiet, M. J., ed. *Nothing Makes You Free: Writings by Descendants of Jewish Holocaust Survivors.* New York: W. W. Norton, 2003.

Buruma, I. *The Wages of Guilt: Memories of War in Germany and Japan.* New York: Farrar, Straus and Giroux, 1994.

Caruth, C. *Unclaimed Experience.* Baltimore: Johns Hopkins University Press, 1996.

Celan, P. *Selected Poems and Prose of Paul Celan.* New York: W. W. Norton, 2001.

Clendinnen, I. *Reading the Holocaust.* Cambridge: Cambridge University Press, 1999.

Cohen, R. A. *Ethics, Exegesis and Philosophy: Interpretation After Levinas.* Cambridge: Cambridge University Press, 2001.

Cole, T. *Selling the Holocaust: From Auschwitz to Schindler. How*

History Is Bought, Packaged, and Sold. New York: Routledge, 1999.

Deak, I., J. T. Gross, and T. Judt, eds. *The Politics of Retribution in Europe: World War II and Its Aftermath.* Princeton: Princeton University Press, 2000.

Delbo, C. *Auschwitz and After.* New Haven: Yale University Press, 1995.

Duras, M. *The War: A Memoir.* New York: New Press, 1994.

Edelman, G. *War Story: A Novel.* New York: Riverhead Books, 2001.

Ehrenreich, B. *Blood Rites: Origins and History of the Passions of War.* London: Virago, 1997.

Epstein, H. *Children of the Holocaust: Conversations with Sons and Daughters of Survivors.* New York: Penguin Books, 1979.

Feinstein, S. C., ed. *Witness and Legacy.* Minneapolis: Carolrhoda, 1999.

Felsen, I. "Transgenerational Transmission of Effects of the Holocaust." In *International Handbook of Multigenerational Legacies of Trauma,* edited by Y. Danieli, pp. 43–68. The Plenum Series on Stress and Coping. London: Plenum Press, 1998.

Figes, E. *Tales of Innocence and Experience: An Exploration.* London: Bloomsbury, 2003.

Finkelstein, N. G. *The Holocaust Industry: Reflections on the Exploitation of Jewish Suffering.* 2d ed. New York: Verso Books, 2003.

Finkelstein, N. G., and R. B. Birn. *A Nation on Trial: The Goldhagen Thesis and Historical Truth.* New York: Henry Holt and Company, 1998.

Finkielkraut, A. *The Imaginary Jew.* Lincoln: University of Nebraska Press, 1994.

Fitzpatrick, M., ed. *Kazimierz Moczarski: Conversations with an Executioner.* Englewood Cliffs, N. J.: Prentice-Hall, 1981.

Flanzbaum, H., ed. *The Americanization of the Holocaust.* Baltimore: Johns Hopkins University Press, 1999.

Foer, J. *Everything Is Illuminated: A Novel.* London: Hamish Hamilton, 2002.

Fogelman, E. *Conscience & Courage: Rescuers of Jews During the Holocaust.* London: Victor Gollancz, 1995.

Frank, A. *The Diary of Anne Frank.* Revised critical edition. New York: Doubleday, 2003.

Fremont, H. *After Long Silence: A Woman's Search for Her Family's Secret Identity.* London: Piatkus, 1999.

Fresco, N. "Remembering the Unknown." *International Review of Psychoanalysis* 11 (1984): 417.

Freud, S. "Mourning and Melancholia" (1917). In *The Pelican Freud Library.* Vol. 11, *On Metapsychology: The Theory of Psychoanalysis,* pp. 245–268. London: Penguin, 1984.

Friedman, C. *Nightfather.* New York: Persea Books, 2002.

Gay, R. *Safe Among the Germans: Liberated Jews After World War II.* New Haven: Yale University Press, 2002.

Goldhagen, D. J. *Hitler's Willing Executioners: Ordinary Germans and the Holocaust.* London: Little, Brown, 1996.

Gourevitch, P. *We Wish to Inform You That Tomorrow We Will Be Killed with Our Families: Stories from Rwanda.* New York: Picador USA, 1999.

———. "The Memory Thief." *New Yorker* (June 14, 1999): 48–68.

Greenspan, H. *On Listening to Holocaust Survivors: Recounting and Life History.* Westport, Conn.: Greenwood Press, 1998.

Grinberg, L., and R. Grinberg. *Psychoanalytic Perspectives on Migration and Exile.* New Haven: Yale University Press, 1989.

Gross, J. T. *Neighbors: The Destruction of a Jewish Community in Poland.* Princeton: Princeton University Press, 2001.

Grossman, D. *See Under Love.* London: Jonathan Cape, 1990.

———. *The Book of Intimate Grammar: A Novel.* New York: Picador USA, 2002.

Gruber, R. E. *Virtually Jewish: Reinventing Jewish Culture in Europe.* Berkeley: University of California Press, 2002.

Halasz, G. "Memories of Silence: Trauma Transmission in Holocaust-Survivor Families and the Exiled Self." In vol. 3 of *Remembering for the Future: The Holocaust in an Age of Genocide,* edited by J. K. Roth and E. Maxwell, pp. 117–126. Houndmills, U.K.: Palgrave, 2001.

———. *Children of Child Survivors of the Holocaust: Can Trauma Be Transmitted Across the Generations?* Paper Presented at the "The Legacy of the Holocaust: Children of the Holocaust" Conference, Jagiellonian University, Cracow, May 24–27, 2001.

Halbwachs, M. *On Collective Memory (Heritage of Sociology).* Chicago: University of Chicago Press, 1992.

Hass, A. *The Aftermath: Living with the Holocaust.* Cambridge: Cambridge University Press, 1995.

Hendry, J., ed. *Interpreting Japanese Society: Anthropological Approaches.* 2d ed. London: Routledge, 1998.

Herman, J. L. *Trauma and Recovery.* New York: Basic Books, 1992.

Hillesum, E. *An Interrupted Life and Letters from Westerbork.* New York: Metropolitan Books, Henry Holt, 1996.

Hirsch, M. *Family Frames: Photography, Narrative and Postmemory.* Cambridge, Mass.: Harvard University Press, 1997.

Hoffman, E. *Lost in Translation: A Life in a New Language.* New York: Dutton, 1989.

Hoffman, E. *Shtetl: The Life and Death of a Small Town and the World of Polish Jews.* London: Secker & Warburg, 1998.

———. "True to Life?" *Time Magazine* (June 14, 1999): 144–145.

———. Review of *The Holocaust in American Life,* by Peter Novick. *New York Review of Books* (March 9, 2000): 19–23.

Homans, P. *The Ability to Mourn: Disillusionment and the Social Origins of Psychoanalysis.* Chicago: University of Chicago Press, 1989.

Hovannisian, R. G., ed. *The Armenian Genocide in Perspective.* New Brunswick, N.J.: Transaction Books, Rutgers University, 1986.

Hrair Dekmejian, R. "Determinants of Genocide: Armenians and Jews as Case Studies." In *The Armenian Genocide in Perspective,* edited by R. G. Hovannisian. New Brunswick, N.J.: Transaction Books, Rutgers University, 1986.

Ignatieff, M. *Blood and Belonging: Journeys into the New Nationalism.* London: Vintage, 1994.

———. *Human Rights as Politics and Idolatry.* Princeton: Princeton University Press, 2001.

Kakar, S. *The Colors of Violence: Cultural Identities, Religion and Conflict.* Chicago: University of Chicago Press, 1990.

Karpf, A. *The War After: Living with the Holocaust.* London: Minerva, 1997.

Kestenberg, J. S. "Transposition Revisited: Clinical, Therapeutic, and Developmental Considerations." In *Healing Their Wounds: Psychotherapy with Holocaust Survivors and Their Families.* Edited by P. Marcus and A. Rosenberg. New York: Praeger, 1989.

Kingston, M. H. *The Woman Warrior.* New York: Knopf, 1976.

Klein, M. *Envy and Gratitude and Other Works 1946–1963.* London: Virago Press, 1988.

Kluger, R. *Still Alive: A Holocaust Girlhood Remembered.* New York: The Feminist Press, 2001.

Kott, J. *Shakespeare, Our Contemporary.* New York: W. W. Norton, 1974.

Krell, R. "Medical and Psychological Effects of Concentration Camps on Holocaust Survivors." In vol. 4 of *Genocide: A Critical Bibliographic Review.* Edited by R. Krell, M. I. Sherman, and E. Wiesel. Somerset, N.J.: Transaction Publishers, 1997.

Krystal, H., ed. *Massive Psychic Trauma.* New York: International Universities Press, 1969.

La Capra, D. *History and Memory After Auschwitz.* New York: Cornell University Press, 1998.

Langer, L. L. *Admitting the Holocaust.* Oxford: Oxford University Press, 1995.

Laub, D. "Bearing Witness or the Vicissitudes of Listening." *Testimony: Crises of Witnessing in Literature, Psychoanalysis and History.* Edited by S. Felman and D. Laub, p. 68. New York: Routledge, 1992.

Lentin, R. *Israel and Daughters of the Shoah: Reoccupying the Territories of Silence.* New York: Berghahn Books, 2000.

Levi, P. *Survival in Auschwitz: The Nazi Assault on Humanity.* New York: Collier Books, 1961.

———. *The Truce: A Survivor's Journey Home from Auschwitz.* London: Bodley Head, 1965.

———. *The Reawakening.* New York: Collier Books, 1986.

———. *The Drowned and the Saved.* New York: Summit Books, 1988.

Levinas, E. *Emmanuel Levinas: Basic Philosophical Writings: Studies in Continental Thought.* Edited by A. T. Peperzak, S. Critchley, and R. Bernasconi. Indianapolis: Indiana University Press, 1996.

Liebrecht, S. *Apples from the Desert: Selected Stories.* The Helen Rose Scheuer Jewish Women's Series. New York: The Feminist Press at the City University of New York, 2000.

Lifton, R. J. *Death in Life: Survivors of Hiroshima.* New York: Random House, 1967.

———. *Home from the War: Vietnam Veterans: Neither Victims nor Executioners.* New York: Simon & Schuster, 1973.

———. *The Nazi Doctors: Medical Killing and the Psychology of Genocide.* New York: Basic Books, 2000.

Linenthal, E. T. *Preserving Memory: The Struggle to Create America's Holocaust Museum.* New York: Penguin Books, 1995.

Margalit, A.. *The Decent Society.* Cambridge, Mass.: Harvard University Press, 1996.

———. *The Ethics of Memory.* Cambridge, Mass.: Harvard University Press, 2002.

Meredith, M. *Coming to Terms: South Africa's Search for Truth.* New York: PublicAffairs, 1999.

Merridale, C. *Night of Stone: Death and Memory in Russia.* London: Granta, 2000.

Milchman, A., and A. Rosenberg, eds. *Postmodernism and the Holocaust.* Amsterdam: Rodopi, 1998.

Milosz, C. *New and Collected Poems: 1931–2001.* New York: Ecco, 2001.

Mitscherlich, A., and M. Mitscherlich. *The Inability to Mourn.* New York: Grove Press, 1975.

Nalkowska, Z. *Medallions.* Evanston, Ill.: Northwestern University Press, 2000.

Nora, P., ed. *Realms of Memory.* 3 vols. New York: Columbia University Press, 1996–1998.

Novick, P. *The Holocaust in American Life.* Boston: Houghton Mifflin, 1999.

Nussbaum, M. C. *Upheavals of Thought: The Intelligence of Emotions.* Cambridge: Cambridge University Press, 2001.

O'Siadhail, M. *The Gossamer Wall: Poems in Witness to the Holocaust.* St. Louis: Time Being Books, 2002.

Orizio, R. *Talk of the Devil: Encounters with Seven Dictators.* London: Random House, 2003.

Overy, R. *Interrogations: The Nazi Elite in Allied Hands, 1945.* London: Allen Lane, 2001.

Pines, D. "The Impact of the Holocaust on the Second Generation." In *A Woman's Unconscious Use of Her Body: A Psychoanalytical Perspective,* edited by D. Pines. London: Virago, 1993.

————. "Working with Woman Survivors of the Holocaust." In *A Woman's Unconscious Use of Her Body: A Psychoanalytical Perspective,* edited by D. Pines. London: Virago, 1993.

Polonsky, A., ed. *My Brother's Keeper? Recent Polish Debates on the Holocaust.* Oxford: Routledge in Association with The Institute for Polish-Jewish Studies, 1990.

Redlich, S. *Together and Apart in Brzezany: Poles, Jews, and Ukrainians, 1919–1945.* Indianapolis: Indiana University Press, 2002.

Reichel, S. *What Did You Do in the War, Daddy? Growing Up in Germany.* New York: Hill & Wang, 1989.

Richmond, T. *Konin: A Quest.* London: Jonathan Cape, 1995.

Ricoeur, P. "Memory and Forgetting." In *Questioning Ethics: Contemporary Debates in Continental Philosophy,* edited by R. Kearney, with M. Dooley. London: Routledge, 1999.

Rosenbaum, A. S., ed. *Is the Holocaust Unique? Perspectives on Comparative Genocide.* Boulder: Westview Press, 1996.

Rosenthal, G., and D. Bar-On. "A Biographical Case Study of a Victimizer's Daughter Strategy: The Pseudo-Identification with the Victims of the Holocaust." *The Journal of Narrative and Life History* 2 (1992): 105–127.

Rosmus, A. *Against the Stream.* Columbia: University of South Carolina Press, 2002.

Scarry, Elaine. *The Body in Pain: The Making and Unmaking of the World.* Oxford University Press, 1985.

Schlink, B. *The Reader.* London: Phoenix House, 1997.

Sebald, W. G. *The Emigrants.* London: Harvill, 1996.

———. "The Natural History of Destruction." *New Yorker* (November 4, 2002): 66–77.

———. *On the Natural History of Destruction.* Translated by Anthea Bell. New York: Random House, 2003.

Segev, T. *The Seventh Million: The Israelis and the Holocaust.* New York: Hill and Wang, 1993.

Sereny, G. *Into That Darkness: An Examination of Conscience.* London: Vintage Books, 1983.

———. *Albert Speer: His Battle with Truth.* Reprint edition. London: Vintage Books, 1996.

———. *German Trauma: Experiences and Reflections, 1938–2001.* London: Penguin Books, 2001.

Shay, J. *Achilles in Vietnam: Combat Trauma and the Undoing of Character.* New York: Atheneum, 1994.

Shengold, L. *Soul Murder Revisited: Thoughts About Therapy, Hate, Love, and Memory.* New Haven: Yale University Press, 1999.

Sichrovsky, P. *Born Guilty: Children of Nazi Families.* New York: Basic Books, 1988.

Sontag, S. *Regarding the Pain of Others.* New York: Farrar, Straus and Giroux, 2003.

Spiegelman, A. *Maus: A Survivor's Tale.* Harmondsworth: Penguin, 1986.

Staub, E. *The Roots of Evil: The Psychological and Cultural Origins of Genocide.* Cambridge: Cambridge University Press, 1992.

Steinlauf, M. C. *Bondage to the Dead: Poland and the Memory of the Holocaust.* New York: Syracuse University Press, 1997.

Suleiman, S. R. "Problems of Memory and Factuality in Recent Holocaust Memoirs: Wilkomirski/Wiesel." *Poetics Today* 21, no. 3 (Fall 2000): 543–559.

———. "The 1.5 Generation: Thinking About Child Survivors and the Holocaust." *American Imago* 59, no.3 (2002): 277–296.

Tec, N. *When Light Pierced the Darkness: Christian Rescue of Jews in Nazi-Occupied Poland.* Oxford: Oxford University Press, 1986.

Todorov, T. *Facing the Extreme: Moral Life in the Concentration Camps.* New York: Metropolitan Books, Henry Holt, 1996.

Wardi, D. *Memorial Candles: Children of the Holocaust.* London: Tavistock, 1992.

Wiesel, E. *Night* (25th anniversary edition). Toronto, New York: Bantam, 1982.

———, ed. *Daughters of Absence: Transferring a Legacy of Loss.* Stirling, Va.: Capital Books, 2001.

Wilkinson, A. "A Changed Vision of God." *New Yorker* (January 24, 1994): 52–68.

Wilkomirski, B. *Fragments: Memories of a Childhood.* London: Picador, 1996.

Winnicott, D. W. *Through Paediatrics to Psychoanalysis: Collected Papers.* London: Karnac Books and The Institute of Psychoanalysis, 1992.

Yerushalmi, J. *Zakhor: Jewish History and Jewish Memory.* Seattle: University of Washington Press, 1982.

Young, J. *Writing and Rewriting the Holocaust.* Indianapolis: Indiana University Press, 1988.

Young, J. E. *The Texture of Memory: Holocaust, Memorials and Meaning.* New Haven: Yale University Press, 1993.

ACKNOWLEDGMENTS

A book such as this is informed by many conversations and encounters, and a full list of people to whom I am indebted would be too long to compile. However, my special thanks go to Helen Epstein, for her collegial help and generosity in sharing insights into a theme with which she is well familiar. I was grateful for the opportunity to explore aspects of the book's subject through several lectures: the 2000 Una's Lecture in the Humanities at the Doreen B. Townsend Center for the Humanities at the University of California at Berkeley; a lecture in the Oxford Amnesty International series on "Human Rights, Human Wrongs" in 2001; the Isaiah Berlin lecture at Wolfson College, Oxford, in 2002; and the 2002 Kristallnacht Commemoration address at the Beth Israel Synagogue in Vancouver, Canada. To the sponsors of all these events, my warm thanks. My appreciation to the team at PublicAffairs for their energy and efficiency at all stages of the publication process. I am especially grateful to Peter Osnos, who has been closely involved with this project from the beginning; and to Kate Darnton, whose enthusiasm and editorial tact have been a support throughout its writing. To my agent, Georges Borchardt, my thanks, as ever.

INDEX